86- sweet & sour salmon fillets

RABBI ABRAHAM J. TWERSKI, M.D. • JUDI DICK

A TASTE OF NOSTALGIA

Tales and recipes to nourish body and soul

Published by

ARTSCROLL

SHAAR PRESS

Photo Credits

Cover, title pages, page 94: Library of Congress

Pages 26, 108, 140, 166, 178, 188, 194: YIVO Institute for Jewish Research

Pages 80, 216, 220: YIVO Institute for Jewish Research and Menakhem Kipnes / Forward Association

Page 128: YIVO Institute for Jewish Research and Engel Photo / Forward Association

Page 244: YIVO Institute for Jewish Research and Alter Kacyzne / Forward Association

Pages 226, 290: YIVO Institute for Jewish Research and Forward Association

We thank Jesse Aaron Cohen of YIVO Institute for his gracious guidance and assistance.

Published by ARTSCROLL / SHAAR PRESS
4401 Second Avenue / Brooklyn, NY 11232 / (718) 921-9000 / www.artscroll.com

Distributed in Israel by SIFRIATI / A. GITLER
6 Hayarkon Street / Bnei Brak 51127 / Israel

Distributed in Europe by LEHMANNS
Unit E, Viking Business Park, Rolling Mill Road
Jarrow, Tyne and Wear, NE32 3DP / England

ISBN: 1-4226-0105-6

Distributed in Australia and New Zealand by GOLDS WORLD OF JUDAICA
3-13 William Street / Balaclava, Melbourne 3183, Victoria / Australia

Distributed in South Africa by KOLLEL BOOKSHOP
Shop 8A Norwood Hypermarket / Norwood 2196 / Johannesburg, South Africa

Printed in the USA by Noble Book Press

In memory
of my mother,

Mollie Lando

מטל סאבל אשת ר' דוד צבי ז"ל

נפטרת עשרה בטבת תשמ"ז

a wife to be admired
a mother to be looked up to
a hostess and *mekarev rechokim*
with warmth and graciousness before it was in style
and, above all, a balabusta and chef par excellence.

She ran a home *"vi es darf tzu zein,"* as it was meant to be — doing the *ratzon Hashem* (will of Hashem) on a shoestring budget — and without any complaints. Her home and her heart were open to all — she was truly an *eishis chayil* to emulate.

Barbara Gold Schaum

בילא נעכא אשת ר' פינחס מרדכי עמו"ש

נפטרת י"ח אדר ב' תשס"ה

a friend to be cherished.

She never complained but lent a sympathetic ear to everyone else's kvetching. She was my closest friend, dearer than a sister. I miss her every day in every way, but the knowledge that she would have gotten a kick out of this book makes me smile.

Acknowledgments

Where to begin?

First and foremost — my heart overflows with gratitude to Hashem Yisbarach for all the many kindnesses with which He has blessed me and my loved ones.

To Rabbi Twerski, for having placed his confidence in me for the past twenty years and for prodding me to undertake this project. It has proved to be the adventure of a lifetime, and I am grateful.

To ArtScroll, in particular Rabbis Meir Zlotowitz, Nosson Scherman and Sheah Brander, for the job of my dreams. It is a privilege to be counted as one of the ArtScroll family.

And, to my colleagues at ArtScroll: Rabbi Avrohom Biderman for his chizuk and for finding the photos that so enhance this book; Sury Reinhold, for her patience and fortitude in deciphering my notoriously illegible handwriting and for typing the recipes; Mrs. Frime Eisner and Mrs. Mindy Stern for their impeccable proofreading. Their eagle eyes saved me from innumerable bloopers.

Eli Kroen for his magnificent cover — I've become so accustomed to his brilliance that it's easy to take for granted. And to Mrs. Tzini Fruchthandler. Her input is evident on each and every page. She is a master at graphics — note the stunning layout — and a balabusta who merits this esteemed title. Her comments and questions clarified my thoughts and compelled me to write and rewrite until we got it right. My appreciation is boundless.

To my close friend and neighbor Hindy Sirkis, whose finishing touch has enhanced every recipe.

To my parents (ע״ה), Dovid Hersh and Mattel (Mollie) Lando — who raised me in a home that may have been lacking in material wealth but was so steeped in all the right values that I never felt I was missing anything. Their mesiras nefesh — for Shabbos, for chinuch habanim and for acheinu b'nei Yisrael was immeasurable and has left its imprint on all their descendants, and IY"H will continue to do so, till time immemorial.

To my children and their families. You have always been my on-target critics and my biggest fans. It's a joy and zechus to be your mother.

An especial thanks to my daughter Miriam who extended herself beyond belief to help formulate the original recipes. To my granddaughter Mati Dick (Lakewood) who ran my test kitchen, quantified recipes and gave suggestions. She was ably assisted by her sister Chaya Gitty. And to my granddaughter Raitzy Godfrey whom I enlisted time and again to help me quantify all the time-consuming recipes. She graciously stood in my kitchen and closed myriad kreplach, etc. without complaint.

To my husband Nochum. Without his encouragement, I would never have undertaken this, or any other project. I am honored to be his wife and I pray the Aibishter will further bless us with children, grandchildren and great-grandchildren who are lomdei Torah, tzaddikim, and baalei middos tovos.

Judi Dick

Adar 5766

Introduction

Another Jewish cookbook? Why?

Fooled you! It's *not* a cookbook. It's a *storybook* with some great recipes.

If you insist on thinking about it as a cookbook, that's o.k., because it is chock full of great recipes. But this is not your typical cookbook. This one is different. It's made with *spices!* No, not those from the spice rack, but the spices of stories from the vast treasury of our Jewish heritage: stories that can make you laugh and stories that can make you think; stories that can nourish the spirit just as recipes nourish the body; stories that can add a unique flavor to food; stories that can extend the enjoyment of a dish far beyond the time when the taste has faded from the palate.

Food has always occupied a pivotal place in Jewish culture. The traditional *Ess, ess, mein kind* (eat, eat, my child) was one of the ways in which Jewish mothers expressed their love for their children. Food was symbolic, as with the special dishes of the festivals, and was also a vehicle of Divine service: "My offering, My food for My fires, My satisfying aroma shall you offer to Me" (*Numbers* 28:2).

It's the attitude that counts! People swear that talking to their plants can enhance their growth. Similarly, the attitude in food preparation may add more taste to the food. While our taste buds may detect only the physical ingredients in the food, our sensitive minds may be able to detect the warmth and caring that went into its preparation.

Nothing communicates as effectively as stories. Associating stories with recipes may animate one's spirit, eliciting a chuckle or providing a thoughtful insight. And the treasury of Jewish folklore abounds in such stories. Relating the story that accompanied the recipe may also stimulate pleasant dialogue among the guests. There is no question about it. Food tastes better when one is in an upbeat mood.

Of course, food is for nourishment, and the more attractive and pleasant tasting it is, the better the digestion. But food can be even more than physically nourishing. The stories, traditions, and folklore associated with food can give it more meaning.

Special days in the Jewish calendar are often associated with certain foods. There are fascinating traditions about these days and about some of the foods.We will note some of these interesting customs and practices.

It is our hope, therefore, that this storybook/cookbook may make the food taste better and the participants feel happier.

Stories

Stories are a powerful method of communication. The Maggid of Dubnow's stories and parables elucidated very profound concepts. Stories are a way to convey concepts not only to children, but to adults as well.

Some stories are about us. That is, an individual can identify with someone or some incident in the story. However, the point in the story may be such that a person will resist identifying himself in the story. When a person is able to apply the story's message to himself, that indicates spiritual progress. So, here is a story about a story.

Shortly before his death, the Baal Shem Tov gathered his disciples and gave each one a mission to accomplish. To one he said, "Your assignment is to travel all over Europe and relate what you saw and heard here." Seeing the disciple's disappointment, the Baal Shem Tov said, "There will come a time when you will know that your mission has been fulfilled, and then you will not have to do any more traveling."

The disciple carried out his assignment faithfully, traveling to Jewish communities throughout Europe, telling stories about the Baal Shem Tov. Once, in an Italian town, he was told that a wealthy nobleman there paid a golden ducat for a new story.

The disciple went to the nobleman's mansion, and was greeted very warmly. However, he was shocked to realize that his mind had gone blank, and he could not recall even one of the many stories he knew. The nobleman said, "You are undoubtedly weary from traveling. Have something to eat and rest overnight. Your memory will come back."

But the disciple's memory did not recover. After two days he told the nobleman that there was no point in his remaining any longer. As he was about to leave, he said, "Something just came to my mind. It is not much of a story, but, as it is the only thing I remember, I will tell it to you.

"One day, the Baal Shem Tov told me that he wished me to accompany him to a town in Turkey. We boarded the wagon, and the Baal Shem Tov told his driver, Alexi, to face backward. The horses then took off at a supernatural speed, and we found ourselves in a town in Turkey. The Baal Shem Tov secured a room in the Jewish quarter.

"This was Easter week, during which Jews barricaded themselves in their homes, because the anti-Semitic passion was intense. The Christians called the Jews 'god-killers,' and in retaliation, killed a Jew during that week.

"Imagine my astonishment when the Baal Shem Tov threw open the shutters, revealing himself to the passing crowd. Soon we noticed a procession led by the bishop. The Baal Shem Tov turned to me, saying, 'Go tell the bishop I wish to see him.'

"I could not believe my ears. Did the Master wish me to be killed? But the Baal Shem Tov was adamant, and, risking my life, I went out and reached the bishop just as he was about to ascend the platform. In a broken voice I told him that the Baal Shem Tov wished to see him. The bishop appeared shaken, then said, 'I will come after the service.'

"The bishop indeed came, and he and the Baal Shem Tov were secluded for three hours. After the bishop left, the Baal Shem Tov said that we could return home.

"That's not much of a story," the disciple said, "but that is all I can remember."

The nobleman broke into tears. He cried out, "Oh, how I have been waiting for you! I recognized you the moment you came here. You see, I was that bishop.

"I was orphaned as a child, and although the community did care for me, I was unhappy with my lot. When the church told me that they would give me whatever I desired if I would convert, I could not withstand the temptation, and I abandoned the faith of my fathers.

"I was bright and diligent, and became a priest. Then I was elevated to the position of bishop. I participated in the persecution of my people, even with the annual killing of a Jew during Easter week.

"The night before you came, I dreamt of my father, who said that it was time to return to my faith. When you appeared, I realized that this was not a coincidence.

"During my meeting with the Baal Shem Tov, I confessed my sins. I did not think there was any possibility of *teshuvah* for me. The Baal Shem Tov said that no person was ever beyond *teshuvah*. He told me to sell my belongings and go to a distant town where I could not be recognized. I was to give much *tzedakah*, observe all the mitzvos scrupulously, and pray to Hashem for forgiveness.

"The Baal Shem Tov said, 'One day, when you will hear your own story, you will know you have been forgiven.'

"When you were unable to remember any stories, I realized that Hashem had not yet accepted my *teshuvah*. I have been praying and crying all day and all night, pleading for forgiveness. Now that you remembered and told me this story, I know that Hashem has accepted my *teshuvah*."

So, this was a story about a story. And the message? When you can identify with a story and can recognize the character faults it describes as being your own, then you will know that you have been forgiven.

We hope you thoroughly enjoy the recipes in the book. As you will see, they are indeed tasty. However, we cannot equal the culinary skills of the water-carrier's wife who served food with a special ingredient.

Toward the end of his life, R' Elimelech of Lizhensk ate very little. His son, R' Elazar, pleaded with him to take more nutrition. R' Elimelech said, "If I could have the soup cooked by the water-carrier's wife, I would eat it."

R' Elimelech once went to visit the water-carrier, who was one of the hidden *tzaddikim*.

"Please serve something for our great guest," the water-carrier asked his wife.

Because of their poverty, the wife found there was nothing in the kitchen to serve. She then put a pot of water on the fire and said, "Master of the universe! I have nothing to serve the great *tzaddik*. But You have everything. Please put some of the fruits of Gan Eden into this pot."

When the water-carrier's wife brought in the "soup," and served R' Elimelech, he said, "Why, this soup has the taste of Gan Eden!"

The taste of Gan Eden is reserved for us after 120 years, but we hope you will find these recipes enjoyable. *Ess gezunt!*

A Spiritual Activity

In Judaism, food has a spiritual status. The meat of the sin-offerings that were brought in the Temple was eaten by the *Kohanim* (priests), and (assuming that the penitent did *teshuvah*) the sin was erased. The Talmud says that inasmuch as we no longer have the Temple, a person's table is equivalent to the Altar. This can be understood in two ways. (1) A person invites the poor to eat at his table, which entails the great mitzvos of *tzedakah* (charity) and *hachnassas orchim* (hospitality), and (2) the person eats with the intent that the food should provide the requisite nutrition that will enable him to do mitzvos.

Providing the needy with food is a great mitzvah. The Talmud relates that the wife of one of the sages was even more meritorious than her husband, because she gave poor people food with which they could overcome their hunger at once, whereas the husband gave them money as *tzedakah*, with which they would have to purchase food. The wife's help was of immediate assistance.

People who are blessed with adequate food should remember that there are families that are destitute. The Torah repeatedly commands us to remember the poor, the widows, and the orphans, and to provide for their needs.

One chassid who was destitute importuned his Rebbe for a *berachah* (blessing) that he be prosperous. The Rebbe said that he would bless him, but first the Rebbe gave the chassid money and said, "You are to buy the finest delicacies, and you must eat them in the presence of your children. However, you may not, under any circumstances, allow the children to eat of this food."

The man did as he was instructed, but when he saw his hungry children looking longingly at the food, he could not swallow it. He would have preferred to eat rocks.

When he returned, the Rebbe said, "I will bless you with prosperity, but how will you be able to enjoy your wealth when you know there are so many people who lack even the essentials of life?"

The chassid did prosper, and gave *tzedakah* lavishly. He rarely ate at home, preferring to eat in the soup kitchen he had funded for the poor. He often slept in the *hekdesh* (the community shelter for the homeless). The Rebbe knew that the only way to truly empathize with the poor is to experience what they feel.

R' Nachum of Chernobyl would travel among towns and villages, raising money to ransom Jews from dungeons in which the *poritzim* (feudal lords) had imprisoned them. R' Nachum was once the victim of an anti-Semitic plot and was imprisoned.

R' Zev of Zhitomir, one of R' Nachum's peers, visited him in prison. He said, "The Torah tells us that Hashem commanded the patriarch Abraham to leave his home and travel to Canaan. Abraham is famous for his *gemilas chasadim* (acts of kindness), providing food and shelter to wayfarers. Hashem said to him, 'What you are doing is indeed praiseworthy, but you really cannot appreciate the needs of a wayfarer unless you have

experienced them. Therefore, leave your home and become a wayfarer yourself; then you will understand their needs.'

"So it is with you, R' Nachum. You have indeed been steadfast in redeeming Jews from prison, but in order to really persevere in this mitzvah, you must experience what it is like to be in prison. That is why you are here."

In the days of yore, it was considered virtuous to fast as an act of penitence. Chassidic authorities said that fasting is virtuous only if it does not weaken a person and curtail his ability to study Torah and do the mitzvos. They were also concerned that a person who inflicts hunger on himself might become vain, thinking, "Look what a *tzaddik* I am." R' Yisrael of Kozhnitz said, "I'd rather that a person pretend that he fasts all week in order that people should think him to be a *tzaddik*, than for him to actually fast all week and deceive *himself* into believing that he is a *tzaddik*." Ramchal (Rabbi Moshe Chaim Luzzatto) in *Mesillas Yesharim* says that true piety is refining one's *middos* (character traits) rather than in fasting.

One of the Rebbes said, "You sinned by doing improper acts with your hands, speaking *lashon hara* (defamatory speech) with your tongue, or listening to *lashon hara* with your ears. You sinned with your eyes by looking at improper things. Why are you fasting and punishing your stomach? It did no wrong."

A man who confessed to having committed a number of sins asked R' Mordechai of Lechovitz what he must do as penance. R' Mordechai said that he would instruct him what he must do, but on the condition that he promise to faithfully follow the instructions. The man pledged to do so, expecting that he would be ordered to fast and engage in self-mortification.

R' Mordechai said, "For the entire year, you must eat the finest delicacies. Avail yourself of the most comfortable furniture for your home. Do not deny yourself any comforts whatsoever. Indulge yourself in every way imagineable At the end of the year, come back to me."

The man did as he was told, but when he ate the delicious food, he thought "What right have I to this pleasure? Because of my sinfulness, I deserve to eat hot coals." When he slept in a comfortable bed, he thought, "I don't deserve this. I should be torturing myself, sleeping on a bed of nails," and he would cry himself to sleep in remorse. The agony he experienced in indulgence was far worse than he would have experienced had he fasted.

My father used to cite the verse, "May goodness and kindness pursue me all the days of my life" (*Psalms* 23:6). He commented: "To be pursued means that one is fleeing from something. But why would anyone flee from goodness and kindness?" The above story illustrates that experiencing goodness and kindness can indeed be agonizing. The psalmist, therefore, said to Hashem, "If You wish to punish me, do so with goodness and kindness."

Eating in order to be in optimum health so that one can properly serve Hashem is a mitzvah. The Baal Shem Tov prayed that he be shown the individual with whom he would share Gan Eden (Paradise). In a dream, the identity of the person was revealed to him.

The Baal Shem Tov traveled to this person's locale and asked to stay in his home so that he could observe how he served Hashem. To the Baal Shem Tov's great astonishment, he did not see the man studying Torah or *davening* with fervor or displaying any manifest acts of devotion. The only unusual thing he noticed was that this man ate a great deal.

"Why do you eat so much?" the Baal Shem Tov asked. "You must know it is not beneficial. Do you really have a ravenous appetite?"

"Not at all," the man said. "I often must force myself to eat. But I eat this much in order that I should be big and strong. You see, my father was once kidnaped by some *goyim*. They employed numerous tactics to force him to convert. My father was a frail person. They beat him mercilessly, until he was not able to tolerate the pain.

"I decided that this would never happen to me. I will make myself so strong that if anyone tries to force me to give up my G-d, I will be able to beat them to a pulp. That is why I eat so much."

The Baal Shem Tov said, "Now I understand this simple person's greatness. Every bite of food he takes is for the sake of *Kiddush Hashem* (sanctifying the Name of G-d)."

Yom Tov — Eruv Tavshilin

As you know, it is permissible to cook on Yom Tov. However, it is permissible to cook only for that particular day. If, for example, Yom Tov occurs on Tuesday and Wednesday, one may cook on Tuesday for Tuesday's meals, but not for Wednesday's meals.

If Yom Tov occurs on Friday, and one wishes to prepare the Shabbos meals, it is permissible to do so with the ritual of *eruv tavshilin* (lit., "a mixing of cooking").

The prohibition of cooking food on one day of Yom Tov for another day is of Rabbinic origin. The sages, therefore, amended their prohibition to enable people to prepare food for Shabbos. Otherwise, if Yom Tov occurred on Thursday and Friday, the food for Shabbos would have to be prepared on Wednesday, and there would be no way to have hot food on Shabbos.

However, the amendment calls for the ritual of *eruv tavshilin.* Before the onset of Yom Tov, one takes a challah (or a roll or a matzoh) and a cooked item (fish, meat, or egg), and designates this as the *eruv.* The *berachah* for the *eruv* can be found in the *siddur.*

There are two opinions in the Talmud concerning this ritual: (1) By setting aside the *eruv*, you will be reminded not to prepare only for Yom Tov and forget about Shabbos, and (2) the food of the *eruv* can be symbolic of having begun the cooking for Shabbos before Yom Tov, so that on Yom Tov you will merely be continuing the preparation.

Usually the rabbi makes an *eruv* for the entire *kehillah*, just in case someone forgot to do so. However, the rabbi's *eruv* can be relied upon for only one time. If one forgets a second time, one may not rely on the rabbi's *eruv.* In that case, one may not cook for Shabbos on Yom Tov, and one should get oneself invited to a friend's home for Shabbos.

Why Round Challahs on Yom Tov?

Although the Shabbos challahs are braided, the Yom Tov challahs are traditionally round.

Some say that the braided challahs on Shabbos symbolize the twelve loaves of the showbread in the Temple. Each challah was braided with six strands of dough, so together there were twelve strands. Since on Yom Tov there is no need to symbolize the showbread (which was offered only on Shabbos), there was no need to braid separate strands.

Others say that the custom of using round challahs began with Rosh Hashanah, and that the circular shape symbolizes infinity, because a circle has no beginning and no end. Since in our Rosh Hashanah prayers we "enthrone" G-d, acknowledging

Him as the Creator and Sovereign of the universe, we have round challahs, representing His infinity. Others say that the circular challahs are reminiscent of a crown, representing the "enthronement." Still others add that the upward spiral shape of the circular challahs indicates our hope that our prayers will ascend to heaven.

Although the symbolism of the circular challahs relates to Rosh Hashanah, the circular shape was extended to all other festivals.

Pleasant Memories

The Torah states, "Abraham was old, he came along with the days, and Hashem blessed Abraham with everything" (*Genesis* 24:1). The usual translation of *ba bayamim*, "he was well along in years," is a free translation. The literal meaning of *ba bayamim* is "he came along with the days," and this conveys an important, not to be ignored, meaning. Your mind does not allow memories to fade, but stores them as treasures.

Scattered throughout the narrative of this book, there are memories of my past. Certainly there were unpleasant episodes in my life, but those can be thrown into the ocean as we do with our sins at *tashlich.* The pleasant memories should be retrieved because they are positive feelings, and *positive feelings are a source of energy.*

I can recall, perhaps when I was 6, sitting with my father Shabbos morning in shul. In that shul, the *chazzan* would recite *Keil Adon,* but not sing it. My father drew me under his *tallis* and sang *Keil Adon* with me. I can remember the warm feeling of my father taking me under his *tallis* when the *Kohanim* said the priestly blessing. That was seventy years ago! But I can summon these moments and enjoy them. Whether we have few or many such memories, whatever we have is stored away in our minds, and we can retrieve them.

Hashem blessed Abraham. He gave him the ability to "come along with the days." We know that the Patriarch experienced much suffering, but he was able to bring his past along with him as a blessing.

You can do that, too. The Yamim Tovim are especially laden with pleasant experiences.

One commentary noted that we refer to the Yamim Tovim as *moadim lesimchah,* festivals *for* joy, rather than as *moadei simchah,* festivals *of* joy. This tells us that the festivals should supply us with joy all year round.

So apply this in two ways: (1) Recall the pleasant events of the Yamim Tovim, and (2) make sure that you maximize the joy of the Yamim Tovim for your children. Pleasant memories, a happy nostalgia, is one of the greatest gifts you can give them.

Abraham J. Twerski

Adar 5766

Foreword

Most recipes from the alte heim did not use expensive ingredients — people had large families and small incomes. Nevertheless, the ingredients they did use were of good quality. My mother always said — "Az mir leigt arayn gutte zachen, nehmt men arois" — If you put in good things, that's what you take out.

So we have rule #1 — good ingredients. To this we must add something that is in short supply nowadays — time. Many of the old-fashioned recipes derived their taste from the long cooking process that mellowed the flavors. In our day we are used to instant gratification and expect things to be done in no time at all. On a day-to-day basis this works, as it should. But for that special occasion where we want to relish a taste of the alte heim (the old country), time is one important element, and in the long run it's a worthwhile investment.

A majority of the recipes are those I learned from my mother. So if a recipe uses the first person — it's me. If it's someone else's recipe, I have given credit where credit is due — but I have prepared all these recipes. They have all been tested and are presented as if you were standing beside me in my kitchen and watching how I make the various foods.

Although the recipes have been placed under specific categories, these are not meant to be menu-plans. Most of them are applicable any time of the year — with the exception of Passover (Pesach). Take the time to read each recipe through from beginning to end before attempting it. This is a good rule of thumb always.

I hope you enjoy reading and making all or some of these. My husband claims that he married me because whenever he came by the house smelled so inviting and the refreshments were

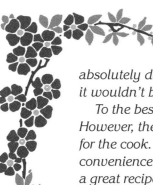

absolutely delicious. (Yes, he did taste the rugelach — he figured if the shidduch didn't work out at least it wouldn't be a total loss.)

To the best of my ability, I have tried to present authentic recipes as they were made in Europe. However, these have been adapted, using modern appliances (mixer, food processor, etc.) to make it easier for the cook. I have also occasionally used canned or ready-made ingredients — sometimes simply for convenience or because by the time I saw my mother making these recipes, she had added them to make a great recipe even more memorable.

Please note the following staple ingredients used in my kitchen, and my comments on the ingredients listed on the recipes:

▸ kosher salt unless otherwise indicated (kosher salt is half as salty as table salt — i.e., 2 teaspoons kosher salt equals 1 teaspoon table salt.)
▸ Idaho potatoes
▸ Spanish onions. Spanish onions are not ideal for sautéeing — they release too much water. Nevertheless, I use only them because of their more intense flavor — it just takes a few extra minutes for the water to evaporate and the sautéeing to begin.
▸ extra-large eggs
▸ all-purpose unbleached flour unless otherwise indicated; 5 lbs. of flour equals 16¼ -17 cups
▸ shortening refers to Crisco™ or other solid vegetable shortening
oil refers to vegetable oil
brown sugar is dark brown sugar unless otherwise indicated
▸ I measure dry ingredients in a measuring cup and liquid ingredients in a glass measuring cup. I look at it at eye level to make sure it's the right amount.

- all cookie sheets are largest size or disposable unless otherwise indicated. All 9"x13" pans are regular or disposable (which are actually 8"x12") unless otherwise indicated.
- cold water is drawn from the tap (not refrigerated)
- margarine and cream cheese should be taken out of the refrigerator and left to soften but not to over-soften
- vanilla refers to pure vanilla extract. If you find pure vanilla is too expensive, use vanilla sugar. Do not use imitation vanilla extract, rather delete the vanilla from the recipe.
- pepper means white pepper. I don't like to use black pepper because of the black specks it leaves in my kugels, even though black pepper may be more to your taste.
- margarine is parve and unsalted
- apples are Cortland unless otherwise indicated
- T = Tablespoon; t = teaspoon
- nut pieces should always be toasted in a preheated 300° oven for 10-15 minutes. Stir often and check as some nuts have a higher fat content and burn easily. Let cool.

Do not be afraid to experiment — that's the beauty of heimishe cooking. If you don't have precisely the right size pot or quite enough of a filling, improvise — you may come up with a winner (when you do, please let me know).

Table of Contents

and Easy Carrots / Bletlach for Lukshen or Blintzes / Potato Chremslach / Onion Soufflé / Cholent Kugel / Vegetable Kugel / Confetti Vegetable Kugel / No-fail Potato Kugel / Sweet Potato Kugel — Eggless / Fricasse / Cholent — Rabachts / Chicken with Duck Sauce / Applesauce / Pear Dessert / Strawberry Fluff / Coffee Ice Cream / Chocolate Nut Sponge Cake / Super Duper Chocolate Cake / Pesach Nut Cake

Carrying cholent to the baker's oven on Friday afternoon, to be kept hot for the Shabbos day meal. Bialystok, 1932

Shabbos

"G-d blessed the seventh day and sanctified it because on it He rested from all His work that G-d created" (*Genesis* 2:3).

Shabbos is not just a day of rest to recharge one's batteries for the coming week. That would make Shabbos subordinate to the workweek. G-d was not exhausted from the work of creation. No, Shabbos is *a blessed and sanctified day*, on which the family eats all the *seudos* together, sings Shabbos songs, and hears words of Torah wisdom. It is a day on which we spend more time in prayer. Free from work and restricted from time-killing distractions, parents and children can get to know each other. Traditionally, parents reviewed with their children what they had learned during the week. Family, close friends and those new to Torah observance are invited, often for meals, and interpersonal bonds are strengthened. Shabbos is a spiritual day.

Why would a spiritual day be celebrated with the gustatory delights of gefilte fish, kugel, chicken soup and roast chicken? This question was posed to the Baal Shem Tov, who answered with a parable:

A prince once committed an offense for which he was banished from the royal palace and exiled to a distant village in the kingdom, where he lived a very austere life. After a lengthy period of time, he received a message from his father that he was pardoned and could return home. This news made him so happy that he could not restrain himself from singing and dancing. However, if he were suddenly to sing and dance, the townsfolk would think he had gone mad. He, therefore, gathered some of the townsfolk together for a party, and provided them with a lavish meal. Satiated with food and drink, they arose to sing and dance, and the prince joined them. The townsfolk were dancing because they were merry with overindulgence, whereas the prince danced because he was returning to the royal palace.

"A person," the Baal Shem Tov said, "is a composite being, comprised of a physical body and a spiritual *neshamah*. On Shabbos and Yom Tov, the *neshamah* wishes to engage in prayer and Torah study to bring it in closer contact with G-d. However, the body does not appreciate this, and is a barrier to spirituality. We, therefore, provide the body with things it can enjoy, so that it, too, will be happy, and will not stand in the way of the *neshamah's* quest for and celebration of spiritual delight."

But we must remember what Shabbos is really all about. The Baal Shem Tov gave a second parable:

A king celebrated the anniversary of his coronation by opening the palace to visitors and providing abundant refreshments for them. A peasant walked by, partook of the food and went on his way. Wise people took the opportunity to go into the palace and see the king.

We partake of the Shabbos delicacies for the reason given by the Baal Shem Tov. However, we should have the wisdom not to be satisfied with this like the peasant, but like the wise men, enter the palace to come close to the king.

And so tradition has transmitted to us many tasty foods for Shabbos and the Festivals. We indeed partake of them, but we should not lose sight of their purpose. Having appeased the body with these delicious foods, we should dedicate ourselves to the spiritual aspects of Shabbos and the Festivals.

Shabbos is ushered in by the lighting of candles. The Talmud says that the candles represent *shalom bayis*, peace and harmony in the home.

Light cannot be confined. If you light a candle for yourself, others can benefit from the light. If you light a candle for others, you can enjoy the light, too. The Shabbos candles should characterize all our actions. We should avoid self-centeredness and behave in a manner that is beneficial to all. We should also realize that when we do something for others, we enrich ourselves.

In some families, it is customary to add a candle for each child. When I discovered this, I was elated that our home was a bit brighter because of my existence. Furthermore, the brightness of my candle did not wane if my report card was not excellent, or even if I misbehaved. The light of my existence was unconditional, and I could understand that my parent's love for me was likewise unconditional.

Women pray at candle-lighting for the health and welfare of the family and for the speedy recovery of those who may be suffering. Candle-lighting time is propitious for prayer. One young man said that he hesitated to look at his mother when she lit the Shabbos candles. "It reminded me of the prohibition to look at the *Kohanim* (priests) when they pronounce the priestly blessing, because the Divine Presence rests on their hands. That's how I felt about my mother. When she prayed before the lit candles, the Divine Presence rested on her."

Although the wife lights the candles, it is recommended that the husband prepare the candles. This is to symbolize that both together bring the light of Shabbos into the home.

We sing *Shalom Aleichem,* welcoming the heavenly angels who visit our home on Friday night and convey G-d's blessings. In turn, we bless our children. How wonderful if all children could understand that blessings flow from their parents! Our generation could certainly benefit from this concept. We then chant *Aishes Chayil,* a Woman of Valor (*Proverbs* 31:10-31), extolling the virtues of the wife and mother .

The *Kiddush* (Sanctification) is then recited over a goblet of wine or grape juice, and we attest that the world was created by G-d in six days. A created world is a world with a purpose, in which each person has a mission. The secular position that the world came into being by some sort of freak accident makes the world a place without an ultimate purpose for its existence. It is meaningless to look for the ultimate purpose of one's existence if the world as a whole has no purpose for existing.

Shabbos is a testimony that G-d created the world for a purpose known only to Him. In this world, I and every other human being have a unique mission. Furthermore, no one else in history, nor all of mankind together, can fulfill my personal mission. Every individual is significant; and I am significant. Shabbos gives meaning to the universe and to my life as well.

There are, of course, varying degrees of the spiritual observance of Shabbos. One *tzaddik*, who did not sleep all of Friday night, explained, "A *shomer* is a guard, a sentry. A sentry dares not fall asleep while on duty. I want to be a *shomer Shabbos*, so I must stay awake."

R' Nachum of Chernobyl was sitting with a group of students on Friday night. After he left the room, the candle went out, and one of the students called in a *Shabbos goy* to relight it. When R' Nachum returned, he groped his way around the room as if in the dark. A candle that was lit on Shabbos, even by a non-Jew, did not provide any light for him.

Preparing for Shabbos

There is a tradition that the husband should assist in the preparations for Shabbos. Many of our *tzaddikim* would assist in the kitchen. It is also customary to sharpen the challah knife on Friday (admittedly a bit difficult with serrated knives).

How can I describe the fragrance in the house of my childhood on Friday morning? You know what a rose smells like, but I challenge you to describe its fragrance. If you have not been in a home where the combined aroma of the challos baking and the gefilte fish and chicken soup simmering fills the air with an intoxicating fragrance, you simply cannot know it nor even imagine it. This was accompanied by the anticipation that in just a few hours, I would be able to dip the fresh, hot challah into the steaming (or if preferred jellied) gefilte fish broth.

I learned the technique of self-hypnosis, and when in a trance, I can take myself back to relive events of the past. I often revisit my home on Friday morning, and can reexperience the unforgettable magic of Erev Shabbos.

Shortly after noon, the table was covered with a white tablecloth and my father would set up the candelabra with the Shabbos candles. Beginning early on Friday the house was pervaded by the Shabbos atmosphere. I know that there are observant families where Shabbos preparations are hurriedly done before candle-lighting time. While this is in full compliance with halachah, they're missing half the fun and much of the beauty.

Friday afternoon, my father took me to the *mikveh* (*ritualarium*). I came to understand that the *mikveh* was a preparation for the sanctity of Shabbos. Many years later, the concept that *mikveh* is a prelude to holiness had an important implication.

It is customary for a father to bless the children before *Kiddush*. The blessing for the sons is, "May G-d make you like Ephraim and Menashe," and for the daughters, "May G-d make you like Sarah, Rebecca, Rachel and Leah." This is followed by the priestly blessing, "May G-d bless you and safeguard you. May G-d illuminate His countenance for you and be gracious to you. May G-d turn His countenance to you and establish peace for you."

It is noteworthy that whereas the blessing for the daughters is that they be like the Matriarchs, the blessing for the sons is that they be like Ephraim and Menashe, rather than like the Patriarchs — Abraham, Isaac and Jacob. This is because Jacob designated that the blessing should be that of Ephraim and Menashe (*Genesis* 48:20).

There is another message in this blessing. Although Menashe was the older of the two, Jacob gave priority to the younger Ephraim. In contrast to the sons of Jacob, who were envious of Joseph's favoritism, Menashe showed no signs of displeasure, even though Jacob said that his younger brother would surpass him. Ephraim and Menashe are thus symbolic of the ideal sibling relationship.

A Divine Reprieve

In spite of his encyclopedic Torah scholarship, the great Gaon of Vilna did not serve as a *posek* in the community. That position was filled by another Torah scholar.

One Friday afternoon, a woman ran into a problem of kashrus in the preparation of the Shabbos food. Since the *posek* lived at some distance, she sent her child to the Gaon, who lived nearby, for a ruling. Inasmuch as it was Friday afternoon and there was limited time to prepare food, the Gaon gave a ruling: the food was not kosher.

When the husband came home, he ran to the local *posek* with the problem and told him of the Gaon's ruling. After some deliberation, the *posek* ruled that the food was indeed kosher.

The *posek* went to the Gaon and said, "My master! I do not have a fraction of your Torah knowledge. However, I am the community authority on halachah. I know that you disagree with me on this ruling, but my authority in the community should not be undermined. I respectfully request that you defer to my ruling, and to demonstrate this, that you accompany me tonight to this man's home and we will both eat of the food that I ruled to be kosher."

The Gaon acquiesced, and that night they both went to the man's home, where they were served the food. Before the Gaon could lift his fork, one of the Shabbos candles sputtered, and a drop of the wax fell into the Gaon's plate. Inasmuch as candles in those days were made of tallow, the food in the Gaon's plate was rendered *tereifah*. The Gaon was thus spared from eating food that he had ruled to be *tereifah*, and the *posek's* authority was not undermined.

When word of this incident spread, the Gaon's followers hailed it as a miracle, due to the Gaon's great *kedushah*. In his profound humility, the Gaon dismissed this, saying, "The Talmud refers to the Shabbos candles as 'lights of *shalom.*' The candle simply fulfilled its function, preserving a peaceful relationship between myself and the *posek.*"

Reason for Gratitude

One Friday night, my wife and I were in Beilinson Hospital in Israel, holding vigil over my grandson who had been seriously injured in an accident. It was with heavy hearts that we ate the food that had been provided for us. I said to my wife, "When we are at home, sitting in comfort at the Shabbos table, free of serious worries and enjoying the Shabbos delicacies, if we don't get up and dance for joy, we are ingrates."

I was reminded of a story. One Friday night, the Baal Shem Tov was in high spirits. After Shabbos, he took several of his disciples and traveled to Apt, where he sent for the bookbinder, Shabsi.

Shabsi approached the Baal Shem Tov with great trepidation. "Tell me what you did this past Friday night," the Baal Shem Tov said.

Shabsi began, "Weeks may go by when no one brings any books to bind. I had not earned any money for several weeks, and on Friday we had no money to buy the bare necessities for Shabbos: candles, wine, food. I told my wife that I refuse to accept any *tzedakah*. If it pleases G-d that we should have a barren Shabbos, then it is all right with me. I left to shul even before noon, to review the Torah portion of the week.

"Having nothing to prepare for the meals, my wife thought that she could at least give the house a thorough cleaning in honor of Shabbos. Unbeknown to me, in a crevice she found a pearl that had been sewn onto her wedding dress many years earlier. She took it to town and sold it, and bought all the provisions for Shabbos.

"Thinking that I would have nothing to eat, I did not rush home after services. When I finally did go home, I was surprised to see that there was light in my house. When I entered and saw the wine and challah on the table, I assumed that my wife had not been able to withstand a barren Shabbos, and must have accepted *tzedakah*. I was disappointed that she had gone against my wishes. My wife read the expression on my face and told me that she had not accepted *tzedakah*, but had found a pearl. I was overjoyed that I would have a proper Shabbos without taking *tzedakah*, and I felt that G-d had arranged that my wife should find this pearl from her wedding dress after so many years. I could not contain my elation. My wife and I danced around the table for a long time. If this was an inappropriate thing for me to do, I am sorry."

The Baal Shem Tov said, "Shabsi, you know that when you come home from shul Friday night, heavenly angels accompany you. When you danced with your wife around the table because of Shabbos joy, the angels danced along with you, and it pleased G-d greatly.

"You merit a great reward. What is your wish?"

Shabsi replied, "We have been married many years, but we are childless. My greatest wish is to have a child."

The Baal Shem Tov said, "This year, you will be blessed with a son who will have a great *neshamah*. You are to name him after me, Yisrael."

That child grew up to be R' Yisrael, the Maggid of Kozhnitz, one of the greatest chassidic masters. He was the reward for feeling the true joy of Shabbos.

When we sit at our Shabbos table in comfort and enjoy the Shabbos delicacies, we should be ecstatic with joy.

The Magic Ingredient of Love

According to tradition, the manna had a magical quality: one could taste in it whatever one desired. There is a magical quality within our means that can affect how we taste our food: that quality is *love*.

One of my favorite stories is that of the disciples of the Baal Shem Tov who one Friday night saw a rather simple person whose face radiated with light. "What is this man's secret?" they asked. "Is he so spiritual a person that his face should shine in this manner?" The Baal Shem Tov replied, "Let's follow him home and see."

The man entered a small hut and greeted his wife with a hearty "Good Shabbos!" Peering through the window, the Baal Shem Tov and his disciples saw a sparsely furnished room that testified to the austere conditions of the household. A wooden table was covered with a plain white cloth, and the two candles shed a warm glow. The man sang *Shalom Aleichem*, welcoming the angels with a lively refrain, then sang *Aishes Chayil* (a Woman of Valor). Then he said to his wife, "Please bring the special wine."

The wife brought two loaves of coarse, dark bread. He washed his hands and recited the proper blessing, then chanted the *Kiddush*. (If one has no wine, one may recite the *Kiddush* on bread.) After he ate of the bread, he said, "We have never yet had such a fine wine! Can you please bring in the fish?"

Moments later the wife served him a small portion of beans. "Hm!" he exclaimed, smacking his lips. "This fish is unusually delicious." He sang a Shabbos song and said, "I'm ready for the soup." The wife appeared with another dish of beans. The man complimented his wife, "This soup is simply superb." He sang another Shabbos song and asked, "Can we have the roast meat and *tzimmis*?" Again the wife served him beans. "How wonderful the roast meat and *tzimmis* are," he exclaimed.

The Baal Shem Tov said to his disciples, "Our ancestors in the desert had the manna, a food from heaven, in which they could taste anything they wished. This man's love for G-d, for Shabbos, and for his wife have enabled him to reach a level of spirituality so lofty that he can taste the finest delicacies in a dish of beans."

Is such a level of spirituality attainable? Even if it is not, it is certainly a far cry from complaining that the food was too cold or lacked salt. At the very least, we can certainly send our compliments to the chef and our gratitude to *HaKadosh Baruch Hu* for that which He has provided.

Satisfied With One's Lot

 story similar to the previous one is told about the great Gaon of Vilna, who said that he learned from an old man and woman to be satisfied with one's lot.

Like many other *tzaddikim*, the Gaon took on a self-imposed exile as penance for his sins. (It defies my imagination to even fantasize what kind of "sins" the Gaon may have had.) He often went without food for days.

One Thursday night, the Gaon arrived in a village and went to the local *beis midrash*, where he spent the night in Torah study. After the morning services, when all the worshipers had dispersed, an elderly woman set some food before her husband, an old blind man. The man said to his wife, "There is someone here who has been studying Torah all night. I don't recognize his voice, so he must be a stranger here." The wife responded, "Yes, there is a man with an angelic appearance here."

"Go fetch him to eat with me," the man said.

Initially, the Gaon refused the invitation, seeing that the food was sparse, but the blind man insisted. "Please, we have more than enough food," he urged.

"How do you support yourself?" the Gaon asked.

The man answered, "My wife goes to the flour mill, and the proprietor allows her to gather the flour that has fallen to the floor. That is enough for us." The wife then served them some bread and gruel.

After they ate and *bentsched* (recited the blessing after a meal), the blind man said to the Gaon, "I want you to be my guest for Shabbos. On Friday, my wife flicks (removes the feathers and hairs) the chickens that people buy for Shabbos, and they give her the chicken feet and gizzards, from which she makes delicious soup. We have a sumptuous meal."

On Friday night, the Gaon came to their meager hut. Townspeople stopped by to wish them "Good Shabbos." They sang *zemiros* and discussed the *parashah*. The old couple were elated to have a *talmid chacham* as their Shabbos guest. The Gaon said that he felt that the *Shechinah* (Divine Presence) was in this joyous, humble hut.

"From this old couple," the Gaon said, "I learned how a person can be happy with whatever he has."

Another Magic Ingredient

That Shabbos is more than just a day of rest, of abstinence from work, that it is a day of *kedushah*, blessed by G-d with incomparable *chein* (grace), can be proven scientifically.

On any weekday, take the exact ingredients for *cholent*, and prepare the *cholent* just as you would for Shabbos. Taste it the next day, and you will find that it simply does not taste the same. *Cholent* prepared on Wednesday and eaten Thursday does not have the same aroma or taste as the *cholent* of Shabbos. If that is not valid scientific proof to the *kedushah* of Shabbos, I don't know what is.

The Talmud says that the Roman emperor asked R' Yehoshua ben Chananyah, "Why do your Shabbos foods have that unique fragrance?"

R' Yehoshua answered, "We have a special spice that makes that fragrance."

"May I have some of that wonderful spice?" the emperor asked.

R' Yehoshua answered, "The name of the spice is Shabbos, and it is effective only for one who observes the Sabbath; but for one who does not observe the Sabbath it is not effective" (*Shabbos* 119a).

A similar incident occurred when R' Yehudah HaNasi invited the Roman emperor, Antoninus, for a Shabbos meal, and served him cold food. Antoninus complimented him on the cuisine. Once he invited Antoninus for a weekday meal, and served him hot food. Antoninus said, "The cold food tasted better."

R' Yehudah said, "Yes, there was a special ingredient."

"Why did you not use that ingredient today?" Antoninus asked. "Surely you're not lacking it."

R' Yehudah responded, "That ingredient is Shabbos. It is not available today."

There is a story about a young man who was seduced by the missionaries and convinced to convert. His family was unable to dissuade him, and the rabbi's efforts were futile. Then a friend said to him, "And will the church give you an egg from the *cholent*?" (In this young man's culture, a hard-boiled egg was an ingredient in the *cholent*.) He promptly recanted and remained faithful to Judaism!

Oneg Shabbos

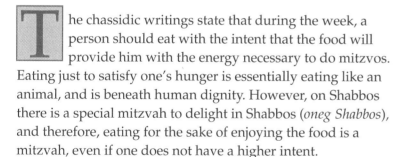

The chassidic writings state that during the week, a person should eat with the intent that the food will provide him with the energy necessary to do mitzvos. Eating just to satisfy one's hunger is essentially eating like an animal, and is beneath human dignity. However, on Shabbos there is a special mitzvah to delight in Shabbos (*oneg Shabbos*), and therefore, eating for the sake of enjoying the food is a mitzvah, even if one does not have a higher intent.

It is customary, before beginning to eat any of the Shabbos foods, to say *lichvod Shabbos kodesh* (this is in honor of the holy Shabbos).

It is traditional to eat egg salad made with onions. The reason for eggs is that they are the traditional food for mourners, and inasmuch as Moses died on Shabbos, we eat eggs as a symbol of mourning for Moses.

The Midrash says that in the manna, one could taste whatever he wished, with the exception of onions and garlic. We use two challos to commemorate the double portion of the manna that was gathered on Friday. Inasmuch as the challos represent the manna, we supplement them with foods containing onions and garlic to provide the tastes that were not found in the manna.

More Precious Than Diamonds

We tell children the Talmudic story of *Yosef Mokir Shabbos* (Joseph who cherished Shabbos), who was rewarded by finding a priceless gem in the fish he bought for Shabbos. However, we must convey to our children that Shabbos is more valuable than gems, and that the true reward for observing Shabbos is "*Shabbos*"!

It has been said that a person who does not take the time to meditate is not much of a human being. The ability to think and contemplate is one of the major distinguishing factors that separate us from lower forms of life. But, given the hectic pace of modern life, who has time to meditate? Even on vacation, many people are in frequent contact with their offices, and the last refuge of respite has been taken from us by the cellular phone. If we were left to our own devices in choosing a period of rest, we would be distracted from meditating 7/24/365.

The Talmud states that G-d said to Moses, "I have a wonderful gift in My treasure house, and I wish to give it to the Children of Israel. Go tell them of it" (*Shabbos* 10b).

Shabbos is indeed a wonderful Divine gift. Shabbos gives us the opportunity to exercise a uniquely human capacity: the ability to meditate. Everything we acquire, even a diamond, is just another possession. Animals, too, have possessions, but they are not able to meditate. Animals have no idea why they live. Human beings can think about the meaning of life, but they must have the time and freedom to think.

Let us teach our children the true value of Shabbos, not only by sharing with them thoughts about Shabbos, but even more importantly, showing how Shabbos can provide us with the dignity of being spiritual people.

Challah:
A Lesson in Sensitivity and Faith

The Friday night meal begins with the *hamotzi* blessing over the challah. Two loaves of challah are covered with a decorative cloth. Why two loaves? Because during our ancestors' forty-year sojourn in the desert, they were sustained by the manna. Every day of the week, each person could gather only one measure, and any excess would spoil by the next morning. However, since manna would not fall on Shabbos, when they gathered the manna on Friday, they found that they each had *two* measures.

The manna symbolism of the challah reminds us that G-d provides a portion for each person, and that greedy accumulation of more than one's share is futile.

But why is the challah covered? Ah! What a beautiful teaching.

In singing the praise of the Land of Israel, the Torah states that it is "a land of wheat, barley, grape, fig, pomegranate, oil-olives and date-honey" (*Deuteronomy* 8:8). Inasmuch as wheat is mentioned before the grape, the rule is that if one partakes of *mezonos* (food made of flour) and of wine, the blessing for the *mezonos* should be recited before the blessing for wine. However, since the *Kiddush* is recited over wine before the meal, the challah *would be humiliated* by being passed over. To avoid the challah "suffering" embarrassment, it is covered during the *Kiddush*.

Of course, the inanimate challah cannot feel humiliation. However, the important teaching of the covered challah is that we must always be sensitive to others' feelings, and assiduously avoid embarrassing anyone.

Why the use of wine or grape juice for *Kiddush?* Some say that it is because of the opinion in the Talmud that the Tree of Knowledge of which Adam sinfully ate was a grapevine. The Arizal said that had Adam, who was created on Friday, waited until Shabbos, he would have been permitted the juice of the grapevine. However, Adam was impatient, and ate the grapes prematurely and without reciting a *berachah* (blessing of gratitude). We, therefore, rectify Adam's sin, as it were, by using wine or grape juice to sanctify the Shabbos, and we recite the appropriate *berachah.* This is also one reason why we begin the *Kiddush* with *yom hashishi* (the sixth day), because it was on the sixth day of creation that Adam ate of the grape.

However, there is also an opinion in the Talmud that the forbidden fruit was actually *wheat.* To satisfy this opinion, we use challah and recite its proper *berachah.*

The challah is also symbolic of the *lechem hapanim* (showbread) that was set in the *Beis HaMikdash* (Holy Temple in Jerusalem) every Shabbos (*Leviticus* 24:5-9). This consisted of twelve unleavened loaves. The showbread miraculously remained fresh all week, and was still warm when it was removed each Shabbos to make room for the new showbread. It is a custom among chassidic Rebbes to have ten small challahs in addition to the two large loaves, to represent the twelve loaves of the showbread. Even without the ten small loaves, it has been said that the two large loaves are each in the shape of the Hebrew letter *vav,* which has the numerical value of 6. Hence two loaves equal the number 12. This is the reason that traditional challos are made from six braids. The *lechem*

mishneh, two loaves, then comprise a total of twelve braids, representative of the *lechem hapanim.*

There is an interesting custom based on the fact that the loaves of showbread that were set on the Table on one Shabbos were eaten by the Kohanim on the following Shabbos. In our home we would use the leftover challah of one Shabbos to make the sweet challah kugel for the next Shabbos.

The Mitzvah of Challah — Message of Hope

In the days of the *Beis HaMikdash,* one of the tithing requirements was to give a portion of the bread dough to the *Kohen* (priest). This tithe was called "challah," and is the origin of the word for the Shabbos bread.

Although we do not give tithes now, it is nevertheless a mitzvah to remove a small portion of the dough, in commemoration of the mitzvah of challah. This small portion is burned, because tithes may not be eaten today.

The reason for this practice is to retain the mitzvah of tithing the challah so that when the Ultimate Redemption occurs and we once again have a *Beis HaMikdash,* we will be accustomed to tithing.

Although it is certainly more convenient to buy challah from the bakery, it is still the practice in many families to bake challah for Shabbos. Whether we bake the challos or buy them, we can greet the Shabbos amid the hope and anticipation of the Ultimate Redemption.

Fish: The Threefold Blessing

I t is traditional to serve fish on Shabbos. Some of the reasons for this practice are:

(1) The letters of Hebrew word for fish, "*dag*," have a numerical value of 7 (*dalet* = 4 and *gimmel* = 3). Inasmuch as Shabbos is the 7th day of the week, a food with the numerical value of 7 is served.

(2) In the account of creation, we find three blessings. "He blessed the fish" (*Genesis* 1:22), "He blessed them "(the human beings, ibid. 1:28), and "G-d blessed the seventh day" (ibid. 2:3). When we eat fish on the seventh day, all three blessings come together. Solomon says, "A string woven of three strands is not easily torn asunder " (*Ecclesiastes* 4:24). Bringing the three blessings together fortifies their power.

There are many varieties of fish. In some families, more than one variety is served. The following story explains one of these customs.

At the table of the Rebbe of Bobov, two varieties of fish are served on Shabbos: marinated fish and gefilte fish.

This practice originated with the Rebbe's ancestor, R' Chaim Halberstam, the *tzaddik* of Sanz. The *tzaddik's* first position as rabbi was in a rather small village, where fresh fish was not always available on Friday. The fish had to be purchased whenever available, sometimes as early as Wednesday. Since they lacked refrigeration, the only way to preserve the fish for Shabbos was to marinate it. If fresh fish happened to be available on Friday, gefilte fish was cooked.

When the *tzaddik* moved to Sanz, fresh fish was always available on Friday. However, since marinated fish had been served regularly on Shabbos, he did not wish to discontinue the practice. Hence many of his descendants serve both varieties.

Farfel: Put the Past Behind You

T he Talmud says that Shabbos is "a semblance of *Olam Haba*," a taste of the delight of the Eternal World.

Certainly, this refers to something that is incomparably greater than the physical delights we experience.

The Midrash cites the phrase in *Genesis* (2:1): "And the heaven and earth were completed," and comments that just as with the onset of Shabbos everything in Creation had been completed and not even the slightest thing was lacking, so should a person feel when Shabbos arrives: everything is complete, there is nothing lacking. There is not the slightest carryover of concern from the previous week. One does not owe any money nor is one worried whether he will receive money owed him. Everything has been paid for. The merchandise one expected has been delivered and is safely stored. One does not worry about where one must go next week. Everything that was to be submitted by a deadline was turned in. The results of the tests one took were received and are favorable. Nothing in one's life is lacking, not even the slightest thing, just as G-d's creation was totally complete.

We may have some difficulty in imagining so blissful a state, but if we could achieve it, it would indeed be "a semblance of *Olam Haba*." Our minds would then be free for total devotion to spiritual pursuits.

Although a person should always have an attitude of *teshuvah*, Shabbos is particularly propitious for forgiveness. The Talmud says that if a person observes Shabbos properly, all his sins are forgiven (*Koheles Rabbah* 4). Inasmuch as a person receives an additional soul (*neshamah yeseirah*) on Shabbos, it is appropriate that one cleanse oneself of all one's wrongdoings in preparation for this enhanced *kedushah*.

To assist us in experiencing this heavenly feeling, my mother would serve *farfel tzimmis* on Friday night, and would refer to it as "Baal Shem's *tzimmis*." The Yiddish word *farfallen* means "it is in the past, over and done with." As my mother served the *farfel tzimmis*, she would say, "Whatever was until now is *farfallen*," as a reminder that we should now put the entire past behind us and not bring any concerns of the workweek into Shabbos.

On Rosh Hashanah, it is customary to eat certain foods whose names are symbolic. For example, we eat a carrot *tzimmis* because in Yiddish the word for carrots is *mehren*, which means "to be fruitful and multiply," and we ask for Hashem's blessing when we eat *mehren*. (In the time of the Talmud, this prayer was said while eating *robia*, which some identify as a legume. *Robia* in Hebrew means "to be fruitful and multiply.") Mother's serving *farfel* followed the same reasoning.

You may enjoy *knaidlach* in your chicken soup, but given the custom of using symbolic foods, many people prefer *lukshen*. Why? Because *lukshen* can be broken up into the Hebrew words *lo kashen*, which means "no hardships." When eating *lukshen* we are reminded to pray for a week free of any hardships.

Kugel: The Secret of Shalom Bayis

A newlywed couple came to Rabbi Yisrael of Kozhnitz. They were each adamant about preserving their respective family traditions, and this resulted in a squabble. In the husband's family, kugel was served at the Shabbos morning *Kiddush* after services, whereas in the wife's family, it was served as part of the Shabbos noon meal. Neither wished to yield.

Rabbi Yisrael suggested that the wife make *two* kugels, one to be served at *Kiddush* and the second during the meal. The second kugel was called the *"shalom bayis"* (harmony in the home) kugel.

My mother always served two kugels on Shabbos: a peppery *lukshen* kugel and a sweet challah kugel. When, as children, we heard the origin of this custom, we absorbed, consciously or subconsciously, the concept that there are ways in which domestic harmony can prevail even when there are differences in opinion. The two kugels may convey a principle of *shalom bayis*. This gives the kugel recipes additional meaning.

(By the way, do you know the origin of the word "kugel"? There is an authentic opinion that it was initially baked in round pans. *Ugal* = round. *K'ugal* means like a circle, i.e., circular in shape. An important piece of trivia, right?)

The Divinely Blessed Kugel

R' Naftali of Ropschitz's wife was extremely frugal, but exceptionally devout. When she *davened*, she was transported into another world.

The rebbetzin would put the bare minimum of *schmaltz* (chicken fat) into the kugel. R' Naftali's entreaties to increase the amount of *schmaltz* in the kugel went unheeded.

One Friday, when the rebbetzin was *davening*, R' Naftali removed the keys from her apron pocket, unlocked the pantry, and put several spoonfuls of *schmaltz* into the kugel. He then returned the keys, and the rebbetzin was completely oblivious to all of this.

Shabbos morning, when she served the kugel, the rebbetzin said, "See! You always criticize me for not putting enough *schmaltz* into the kugel. But look at the Divine blessing. The kugel is dripping with *schmaltz!*"

R' Naftali nodded. "It is indeed a Divine blessing," he said. "We merited this blessing by virtue of *deine tefillos un meine maasim tovim* — your fervent *davening* and my good deeds."

Recipe or Prescription?

This may read like a recipe, but it is actually a prescription, written by a great physician, the Rambam.

"Take the roots of Shabbos, the cores of praise, gratitude, joy and faith, remove the kernels of anguish and worry, and take the blossoms of knowledge and wisdom, and the roots of patience and frugality, and crush them in the pestle of meekness, and cook them in the vessel of humility. Knead them in pleasant speech, and mix all with water of grace and kindness. Let the person suffering from despair drink two spoonfuls every morning and evening, together with three spoonfuls of waters of clear-thought. Purify it from the residue of anger and irritability, and combine all with the essence of acceptance of the Divine will, and the patient will become calm and tranquil."

Sacrificing to Observe Shabbos

Moses Montefiore was one of the wealthiest men in Great Britain. He had many transactions with a number of the British lords with whom he had a close business relationship. Every Friday afternoon, he closed his office, knowing that this might result in his losing lucrative deals.

One Friday night, when Montefiore and his family were at the Shabbos table, a messenger came from one of the lords stating that there was an unusual opportunity to close on a business deal that would bring them both a huge profit, and the lord wanted Montefiore to promptly come to his manor. Montefiore told the messenger that he could not possibly come, because he does not engage in business activities on Shabbos.

A bit later, the messenger returned with an envelope, saying that the lord had sent an important message. When Montefiore explained that he does not open letters on Shabbos, the messenger opened the envelope and read the content, which was a firm statement to Montefiore that if he does not promptly comply with the request to come to the manor, the lord is severing all business ties with him. This would constitute a catastrophic loss for Montefiore, not only of revenue but also of the goodwill of the lord and his peers.

Montefiore told the messenger to relay to the lord that he is indeed grateful for the lord's confidence in him and that he greatly values their relationship, not only on a business level, but also on a personal level. However, he respectfully refuses the request to come to the manor on Shabbos.

On Sunday, Montefiore was again summoned to the lord's manor. On arrival, the lord greeted him warmly and told him that there never was an important transaction on Friday night. What happened was that in a discussion with several other lords, they accused the Jews of having an insatiable desire for wealth, and insisted that the Jews would set aside their most cherished principles in order to make more money.

"I concocted the story about a lucrative deal only to test you, and I am thrilled that you withstood the test; it enabled me to prove your integrity to the other lords."

The following story was related by R' Simchah Kook.

In the early 1900s, the Jews who immigrated to the United States found it extremely difficult to find jobs that did not require them to work on Shabbos. Unfortunately, many could not withstand the financial deprivation and succumbed. Those who kept Shabbos did so with *mesiras nefesh.*

One immigrant with a large family was dismissed from job after job because he refused to work on Shabbos. When he could not afford to pay the rent, he was evicted. Not having anywhere to go, he was put out on the street on a cold winter day with his few belongings. He and his wife went to look for shelter, leaving the children with their possessions. A passerby, hearing the children talking Yiddish, was curious as to what was going on, and the children told him that they had been evicted because their father refused to work on Shabbos and therefore could not pay the rent.

This man was quite wealthy, and was deeply touched by the family's plight. He waited for the parents to return, and gave them $500, a considerable sum in those days, to relocate. The mother asked him, "Do you observe Shabbos?" and when he answered in the negative, she said, "Thank you for your generous offer, but we are sacrificing our lives for Shabbos, and we cannot take money that was earned in violation of Shabbos."

When the man returned home and told his wife about the encounter, she said, "Do you remember when you first began to work on Shabbos, and you told me it would be only temporary and that you would observe Shabbos again? Well, you never kept your word, and you did not stop working on Shabbos. But here you have a family that is out in the cold, and Shabbos means so much to them that they would not take your money. If

they can sacrifice so much for Shabbos, that should be a lesson for you. As for me, I will not stay in this house any longer unless you start observing Shabbos."

Both families merited to see their children become Torah scholars.

(adapted from *Aleinu Leshabe'ach, Vayikra*)

The Lost Shabbos

The Talmud says that Shabbos is *mei'ein Olam Haba*, a taste of Paradise. R' Baruch of Mezhibozh, a grandson of the Baal Shem Tov said, "I would gladly exchange ten *Olam Habas* for one Shabbos." We can only imagine the spiritual bliss of the Baal Shem Tov and his holy disciples on Shabbos.

One time, the Baal Shem Tov was traveling, and was lost in the forest. Try as he might, he could not find his way out of the forest even after a few days. Realizing that it was already Friday, the Baal Shem Tov agonized that he would not be home or with a *minyan* for Shabbos.

As he wandered, he saw a small hut in the distance. He approached and knocked on the door. The door was opened by a man who said in a gruff voice, "What do you want here?" The Baal Shem Tov explained that he was lost in the forest and hoped that he could stay in this hut for Shabbos.

"No, you can't stay here," the man shouted, "I don't like your kind. Go away," and slammed the door in his face.

The Baal Shem Tov knocked on the door again and pleaded with the man. "Please! One Jew must have mercy on a fellow Jew. Let me stay here for Shabbos."

"All right," the man said, "but I don't want you in my house. You can stay in the shed, and make sure you don't disturb me." The Baal Shem Tov thanked him, and put his few belongings in the shed. There was a small lake nearby, and the Baal Shem Tov immersed himself in this *mikveh* as was his custom prior to Shabbos.

Friday night, the Baal Shem Tov *davened* with his usual devotion, singing the prayers aloud. The man came to the shed and said, "I told you I did not want to be disturbed. Your singing bothers me. Keep quiet!" The Baal Shem Tov prayed silently.

After *davening*, the Baal Shem Tov took the bread he had with him and recited *Kiddush* over it. As he began to sing the Shabbos *zemiros*, the man appeared and shouted at him, "Didn't I tell you to keep quiet? Your singing irritates me."

The Baal Shem Tov spent the entire Shabbos under these sorry conditions, accepting upon himself the righteousness of the Divine judgment. When Shabbos was over, the man appeared, this time dressed in beautiful Shabbos clothes. He spoke softly and respectfully, "Will the Master please come into my humble home?"

The Baal Shem Tov was bewildered by this. When he entered the hut, the man's wife said to him, "Does the Master not recognize me? I was an orphan, and I worked in the Master's kitchen. One Erev Shabbos, the Master's wife was combing my hair, and when she pulled it, I exclaimed, 'Stop! You're hurting me!' And she shouted at me to keep quiet. The Master was there and said nothing. The Heavenly Tribunal decreed that because the Master did not intervene to defend an orphan, he had forfeited his *Olam Haba*.

"My husband is one of the hidden *tzaddikim*, and he prayed that the Master not lose his *Olam Haba*. I forgave the Master wholeheartedly. The Heavenly Tribunal then said that the Master should be deprived of the *oneg* of one Shabbos, which is *mei'ein Olam Haba*, and his *Olam Haba* would be restored. My husband prayed that you be lost in the forest and have to spend Shabbos with us, so that he could carry out the judgment of the Heavenly Tribunal, and the Master's *Olam Haba* would be restored."

The Baal Shem Tov thanked the couple profusely. He and the hidden *tzaddik* shared a *Melaveh Malkah* meal, and the two spent the entire night in the study of the secrets of the Torah.

The Sign on the Store

T he Torah says that Shabbos is a "sign" between Hashem and Israel (*Exodus* 31:17). What is the significance of Shabbos being a sign?

The Talmud gives Shabbos extraordinary importance, to the point that if someone keeps Shabbos faithfully, he can be forgiven even if he had transgressed the sin of *avodah zarah* (idolatry).

The Chafetz Chaim explained: A proprietor may close his store. However, if the sign on the store remains, there is reason to believe that he will reopen. If the proprietor removes the sign, it is obvious that he has no intention of ever reopening.

So it is with Shabbos. Even if a person has deviated from observance of the mitzvos, as long as he keeps Shabbos, there is a good likelihood that he will return to Torah observance. Shabbos is the "sign" whose presence indicates that one has not given up. If one violates Shabbos, that is equivalent to removing the sign on the store. It means that one has no intention of returning to *Yiddishkeit*.

A House on Fire

R' Yosef Chaim Sonnenfeld, rabbi of Jerusalem, was once told that in a certain home there was cooking taking place on Shabbos. He quickly ran to the house, burst in and shouted, "*Gevald*! It's the holy Shabbos."

The perpetrator said to the rabbi, "If you wish to reprimand me, is it not rude of you to enter my home without knocking?"

R' Yosef Chaim retorted, "Decorum has its place. If a house is on fire, you don't observe social amenities. You do whatever is necessary to prevent the fire from destroying the house. I heard that there was a fire in your house. That's why I rushed in."

Shabbos Is Greeted With Joy

The Shpoler Zeide, one of the great chassidic masters, would come into the kitchen Friday afternoon to make sure that everything was completed well ahead of sunset. One Friday, the sky was covered with thick clouds, and the sunset was not visible. Although the *tzaddik* had taken precautions to finish everything on time, he was bothered by the thought that perhaps he had miscalculated, and as a result of the deep cloud cover, might not have stopped work early enough.

Although the *tzaddik* was always in a cheerful mood, this Friday he was solemn. He was concerned that he may have lit the candles too close to sunset. "Woe is me!" the *tzaddik* said. "I may have violated the Shabbos."

The rabbis who were the *tzaddik's* Shabbos guests assured him that there was no reason for worry. He had lit the candles long before sunset. "How can you be so sure?" he asked. "When the sun is not visible, one's calculation of sunset might be in error." One of the guests cited the Talmudic maxim that G-d protects a *tzaddik* from an inadvertent transgression.

"That is no consolation," he said. "I am not a *tzaddik*."

Noticing R' Raphael of Bershad, his dear friend, among the guests, the Shpoler Zeide said, "Raphael, you can help me. What can I do if I think I may have desecrated the Shabbos?"

R' Raphael responded, "Violation of Shabbos is a grave sin, and if one suspects that he has violated the Shabbos, one must do *teshuvah*. The first step in *teshuvah* for violating Shabbos is to honor the Shabbos by greeting it with joy. It is forbidden to be sad on Shabbos. The Midrash states that Hashem said to Moshe, 'I have a special gift in My treasury, it is called Shabbos. Go tell the Children of Israel that I wish to give it to them.' We are the recipients of this wonderful gift that Hashem gave us because of His love for us. How can we not rejoice?"

The Shpoler Zeide said, "Raphael, you are a true friend. You did not try to console me with empty reassurances. I will rejoice with Shabbos, and I will do *teshuvah* for a possible transgression."

We can be assured that the Shpoler Zeide did not violate Shabbos. He was indeed among the *tzaddikim* about whom the Talmud says that Hashem protects them from an inadvertent transgression. This story shows us: not only the *tzaddik*'s profound humility, but also teaches us two lessons how important it is to have *simchah* on Shabbos, and that *teshuvah* can be achieved with joy.

Yom HaShishi's Pickles

osher dill pickles made commercially can be quite tasty, but for anyone who ate *Yom HaShishi's* pickles, they are a distant second best.

Who was *Yom HaShishi?* His real name was Mordechai P., and if you called him "Yom HaShishi" to his face, you would be taking your life in your hands.

Giving people nicknames is not permitted in halachah, especially if they are uncomplimentary. Most people are probably unaware of this, and therefore, among Eastern European Jews, it was common practice to do so.

I don't know why Mordechai took offense at being called *Yom HaShishi*. He operated a shop where he bought scrap metal and rags from the peddlers. One time a peddler told him that he had brought his wares to the shop on Friday afternoon, but had found it closed. "Of course." Mordechai said. "When it comes Friday noon, I close the shop. I go to the *shvitz* (Turkish bath) and by me it's *Yom HaShishi* (the first two words of the *Kiddush* inaugurating Shabbos)." The peddler spread the word, and Mordechai was labeled *Yom HaShishi* unto eternity.

It is tragic that so much of the generation that followed these people has been lost to *Yiddishkeit*. Unfortunately, Mordechai's grandchildren have probably never even heard the words *Yom HaShishi*.

Mordechai's unchallenged skill was putting up dill pickles and sharp peppers. I still follow his recipe for pickles (see page 66) but have been unsuccessful in duplicating the peppers. Mordechai claimed great curative powers for his peppers. He had little use for scientific medicine. The best remedy for a cold (or for any other malady) was hot tea and sharp peppers. "This cleans out your brain," he said. Whether it does so or not is questionable. However, it is certainly a powerful decongestant.

When Mordechai failed to show up in shul one Shabbos, I visited him and found him to be sick with a blood clot in his leg. His nephew was a leading internist, who had prescribed medication for him. Mordechai refused the medication, resorting instead to hot tea and peppers, and recovered completely.

Mordechai's family had genes for longevity. I knew several of his cousins who had celebrated their 100th birthdays. Mordechai's birthday was the night of the second Seder, and he would go into a little dance to celebrate. When he was 85, he said he was a Bar Mitzvah, because 8 + 5 = 13. At 88 he claimed he was a "sveet sixteen."

When Mordechai was 95 he suffered a heart attack and was hospitalized. He was treated with state-of-the-art medications, but did not survive. Who knows? Perhaps if the doctors had known that his physiology responded best to hot tea and peppers, Mordechai, like his cousins, would have exceeded 100 years.

Mordechai fancied himself an authority on, well, almost everything. He would gloat over his triumph in a legal altercation. Mordechai's neighbor disputed his right to the use of the driveway for peddlers to deliver their wares. The driveway had been used for years by the previous owner of the property.

Mordechai would relate dramatically, "I valked into the court, and there was the judge and the lawyers. I vent straight to the judge and I said, 'Who here is bigger than the law?' Everyone stopped and looked. I said, 'The law says that when you use a driveway for seven years, it becomes a republic!' Sure, I von the case."

Erev Shabbos in My Parents' Home

In my parent's home, from Thursday afternoon straight through until licht tzinden (candle-lighting time) was definitely Erev Shabbos. My mother had a small — actually a tiny — kitchen and no freezer space to speak of. The old-fashioned refrigerator had a freezer section that could hold two trays of ice cubes and that was about it.

Every Thursday was cleaning day. The last task was to wash and wax the kitchen floor. Linoleum in those days was definitely not easy maintenance and since an entire day of cooking lay ahead, when the wax had dried we spread newspapers over the floor. Friday was the day we shuffled through the layers of newspapers, but they served a purpose. Just before Shabbos, the torn and splattered sheets were removed and thrown down the incinerator chute, and voilà — a sparkling clean and shiny kitchen floor was revealed lichvod Shabbos.

*It's possible that my memory is not 100 percent accurate, but I'm willing to bet that the whole block relished the warm and inviting smells that issued from my mother's kitchen all day Friday. How my mother ever produced such vast quantities in such a small space and in such record time is still a wonder. There was a mixer, but not with a dough hook; and a blender or food processor was not in existence. Nonetheless by the time Shabbos rolled around, the table was bedecked with the tastiest challos imaginable. My mother made the fluffiest, whitest gefilte fish, using ground whitefish and pike. She never used carp as it made the fish dark and she prided herself on how white her fish was. One guest innocently inquired as to how her fish stayed so white and my mother jokingly responded, "Why — I add bleach, of course." Nowadays my husband teases me — how much bleach did you put in this week, it's so white. (Do **not** use bleach — it is just a joke.)*

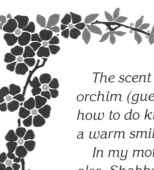

The scent of my mother's chicken soup would waft through the hallways and our many Shabbos orchim (guests) let their noses lead them to the right door. Nowadays there are various seminars on how to do kiruv (outreach), but I'm telling you, nothing beats a hot tasty Shabbos meal served with a warm smile.

In my mother's house the Shabbos menu was standard and traditional and that is how I make it also. Shabbos is Shabbos and fancy new foods definitely have a place. But the traditional food never becomes monotonous. Crisp roast chicken, farfel and hot potato kugel always tasted the way they were made — with lots of love and the special taste of the spice of Shabbos.

Many friends and neighbors would come after the meal, especially on the long winter Friday nights for tea, strudel and mother's delicious apple pie, which was never made in a pie pan but in a deep 12x18 inch pan, and there was never a crumb left for the next day. All this enjoyed while the next day's cholent bubbled merrily on the blech.

Ah, Shabbos. Nothing was ever too hard to do because it was done with an appreciation of the gift of menuchah, the gift Hashem gave to His chosen people.

Challah

Most Jewish housewives in Europe made challah. The recipes were similar but slightly different. The basic challah ingredients are the same, with each balabusta making subtle changes. This varied according to family and location, with some preferring sweet challah (dough as rich as cake), others more plain, and still others an eggless water challah. All are delicious and I'll give you one of each: extra rich, mine; less sweet, from my friend Hindy Sirkis; and water challah from my daughter-in-law Raizy in Eretz Yisrael.

Challah dough is very forgiving — you can play around with the amounts and still get a workable dough — so if one recipe is too rich or a different one is too dry — adapt it and make your own — and you'll have a family classic to pass on for generations.

I think making challah is my most enjoyable adventure in the kitchen. I'm never too lazy to put up a challah dough. My mother always said that that's because I never really grew up and this is my play-dough. It could be that she is right.

*All of the recipes that follow are made with 5 or more pounds of flour — I also give the very rich recipe using only 8 cups of flour so you can try it (do **not take challah** on 8 cups of flour). Consult a rabbi for the amount of dough required to take challah and what amount permits making a berachah.*

Challah Clues:

Here are a few things I've learned over the years and adapted.

▸ Yeast dough needs time. Let it take its time and you will be rewarded with delicious results. When substituting dry yeast for fresh, 2½ Tablespoons dry yeast equals 4 oz. fresh yeast; 3 packets (1 strip) dry yeast equals 4 oz. fresh yeast.

▸ Using less yeast makes the dough take longer to rise, but the slower rising results in a better challah. My dough equals less than 5 quarts at first, but rises to fill a 12-quart pot.

▸ I no longer proof my yeast, but add it to the bowl of the mixer with the other ingredients. Take care that the salt doesn't touch the yeast.

▸ You can use all-purpose flour, high gluten flour, or a mixture of both. Any one is fine. Sift the flour; the result is a lighter challah.

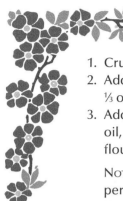

1. Crumble yeast into a mixing bowl of a mixer fitted with the dough hook.
2. Add all the sugar, then ¼ of the flour. Turn the mixer to low and slowly add ⅓ of the water. Let it beat for 1 minute.
3. Add the eggs one at a time, alternating with some of the flour. Then add the oil, alternating with more flour, then add the salt, and finally, the remaining flour, alternating with the rest of the water. Knead for 12-14 minutes.

    NOTE: Trust me, the longer it kneads, the better the dough. I check it periodically — if the dough is adhering to the sides of the bowl, I add flour ⅛ cup at a time but not more than 1 cup extra in total. The 8-cup version of the very rich challah recipe never needs extra flour; the dough is perfect.
4. Transfer dough to a well-greased 12-quart pot or bowl and cover with plastic wrap. Let this rise for 1-1½ hours until it fills the bowl.

    NOTE: It is important to cover the dough. The plastic wrap keeps the dough from drying out. I know that many people place their dough in a white plastic garbage bag to rise — but I'm not convinced that a garbage bag is safe for food.
5. Punch down the dough and let it re-rise for ½-¾ hour.

    NOTE: Many people skip this stage; it is not absolutely necessary and may be omitted, but the extra rising allows the gluten in the flour to expand.
6. Punch down again and take *challah* if applicable. Divide and shape into desired number of challah loaves and/or bilkahs (rolls). (See pages 52-53 for braiding instructions and diagrams.)

Ingredients:

Very Rich Challah: (Small Batch)
2 oz. fresh yeast
¾ cup and 1 Tablespoon sugar
8 cups flour
2 cups warm water
2 eggs
½ cup oil
1¼ Tablespoons kosher salt

Very Rich Challah: (X-Large Batch)
3-4 oz. fresh yeast
2-2¼ cups sugar
5 lbs. plus 6-7½ cups flour
*   (24 cups)*
6 cups warm water
6 eggs
1½ cups oil
4 Tablespoons kosher salt

7. Place on parchment paper-lined cookie sheets, leaving room to expand. Let shaped challah rise until doubled in size, 45 minutes to 1 hour.
8. Brush with egg wash; sprinkle with sesame or poppy seeds if desired.

   NOTE: For challos with a dark mahogany color, brush the challahs with the egg wash about 15 minutes before ready to bake. After the wash dries, brush it on again.
9. Bake in preheated 350° oven about 35 minutes for challah, 25 minutes for rolls. Tap bottom of challah; you should hear a hollow sound that will assure you that they are done. Cool on a rack.

NOTE: Freezes well. Now for an unbelievable hint — I read this many years ago and it really works. Wrap the challah well in foil and place in a plastic bag. Freeze. When you remove the challah from the freezer, defrost **in** the bag, **in** the foil, for 2-3 hours. Then remove from bag, make a small slit in the foil, and set in a preheated 350° oven for 12 minutes (in the foil) to steam dry. Remove from oven, remove foil, and set on a rack to cool. It will taste totally fresh. The moisture that is released when the challah defrosts came from the challah originally, and this method puts it back without drying the challah.

YIELD: 20-24 bilkahs or 8-12 challahs. The small-batch recipe of Very Rich Challah yields 2-3 medium challahs and is great for first-time yeast bakers to experiment with.

Ingredients:

Less Rich Challah:
2-3 oz. fresh yeast
1¼ cups sugar
5 lbs. flour
35 oz. (4⅓ cups) warm water
3 eggs
⅓ cup oil
4 Tablespoons kosher salt

No-Egg Water Challah:
2½ Tablespoons dry yeast
1½ cups sugar
6 lbs. (5 lbs. + 3⅓-3½ cups) flour
6½ cups warm water
½ cup oil
4 Tablespoons kosher salt

Egg Wash:
1 egg, beaten
½ Tablespoon sugar

sesame or poppy seeds
   (optional)

Braiding/Shaping Challah

A six-strand braided challah is traditional, since the 12-strand total is symbolic of the 12 loaves of lechem hapanim that were brought in the Beis HaMikdash every Shabbos.

All of these doughs hold their shapes. I never make challah in pans but if you're leery, a pan won't hurt.

Braiding Traditional Six-Strand Challah:
This is easier to do than to say and it really works. After a few tries it will flow automatically. The result will be a beautiful braided challah.

1. Using the amount of dough for one challah, divide dough into 6 pieces. On a lightly floured surface roll each piece into a 12″ (or shorter) strand. Rolling each strand in a small amount of flour will help define the shape. Don't make the ropes too long; shorter and fatter is better. If the strands are long and thin, the challah will be long and thin. If the ropes are short and fat, the challah will be high and full.
2. Place the lightly floured strands one next to the other. In your mind, number the strands 1-6, going from left to right.
3. Pinch the strands together at the top. (Diagram A)
4. Move left outer strand (#1) to the top, right. (Diagram B)
5. Move right outer strand (#6) to the top, left. (Diagram C)

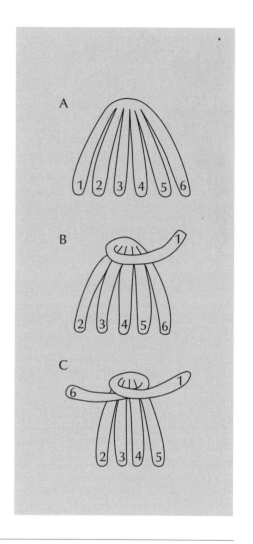

6. Bring right outer strand (#1) down to center, crossing over 2 strands (between #3 and #4). (Diagram D)
7. Move strand #2 to the top right (it will now be in place of the strand #1 you just moved down). (Diagram E)
8. Bring strand #6 over 2 strands to the middle. (Diagram F)
9. Move #5 to the top left (to replace strand #6 you brought down). (Diagram G)
10. Continue in this pattern, moving right outer strand to the middle, then replacing with opposite strand until all the ropes are used up. Pinch ends together and tuck under.

Shaping Round Challah:
1. Make a rope 18"-24" in length, thicker at one end, tapered at the other.
2. Wind the entire rope around the thicker end of the strand (#1) so the thick part is the center of the challah. (See diagrams below)
3. Tuck the end (#2) under and press to seal. This challah will not topple or be lopsided.

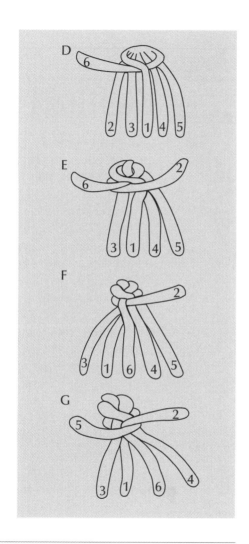

Gefilte Fish

A well-seasoned tasty loaf of frozen store-bought gefilte fish definitely serves us well, but it does not compare to the taste of freshly made individual portions. Is it worth the time and effort? I believe so, but you decide.

A well-seasoned tasty loaf of frozen store-bought gefilte fish definitely serves us well, but it does not compare to the taste of freshly made individual portions. Is it worth the time and effort? I believe so, but you decide.

There are a wide range of recipes for gefilte fish — literally gefilte. I still remember my mother cutting the fish skins into thin strips and placing each portion of the chopped mixture into a piece of skin — thus, gefilte, stuffed. My mother was a Galicziener, and made her fish from a mixture of ground whitefish and pike — not too sweet and not too salty — it was just right. Other recipes use carp, buffalo carp, or other varieties of fish — nowadays salmon gefilte fish is popular.

When I make fish for Pesach and Succos I use 100 pounds or more. I usually get between 50-60 loaves (1½ lbs. each) from a batch —enough for all my kids and their families. It's great — but both my husband and I agree that gefilte fish cooked as individual portions is another experience altogether. So maybe once you'll try it the way my mother always (and I frequently) made it.

1. Clean skins, bones, and heads of fish.
2. Use the biggest pot you own. (I use a 16-quart — my mother taught me the bigger the pot, the less mess to clean up on your stovetop). Put in all the broth ingredients except the carrots.
3. Bring to a boil, skimming the foam that accumulates. Let this broth simmer for ½-1 hour. Add carrots.

Ingredients:

Fish Broth:
fish skins, bones, and heads (optional)
10 cups water
2 onions, peeled and sliced
2 Tablespoons kosher salt
2 Tablespoons sugar
2 whole carrots, peeled

(Ingredients for fish mixture can be found on facing page)

4. While the broth is simmering, place all the fish mixture ingredients into a mixing bowl and mix (using beaters or dough hook), for 8-10 minutes, adding water as needed.
5. Fill a second bowl ¾-full of water.
6. Dip your hands in the cold water and scoop up ⅓-½ cup of the mixture. Shape the fish into an oval about 3″ long. Keeping your hands wet, transfer the ovals from one hand to the other, forming a smooth oval shape. Place the oval into the simmering broth. Repeat with the remaining mixture, placing each oval into the broth. The pieces can touch but should not be on top of each other. Bring to a boil again, then lower to a moderate simmer and cook for 50 minutes.
7. Remove fish carefully, using a slotted spoon. Remove carrots and slice on the diagonal, about ¼″ thick. Refrigerate until serving.
8. To serve, garnish each portion with a carrot slice. Serve with store bought or homemade horseradish (chrain), see page 261.

NOTE: If you want *fargliverte fish yoch* (jelled fish sauce), boil the remaining broth until it is reduced to a quarter of its original amount. This works better if you add a carp head or 3-4 slices of carp to the liquid. Carp bones have a miraculous jelling quality. Strain and pour into a container. Refrigerate. My husband and two of my sons-in-law relish this.

YIELD: 16-24 servings, depending on size of ovals

Ingredients:

Fish Mixture:

4 lbs. total whitefish and pike, whole (using carp makes the fish darker and requires a longer cooking time), to be ground after cleaning (this yields 2¾ lb. ground fish)

2 medium onions, ground

4 eggs

4 Tablespoons kosher salt or 2 Tablespoons table salt

4 Tablespoons sugar

1-2 teaspoons pepper

3 Tablespoons matzoh meal (optional)

¾ cup water, or more as needed

Falsche Fish Croquettes

Rabbi Twerski writes:

What do you do when one of your guests advises you that he / she does not eat fish? Not serving them anything while others are eating fish will make them feel awful. Serving them sautéed mushrooms instead of fish might cause the other guests to raise their eyebrows, "Why is he / she so special? Why didn't I get sautéed mushrooms?" A dilemma.

There is a solution. Falsche fish. * These look like gefilte fish balls, but they are made of ground chicken breast. Well, O.K., they don't look exactly like gefilte fish. They're really chicken burgers, but they're close enough to the appearance of fish so that your pisceophobe guest will not feel conspicuous.*

1. Beat the eggs in a bowl.
2. Add water and all the other ingredients except for the matzo meal, including the ground chicken breast. Mix thoroughly. If mixture is very loose refrigerate for two hours or add matzo meal or bread crumbs as needed.
4. Heat the oil in a large frying pan.
3. Wet hands and shape the batter into oval-shaped patties. Place in heated oil and fry until golden.

*NOTE: See also Traditional Falsche Fish (page 260).

*NOTE: See also Traditional Falsche Fish (page 260).

YIELD: 10-12 patties

Ingredients:

2 eggs
4 oz. water
1 teaspoon onion powder
1 teaspoon garlic powder
2 teaspoons kosher salt
1 Tablespoon potato starch
¼ teaspoon white pepper (optional)
2 lbs. ground chicken breast
3-4 Tablespoons matzo meal or bread crumbs (optional)

4-6 Tablespoons oil, for frying

Bubbie's Chicken Soup

Chicken soup recipes vary slightly from region to region. Every one of them evokes memories of home and motherly (and grandmotherly) love. No wonder it's known as "Jewish penicillin." A hearty bowl of soup can cure almost any ailment. The title says "Bubbie's" but we could say "Zaide's." This is how Rabbi Twerski makes his favorite chicken soup.

1. Fill a 12-quart or larger pot with the water, neck bones, and beet. Bring to a boil and cook for 15 minutes.
2. Add chicken bones, onions, carrots, kohlrabi, parsley root, celery stalks, celery root, and salt to taste. Simmer for 2 hours.
3. Add zucchini and leek. Simmer for 30 minutes. If desired, add dill and chicken soup mix during the last 60 minutes.
4. Allow to cool. Remove solid ingredients and reserve for another use. Strain soup through fine sieve.

YIELD: 5 quarts

Ingredients:

5 quarts water
1 package beef or veal neck bones (approx. 2 lbs.)
1 medium beet, peeled
1 package chicken bones (approx. 2 lbs.)
2 large onions, halved
4 large carrots, peeled
1 kohlrabi, peeled
1 parsley root, peeled
2 stalks celery
3"x3" piece of celery root
salt to taste
1 small zucchini
1 leek, trimmed and washed
4 sprigs dill (optional)
4 teaspoons chicken soup mix (optional)

Mommy's Chicken Soup

This is the way my mother made her chicken soup and the way I make it to this very day. The sole difference is that my mother used chicken quarters (which were eaten at the Friday night seudah) and I use chicken bones.

1. Place bones and water into a big pot — I use a 16-quart pot so I won't have a messy stovetop — bring to a boil and skim until the foam that rises to the surface is no longer dark.
2. Add the rest of the ingredients except the dill.
3. Lower the heat and simmer for an additional hour or longer, adding dill in the final half hour.
4. Cool slightly and strain.

NOTE: I strain my soup by lining my strainer with paper toweling and pouring the soup through — I learned this from my daughter-in-law Fraidle and the soup is clear and gorgeous.

VARIATION: If you like, you can add 2-3 potatoes to the soup, although it may turn cloudy. We love potato and carrots mashed together with a little soup.

YIELD: 5 quarts

Ingredients:

4½ lbs. chicken bones
5 quarts water
1 zucchini
5 stalks celery
5 large carrots, peeled
1 whole ripe tomato
6 cloves garlic
1 parsley root, peeled
1 parsnip, peeled
dill (optional)

Matzoh Balls – Knaidlach

I nearly left this recipe out, on the assumption that everyone knows how to make knaidlach. But on deeper reflection, although the variations are minimal, there are great knaidlach and the greatest knaidlach. The very best use seltzer (I'm not sure this was available in Europe) in place of water and chicken schmaltz (page 263) in place of the oil. But they are terrific in any case. This does not need a mixer — just a bowl and a fork. If you have an over-abundance of chicken soup, the matzoh balls can be cooked directly in chicken soup. However, they absorb so much of the liquid that most cooks hesitate to use their soup for cooking the knaidlach.

1. Beat the eggs until well mixed.
2. Add the oil, water, and seasonings. Beat until smooth.
3. Slowly beat in the matzoh meal, making sure there are no lumps.
4. Place mixture into the refrigerator for at least 20 minutes.
5. In the meantime, bring the 6 quarts of water to a boil in a large (at least 8-quart) pot. Add salt.
6. With wet hands form the cold mixture into walnut-size balls and drop into boiling water. When all the balls are formed, lower heat to a rolling simmer and cook for 20 minutes. Drain and serve or freeze for later use.

YIELD: 16-20 knaidlach

Ingredients:

Mixture:
4 eggs
⅓ cup oil or schmaltz
½ cup water or seltzer
1 teaspoon kosher salt
¼ teaspoon pepper
1 cup (or a bit less) matzoh meal

To Cook:
6 quarts boiling water
1-2 Tablespoons kosher salt

Lima Beans

Lima beans are a traditional accompaniment to the Friday night seudah. This is Mrs. Zaidman's recipe.

1. Place lima beans in a saucepan. Add twice the amount of water as beans (example: use 2 cups of water for 1 cup of beans). Bring to a boil. Cook for 5 minutes.
2. Drain the beans. Refill the pot with the same amount of water. Add drained beans, salt, and sugar.
3. Cook for one hour or to desired tenderness.

Ingredients:

medium lima beans (not baby, not jumbo)
water (see recipe)
½ teaspoon salt, or to taste
½ Tablespoon sugar, or to taste
pepper (optional)

Roast Chicken

The traditional Friday night seudah used roast chicken for its main course. My mother's was delicious but rather basic. She would use one or two whole roasting chickens, usually 5-6 lbs. each. She rarely stuffed the chicken but invariably roasted 1-2 helzels (see recipe on page 184) on the side and often put potatoes and/or carrots in the roasting pan to be cooked in the chicken juices.

1. Preheat oven to 425°.
2. Place the onions into a roasting pan.
3. Make a paste of the paprika, garlic powder, salt, and water. Rub all over the surface of the chicken and, if there is any left, inside the cavity.
4. Place the chicken on the onions. If desired, add the vegetables. Make sure the vegetables are cut into small chunks; if they are too big they will not be fully cooked by the time the chicken is ready.
5. Cover the roasting pan and roast in preheated oven for 1 hour. Uncover. If the chicken is not browned and crispy, bake uncovered an additional 10 minutes. There will be plenty of gravy. Do not overbake.

YIELD: 4 servings

Ingredients:

3 large onions, cut into small chunks
2 Tablespoons paprika
2 Tablespoons garlic powder
½ Tablespoon salt
water to moisten
1 4-5 lb. chicken, whole
2-3 potatoes, cut into small chunks (optional)
2-3 carrots, cut into small chunks (optional)

Stuffings for Chicken

Both Mrs. Zaidman and my daughter Rachael gave me this stuffing recipe. I've used it frequently and it's always just right.

Stuffing I:
1. Sauté onion and celery.
2. Squeeze the water out of the challah. Shred the challah. Add to onion-celery mixture. Add spices, then beat in the egg. Add matzoh meal. Thoroughly knead everything together.
3. If using a whole chicken, stuff the cavity. If using quarters, lift the skin and place stuffing between the chicken and the skin.

YIELD: stuffing for 4-6 chicken quarters or one whole (not cut up) chicken.

Stuffing II:
My daughter Miriam's sister-in-law Nechama Weintraub gave her this recipe for stuffing. It's easy and tasty.

1. Combine ingredients, kneading by hand until smooth. If the filling is very thick, add an additional ¼-⅓ cup of water.
2. Stuff the cavity of a whole chicken or divide and place under the skin of several chicken quarters.

YIELD: stuffing for 4-6 chicken quarters

Ingredients:

Stuffing I:
1 medium-large onion, diced
2 large stalks celery, diced
½ of a bilkah (challah roll), soaked in water
salt to taste
pepper
oregano (optional)
parsley flakes
1 egg
2 Tablespoons matzoh meal or matzoh ball mix

Stuffing II:
1 cup bread crumbs
2 Tablespoons flour
¼ cup corn flake crumbs
2 Tablespoons melted margarine
1 egg
1 small onion, grated
½ cup water, or more as needed
salt to taste
pepper to taste
paprika

Friday Night Farfel

Rabbi Twerski has fond memories of the farfel his mother invariably made for the Friday night seudah. Although my mother didn't serve farfel every week, it definitely was an oft-repeated favorite. Farfel was also served on Rosh Hashanah due to the play on words between farfel and farfallen, as in "zul di sonim veren farfallen" — may the enemies be destroyed. The farfel I remember was made using "egg-barley," a barley-shaped noodle product. Nowadays there are many products on the market, from heimishe farfel to couscous, which can be made in the same fashion and provide variety to the Shabbos table.

1. Place the onion and oil into a 3-quart pot and sauté until the onion is just beginning to color.
2. Add the farfel to the onions and toast over a low flame until lightly browned.
3. Carefully add the hot water (or soup). Add the spices.
4. Cover the pot and bring to a boil, and then lower the heat and simmer for 20-30 minutes until all the liquid is absorbed.
5. Serve immediately or keep warm in a low oven for up to 30 minutes.

VARIATION: If desired, mushrooms may be added to this dish. If using fresh mushrooms, chop them into ½" cubes. In step 1 sauté them with the onion until any liquid released has evaporated. Alternatively, if using canned mushrooms, add them before step 4.

YIELD: 6-8 servings

Ingredients:

1 Spanish onion, diced
¼ cup oil
2 cups farfel
4 cups boiling water or chicken soup
salt to taste
pepper if desired

Optional additions:
mushrooms, ½ lb. fresh or 1 (8-oz.) can, well drained

Cucumber Salad

My mother would slice her cucumbers very, very thin. She would salt them and let them sit for ½-1 hour and then squeeze out the liquid and discard it. She would then add the rest of the ingredients. Over the years, I've dropped the first step and we have developed a liking for a firmer, crisper salad. Both methods are good. I provided specific amounts, but tastes vary, so play around with the recipe until it meets your liking.

1. Place the cucumber and onion slices in a bowl.
2. Combine the vinegar, sugar, and salt and pour over the vegetables. Toss to coat well.
3. Refrigerate at least 2-3 hours before serving.

YIELD: 1½-2 quarts

Ingredients:

3 large cucumbers (not kirbies), peeled and sliced thin
1 large onion, sliced thin
⅓-½ cup vinegar
⅓-½ cup sugar
2½ Tablespoons kosher salt

Calf's Foot Jelley – Petcha

Gala, petcha, galaretta — so many names for one simple delicacy. My mother-in-law made petcha using chicken feet. This is an acceptable method but real authentic petcha is made from beef or veal knee bones (the butcher sometimes labels these as "jelly bones"). This is my neighbor Hindy Sirkis' recipe. Her daughter Raizy Bristowsky made it for me in her test kitchen. What's to say — if you love it — you love it. If you don't — it's because you never tasted this one.

1. Place the bones into a 5-quart pot. Add just enough water to cover the bones. Add salt and garlic cloves. Bring to a boil and with a spoon remove the scum that rises to the surface.
2. Cover the pot and simmer for 8-9 hours over the lowest possible heat. The longer it cooks, the easier to work with and the better it is. Remove from heat and cool for ½-1 hour.
3. Remove bones from liquid. Separate meat from the bones. Put meat and liquid through a grinder or a Foley mill.
4. Pour liquid into a pan. Taste and adjust flavor
5. Refrigerate and allow to congeal. Remove the fats that rise to the surface.
6. Cut into portions and serve. This can also be frozen. To serve, reheat and then let it jell once more.

YIELD: 6 2"x3" pans, ¾ full

Ingredients:

4 lbs. knee bones
water
2 Tablespoons kosher salt
9 whole cloves garlic, peeled

Egg Kichel – Eyer Kichel

Egg (Eyer) Kichel are plain biscuits that were usually served at Kiddush time on Shabbos morning with herring. My mother was a pro at making these — they were a regular Shabbos staple in our home. Hers were beautiful and had a round cupped shape. I made them myself several times many years ago, but dropped them from my repertoire because — si lost zich essin — they called to me to munch on them. To my dismay, I could not find my mother's recipe when I was putting together this collection. So one Friday morning in the middle of the summer, I tried 7 different recipes — adjusting and readjusting until I finally got the taste but I still couldn't quite get the shape. These came closest in shape and in taste.

1. Preheat oven to 400°.
2. Beat first four ingredients until smooth. (This can be done by hand.) Add flour and mix until the flour is incorporated. It will still be sticky at this point.
3. Turn out onto a heavily floured kneading board and roll into a 10"x14" rectangle. Let rest. Roll dough again until ⅛" thick. Cut into circles with a 3" cookie cutter (my mother used the rim of a glass).
4. Put circles on greased cookie sheet. Brush with oil. Bake until brown at the edges. Cool and store in airtight container.

YIELD: approximately 3 dozen kichel

Ingredients:

3 eggs
1 teaspoon salt
1 Tablespoon schnapps
2 Tablespoons oil
1¾ cups flour

additional oil, for brushing

Cholent Kugel

This is my mother's cholent kugel, but she never measured. It seemed to me that she never did the same thing twice, but it always came out tasting the same. Her original recipe was slightly different, but she changed it to use cornflake crumbs many years ago. Although cornflake crumbs were not a kitchen staple in Europe, it's worthwhile not to be so authentic sometimes. Many years ago, my daughter Miriam had the patience to perfect the quantities.

1. Put oil, potatoes, and onion in bowl of food processor fitted with the S-blade. Process until smooth.
2. Transfer to a large bowl and add the rest of the ingredients. Mix thoroughly.
3. Form 2-3 rolls, depending on the size desired, by placing the mixture on a sheet of aluminum foil. Roll with foil into a cylindrical shape and seal ends.
4. Place on top of cholent (but do not submerge) at least one hour before Shabbos, or freeze for future use.

VARIATION: I make this kugel using a little less oil or else a little bit more flour to stuff a whole chicken, or, in larger quantities, to fill a whole breast of veal in which a pocket has been made (see page 159).

YIELD: 2-3 rolls

Ingredients:

1 small onion
3 potatoes (about 2-2½ lbs.)
1 cup cornflake crumbs (I prefer to crush my own cornflakes; this gives the kugel a better texture and consistency — but measure after crushing)
¼-½ cup oil
1 cup flour
1½-2 Tablespoons paprika
1 Tablespoon kosher salt
pinch of pepper
garlic powder, to taste (optional)

Potato Kugel

This is another one of Mrs. Zaidman's specialties. I'm including it because it is slightly different. It contains a cup of water, which makes the kugel particularly light and fluffy.

1. Preheat oven to 450°.
2. With a fork, beat eggs in a mixing bowl.
3. Grate potatoes and onion. Add to beaten eggs. Add rest of ingredients. If you heat the oil in the pan, add it carefully to the batter. Stir thoroughly.
4. Pour mixture into a 10"x13" pan. Bake at 450° for 2 hours.

YIELD: 1 10"x13" pan

Ingredients:

10 eggs
10 large potatoes
1 large onion
1 cup oil
   — can be heated in pan first
1 cup water
salt to taste
pepper to taste
pinch of sugar

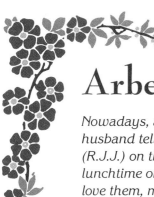

Arbes – Nahit

Nowadays, arbes are customarily served at a shalom zocher, but my husband tells me that when he was in Yeshivah Rabbeinu Yaakov Yosef (R.J.J.) on the Lower East Side, he bought hot arbes from a peddler during lunchtime on schooldays. These are an acquired taste — and those who love them, munch on them the way one munches on salted peanuts.

Ingredients:

1 lb. chickpeas
salt to taste
pepper to taste
water (see instructions)

1. Soak chickpeas in lukewarm water overnight. (I add 2 Tablespoons kosher salt to the water — don't ask why, but my mother did, so I do). Use water at least 3 times the volume of the peas — about 6-8 cups. Drain.
2. Check the peas and discard those with holes, shriveled seeds, or other unappetizing morsels.
3. Cook in salted water that covers the peas by about 1". When the water comes to a boil, remove the *schaum* (foam) that rises to the surface. Lower heat and cook at a rolling boil until the arbes are tender but have not lost their shape.
4. Drain and spread on a towel (I use an old white cotton tablecloth) so that all the excess moisture will be absorbed.
5. Sprinkle immediately with pepper and roll the *arbes* back and forth in the towel. Taste the *arbes*. (There may be enough salt from the cooking.) If desired, add salt and more pepper.
6. Serve hot, cool, or at room temperature.

YIELD: 2 quarts

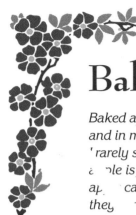

Baked Apples

Baked apples are homey, tasty, and satisfying. My mother made them often, and in my house I make a batch almost every Erev Shabbos during the winter. I rarely serve dessert since we're all so full after the seudah, but a warm baked apple is just right. When I'm really lazy — more often than not — I fill the apple cavities with honey poured straight from the jar and bake at 350° until they soft but still hold their shape. I pour the syrup back into the cavities. This recipe is even better.

1. Preheat oven to 350°.
2. Core the apples carefully so you don't cut through the bottom. Some people peel the top third of the skin from the apple but I just make a few slits around the top edge. Place the apples in a pan.
3. Combine raisins, almonds, and honey. Fill the cavities. Pour a thin layer of water on the bottom of the pan.
4. If desired, sprinkle apples with sugar and cinnamon.
5. Bake 30-40 minutes, until the apples are soft but not falling apart. If you're not too lazy (I am), you can baste the apples every 10 minutes or so with the liquid in the pan.

NOTE: Baked apples are yummy when eaten warm (I keep them on the *blech*), at room temperature, and even cold from the refrigerator.

YIELD: 6 servings

Ingredients:

6 baking apples (I use Cortland)
6 Tablespoons raisins
6 Tablespoons slivered
   almonds, toasted
6 Tablespoons honey
1 Tablespoon sugar (optional)
½ teaspoon cinnamon
   (optional)

Apple Pie

*The quantities given in this recipe are perfect for a deep dish pie-pan, but I always make extra dough. The leftovers, rolled out **very** thin and sprinkled with sugar and cinnamon, make the crispest, crunchiest sugar cookies. This recipe doesn't need a mixer. I beat everything with a fork in a mixing bowl. My granddaughter Mati, in Lakewood, is a pro at this and her pies are as beautiful to look at as they are scrumptious to eat.*

1. Preheat oven to 350°. Lightly grease and flour a 9"-10" deep dish pie-pan.
2. Beat eggs and sugar together until sugar dissolves. Add the next five ingredients in the order listed, and stir until a soft dough forms.
3. Divide dough into 2 pieces, one slightly larger than the other.
4. On a well-floured board, roll out the larger piece until it is very thin. I roll the dough around my rolling pin, lift it, and unroll over the pan, fitting it into the botton and up the sides of the pan. Paint the dough with jam.
5. Mix apples with remaining filling ingredients and mound into pan.
6. Roll out the second piece of dough and place over the filling.
7. If desired, lightly smear crust with oil and sprinkle with sugar or sugar/cinnamon mixture.
8. Prick crust with a fork or make a few slits to allow steam to escape.
9. Bake on lower rack until lightly browned, about 45 minutes to 1 hour.

YIELD: 12-16 servings

Ingredients:

Dough:
3 eggs
½ cup sugar
slightly less than ½ cup oil
½ cup orange juice
3¼-3½ cups flour
1½ teaspoons baking powder
pinch of salt

jam

Filling:
3 lbs. apples (I use Cortland), peeled, cored, and cut into chunks
½ cup sugar
2 Tablespoons cinnamon
1 cup cornflakes, crushed
1 can crushed pineapple, drained (optional)

Optional Topping:
oil for smearing
1-1½ Tablespoons sugar or 1-1½ Tablespoons sugar/cinnamon mixture

Falsche Mandlebroit

A hands-down favorite, my mother made it every week. The batter has no almonds, therefore falsche (imitation). The taste is derived from almond extract.

1. Preheat oven to 350°. Line 2 cookie sheets with parchment paper.
2. Beat the eggs, sugar, and oil until creamy. Add orange juice, flour, and baking powder.
3. Remove ¼ of the batter to another bowl and add cocoa and almond extract to this. Mix until well combined. Set aside.
4. Spoon ¼ of the white mixture onto a well-floured kneading board. Pat into a 6"x15" rectangle shape.
5. Spread ¼ of the chocolate mixture along one long edge of the dough and roll over onto itself so the chocolate is enclosed.
6. Place seam-side-down, on a cookie sheet, leaving room for expansion. Repeat with remaining mixtures. By hand, stretch each log (2 per cookie sheet) to the length of the sheet.
7. Bake for 25-35 minutes until light brown. Cool on rack.
8. Using the back of a spoon, cream margarine and confectioners' sugar, adding water a drop at a time to form a thick but spreadable white glaze.
9. Using ¾ of this mixture, glaze the tops of the logs. Mix cocoa and extract into remaining glaze; spread chocolate glaze down the center of strips.
10. Cut into ½"-¾" slices on the diagonal. Store in covered container.

YIELD: 4 logs each yielding 15 slices

Ingredients:

Dough:
5 eggs
1 cup sugar
1 cup oil
½ cup orange juice (or 1 whole grated orange)
6 cups flour
2 Tablespoons baking powder
1 Tablespoon cocoa
¾ teaspoon almond extract

Glaze:
4 Tablespoons margarine
2 cups confectioners' sugar
water to form thick but spreadable paste
1 Tablespoon cocoa
drop of almond extract

Streussel Cake

This basic cake recipe goes very far and is both tasty and filling. It's great with a glass of cold milk or a cup of hot tea. If you want an exceptionally light cake you can beat the ingredients together by adding one ingredient at a time in the order listed — but it comes out almost as good when everything is dumped into the mixing bowl at once.

1. Preheat oven to 375°.
2. Beat all the batter ingredients together. Set aside.
3. Prepare the streussel by mixing all the streussel ingredients together until they become a crumbly mixture.
4. Pour half the batter into a greased and floured 10"x15" pan.
5. Sprinkle half the streussel over the batter in the pan. Then carefully pour on the rest of the batter. Sprinkle the surface with remaining streussel mixture.
6. Bake for 45 minutes or until it tests done.

YIELD: 1 10"x15" pan

Ingredients:

Batter:
3 eggs
2¼ cups sugar
¾ cup oil
1½ cups orange juice
4½ cups flour
2 Tablespoons baking powder
1 teaspoon salt

Streussel:
1½ cups brown sugar
6 Tablespoons flour
6 Tablespoons melted
    margarine or oil
1½ cups ground nuts
2 Tablespoons cinnamon

Selling herring in Otvosk, Poland, 1927

Shalosh Seudos

On Friday, the Israelites in the desert received a double portion of the manna, and they put some of it away for Shabbos. Moses said, "Eat it this day, for this day is Shabbos to Hashem. This day you will not find it in the field" (*Exodus* 16:25). Because Moses used the term "this day" three times in regard to eating on Shabbos, the Talmud derived that there should be three meals on Shabbos.

Traditionally, the Shabbos meals are accompanied with *zemiros* (Shabbos songs) that celebrate the praises of Hashem and the holiness of Shabbos. The Midrash quotes King David: "Master of the universe! See how different Your nation is. Other nations celebrate their feasts with levity, while Your nation, when they eat and drink, sings Your praises" (*Sefer HaManhig, Shabbos* 61).

Celebrating Shabbos with three meals is of such merit that the Talmud says, "Whoever observes the three meals of Shabbos is spared from three forms of punishment: the anguish prior to the coming of Mashiach, the judgment of *Gehinnom*, and the war of *Gog U'Magog*. Furthermore, his prayers are answered" (*Shabbos* 118a). Of course, this refers to observing the three meals with the appropriate *kavannah* (intent), *kedushah* (holiness), and *divrei Torah* (words of Torah).

Shabbos afternoon, usually after *Minchah*, is the time for the third meal, generally a token meal, consisting of challah and fish. (Of course, one may serve a full meal if one wishes.)

Among chassidim, this third meal, *seudah shelishis*, is eaten in the dark. According to Kabbalah, this time is the zenith of Shabbos, and is especially propitious. Sitting in the dark, where there are no distractions, is conducive to meditation.

This meal is commonly referred to as *shalosh seudos*, which means "three meals." *Divrei Emes* explains that the first two *seudos* of Shabbos — Friday night and Shabbos noon — are full meals that one eats when hungry. There is no indication that one is eating primarily to fulfill a mitzvah. However, the third meal, a token meal eaten when one is not hungry, is obviously intended to fulfill the mitzvah of three meals on Shabbos. This indicates that the first two meals were also in honor of Shabbos. Therefore, the third meal is called *shalosh seudos*, because it encompasses all three meals. Chassidic Rebbes usually give a discourse on Chassidus at *seudah shelishis*.

The Sincerity of the Simple Folk

One Shabbos, the Baal Shem Tov had many guests, including simple, unlearned people, to whom he showed special affection. The Baal Shem Tov and his disciples were having *seudah shelishis*, and he was giving a profound discourse on the hidden meanings in Torah. In an adjacent room, the simple, unlearned folk were reciting *Tehillim*.

Some of the disciples thought, "How fortunate we are to be with the Master and receive his profound teachings, not like the unlearned people who cannot understand this."

The Baal Shem Tov instructed his disciples to close their eyes and place their hands on their neighbors' shoulders, and he placed his hands on the shoulders of the disciples sitting to his right and left, thus completing a circle. The disciples felt themselves being transported to celestial worlds, where they heard verses of *Tehillim* being recited in heartrending tones: "Master of the Universe! Return us to You, our Salvation. Nullify Your wrath over us." Another voice pleaded, "My soul thirsts for You. My flesh pines for You." Yet another cried, "All I ask is to dwell in the House of Hashem." The disciples wondered — from where were such devoted prayers coming? Who could be reciting *Tehillim* with such pure passion for Hashem? Would that we could rise to a level of devotion so pure.

The Baal Shem Tov then told the disciples to open their eyes. "The verses of *Tehillim* that you heard were those recited by the simple, unlearned folk, who pour out their hearts to Hashem in sincerity and purity." They then understood why the Baal Shem Tov showed these people such great affection.

Holding Onto Shabbos

It is customary to prolong *seudah shelishis* to show that we are reluctant to part with Shabbos. The Talmud says that with the onset of Shabbos, Hashem gives us an additional *neshamah*, which leaves us at the close of Shabbos (*Beitzah* 16a). We extend Shabbos to retain this special *neshamah* a bit longer. Among chassidim, *seudah shelishis* may be prolonged far into the night, because the Midrash says that the souls who are confined to *Gehinnom* are given a reprieve on Shabbos. This reprieve lasts as long as some Jews are still observing Shabbos. Extending the Shabbos is doing a *chesed* to these souls.

Gefilte Fish à la Twerski

Rabbi Twerski reminisces:

Gefilte fish is a traditional Shabbos dish, and is a favorite of many people. What may not be widely known is that gefilte fish is the solution to a halachic problem. One type of work that is forbidden on Shabbos is bo'reir *(sorting). This presented a problem with fish, which is often very bony. One may not remove the bones from the fish, and it is cumbersome to remove the fish from around the bones. The solution was to de-bone the fish and grind it before Shabbos. The ground fish evolved into what we know as gefilte fish.*

As a child, I used to accompany my nanny, Leah, to the fish market. Incidentally, the floor in a fish market or a butcher shop was always covered with sawdust. There must have been a good reason for this, just as there must have been a good reason for covering the floor with newspapers after washing it. Times have changed. No sawdust, no newspaper.

The proprietor would take out a fish and, in an idiom that sounds reasonable in Yiddish but sounds terrible when translated literally, ask Leah, "Do you want your head split in two? Should I cut you up in slices?"

Leah would fillet the fish and grind it with a hand grinder. Food processors were not around yet. Then she would use the hock-messer *(chopping knife) to further chop and mix the fish in a large wooden bowl. After adding the necessary ingredients, she would shape the fish into oval balls and cook them in a home-made broth.*

All that is past history. (See, however, page 54). Today one buys a loaf of frozen gefilte fish. I wonder, what are we doing with all the time that modern conveniences save us?

Here is Rabbi Twerski's recipe using a loaf of frozen gefilte fish. There are different regional varieties, just as there are different regional dialects: Russian, Polish, Hungarian, Galicianer. Some prefer sweeter fish, some more peppery. Here is a basic recipe. Add or subtract sugar and pepper to your personal taste.

1. Put the water into a pot that will hold the fish loaf.
2. Bring water to a boil, add ingredients (except dill). Bring to a boil again, then reduce heat to a low boil. Cook for 1½ hours. If desired, add 3 sprigs of dill during the last 10 minutes of the cooking.

YIELD: 8-10 slices

Ingredients:

4 cups water
1 loaf frozen gefilte fish
1 large onion, peeled
3 carrots, peeled and thinly sliced
2 stalks celery
1 parsley root, peeled
2 teaspoons sugar
2 teaspoons kosher salt
½ teaspoon white pepper, or to taste
dill (optional)

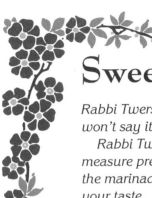

Sweet and Sour Fish

Rabbi Twerski brought a sample of this fish to my house one Sunday. I won't say it led to a fight, but we all wanted more.

Rabbi Twerski writes: No matter how hard he tried, he could not measure precisely. He suggests that you use the quantities listed, then taste the marinade, adding brown sugar, lemon juice, and salt as needed to suit your taste.

1. Prepare the marinade. In a 4- or 5-quart pot, boil onion slices in one cup of water for 3 minutes. Add brown sugar, honey, salt, and lemon juice. Stir; after cooking one minute, taste and adjust ingredients as needed.
2. Let the marinade cool. Add the salmon fillets and refrigerate in the pot for 3 hours.
3. Remove the pot from the refrigerator. Bring to a slow boil. After 20 minutes, add raisins, bay leaves, and pickling spice. Cook 5 minutes longer; remove from heat. Remove bay leaves.
4. Serve immediately or at room temperature. Store the fish slices in the marinade. It will keep in the refrigerator for one week.

YIELD: 6 servings

Ingredients:

6 1½" slices salmon fillet
1 medium-size onion, thickly sliced
1 cup water
1 Tablespoon brown sugar
1 Tablespoon honey
juice of 1 fresh lemon
1 teaspoon kosher salt
¼ cup raisins
6 bay leaves
12 whole allspice

Vegetarian Liver

This is another one of the excellent recipes that I got from my cousin Barbara Schaum. She was the best friend I ever had and many of my favorite recipes come from her kitchen. In Europe vegetarian liver was very often made with mushrooms, which grew wild and were plentiful and cheap. Canned vegetables may not be authentic — but this recipe is fast, easy, and delicious.

1. Drain the beans and peas in a colander.
2. Sauté the onions in oil until golden.
3. In the bowl of a food processor fitted with the S-blade, process the sautéed onions, green beans, green peas, eggs, and walnuts until smooth.
4. Chill, taste, and season with salt and pepper.

YIELD: 2 lbs.

Ingredients:

5 medium onions, diced
¼-⅓ cup oil
1 (16-oz.) can cut green beans, drained
1 (16-oz.) can green peas, drained
6 hard-boiled eggs
3-4 oz. shelled walnuts, either pieces or ground
salt to taste
pepper to taste

Lisa's Challah Kugel

European housewives were thrifty to a fault; nothing went to waste. Any leftover challah was recycled to make the following Shabbos' yummy challah kugel. This recipe is an updated version of the old-fashioned challah kugel. It's Rabbi Twerski's daughter-in-law Lisa's specialty.

1. Remove the crust of the challah and set aside for another use.
2. Soak challah in warm water for 10 minutes. Remove and squeeze out the water. Add remaining ingredients to the challah. Mix until smooth. (Best when kneaded by hand.)
3. Transfer to desired pan (may be baked in 9" pan or as cupcakes) and bake at 350° until brown on top.

VARIATION: At the end of step 2, thinly sliced Granny Smith apples can be added to the batter. Before baking the kugel, sprinkle the top with cinnamon and sugar.

YIELD: 1 9" pan or 12 cupcakes

Ingredients:

1 medium challah or equivalent in challah slices
5 eggs
2 teaspoons vanilla
¾ cup oil
1 (3-oz.) package parve instant vanilla pudding

Sweet Lukshen Kugel

This is my family's absolute favorite. Some like it hot, some like it cold — some even like it 9-days-old. I put a lot of fruit into my kugel but you can use less or more, or even leave it out. Not everyone loves raisins, but I put them in anyway. Those who don't like them pick them out.

1. Preheat the oven to 375°.
2. In boiling salted water, cook the noodles *al dente* according to package directions.
3. While noodles are cooking, peel, core, and cut the apples and/or other fruits into small chunks.
4. Drain the noodles and put into a large bowl.
5. Add the sugar, fruits, raisins, vanilla, and cinnamon. This will cool the noodles a bit; then add the eggs one at a time, mixing well after each addition until loose and creamy. If the mixture seems too thick, add the extra egg. Taste and adjust flavor. There should be enough salt since the noodles were cooked in salted water, but you may need a bit more.
6. Pour oil into a 9"x13" pan and place in oven briefly to heat.
7. Carefully remove pan and pour heated oil into the mixture. Mix thoroughly.
8. Transfer the mixture to the pan and bake for about 1 hour until the top is browned and crunchy.

YIELD: 1 9"x13" pan

Ingredients:

1 lb. noodles (I use a combination of wide and medium)
salt
2 large apples and/or other fruits, such as peaches, grapes, etc.
¼ cup oil
1 can pineapple tidbits, well drained
¼-⅓ cup sugar
⅓-½ cup raisins
1 teaspoon vanilla
1-2 teaspoons cinnamon
4-5 eggs

Potato Salad

Any time my sons-in-law come for Shabbos, I'm sure to include this on the menu. My family claims that this recipe can make a potato-salad fan out of anyone. The potatoes may be any size — small to large. But they should all be about the same size so that they are done cooking at the same time. The quantities given for the vegetables can vary. My granddaughter Mati Dick loves the vegetables and I double the amount when I make this for her family.

1. Cook the potatoes in salted water until soft but not mushy. (A fork inserted into a potato should go in easily).
2. While the potatoes are still warm, peel and dice into medium cubes. Place cubed potatoes into a large bowl and dredge with 2 Tablespoons of kosher salt and flip them over. Sprinkle an additional 1-2 Tablespoons kosher salt over the potatoes. Shake the bowl so that all the potatoes are coated with salt. Do **not** skip this step. It makes a world of a difference.
3. Add the prepared vegetables to the potatoes.
4. Prepare the dressing. Combine mayonnaise, vinegar, and sugar. Taste — if it's tangy enough, sweet enough — according to your taste. **Do not add salt.** There should be enough salt on the potatoes.
5. Pour the dressing over the vegetables and mix well. Adjust seasonings. Refrigerate (although my daughter-in-law Fraydel says it's even better while still warm).

YIELD: 2 quarts

Ingredients:

3 lbs. red potatoes, unpeeled
2 stalks celery, diced fine
1 medium onion, diced fine
2 carrots, shredded
½ green pepper, diced fine
½ red pepper, diced fine
3-4 Tablespoons kosher salt, see recipe

Dressing:
⅔-¾ cup mayonnaise
½ cup vinegar
⅓-½ cup sugar

Fresh Fruit Soup

I make this in a huge pot early in the summer. It freezes wonderfully and is refreshing for shalosh seudos. The quantities are irrelevant — use whatever fruits you like or can get at a reasonable price. Use slightly soft (but not spoiled) fruit in season. When I put the soup into containers, there is always excess liquid; I pour this into ices molds and give my einiklach (grandchildren) frozen fruit pops when they come to swim in my kiddie pool. What an easy way to build loving memories!

1. Wash and pit the fruit. Do not peel. Cut peaches, plums, nectarines, and apricots into chunks and halve the grapes and cherries.
2. Place the fruit into a pot large enough to hold it and still have 3-4 inches until the rim. Add water to 1-1½ inches **below** the fruit. (The fruit will release its own juices.)
3. Bring to a boil. (Be careful — the liquid can boil over — that's why I suggest a **big** pot). Lower the heat and simmer for 5 minutes. Remove from heat.
4. Taste the liquid. It will probably be too tart. With heat **off**, add sugar ¼ cup at a time until it's to your liking. It's better undersweetened than oversweetened.

NOTE: Nowadays I sometimes use packaged gel desert in place of some of the sugar. This adds color (especially when cherries aren't available) and slightly thickens the soup.

YIELD: will vary according to the amount of fruit used

Ingredients:

peaches
plums, several varieties
nectarines
apricots
grapes, red and green
cherries
sugar to taste
1-2 packages raspberry gel
    desert, (optional)

1-2-3-4 Cake

This cake gets its name from the listing of ingredients. It's as simple to make as it is to remember. Recently there has been a big tumult regarding the extensive use of margarine. This cake uses only oil, and it also makes great cupcakes. I'm listing the ingredients in the 1-2-3-4 order even though they aren't incorporated in that order.

1. Preheat oven to 350°.
2. Beat eggs and sugar together until sugar is dissolved and the mixture is light and lemon-colored. Add oil and beat until incorporated.
3. Sift flour and baking powder together and add to egg mixture, alternating with the juice.
4. Pour half the batter into a greased and floured 9"x13" pan. Combine the ¾ cup sugar and the cinnamon. Sprinkle batter with half the sugar/cinnamon mixture and, if desired, all the nuts. Pour the remaining batter on top and sprinkle with the rest of the sugar-cinnamon.
5. Bake for 45 minutes to 1 hour until a toothpick inserted into the cake comes out dry.

YIELD: 1 9"x13" pan

Ingredients:

1 cup oil
2 cups sugar
3 cups flour
4 eggs
1 Tablespoon baking powder
1 cup orange juice or apricot nectar

¾ cup sugar
2 Tablespoons cinnamon
½ cup chopped walnuts or pecans (optional)

Carrot Cake

This is rich and dense, similar to a honey cake. It is repeatedly a winner. I've been making this recipe for over 40 years. In the beginning I made it only when I could cajole my husband into grating the carrots. Now that a food processor has become a kitchen staple, I whip it up all the time.

1. Preheat oven to 350°. Grease and flour a 9"x13" pan.
2. Beat eggs and sugar until well combined. Add oil and mix thoroughly.
3. In a bowl, combine the flour, baking powder, baking soda, and salt.
4. In a bowl, combine the grated carrots and apple.
5. Add the dry ingredients to the egg mixture alternately with the carrot/apple mixture, beginning and ending with the dry ingredients.
6. Mix in the nuts and raisins.
7. Pour the mixture into the prepared pan and bake for 1 hour or until tester comes out dry. Do not overbake.

YIELD: 1 9"x13" pan

Ingredients:

4 eggs
2 cups sugar
¾ cup oil
2¼ cups flour
1 teaspoon baking powder
1 teaspoon baking soda
½ teaspoon salt
6 medium carrots (¾ of a pound), grated fine
1 large apple, grated fine
¾ cup chopped walnuts or pecans (half the nuts can be ground)
¾ cup raisins

On the streets of Cracow, 1917

Melaveh Malkah

In contrast to the delicacies of the Shabbos *seudos*, the menu of the *Melaveh Malkah seudah* on Shabbos night was rather simple. *Melaveh Malkah* means "escorting the queen," referring to parting with "Queen Shabbos." In *der alter heim* the usual menu consisted of herring, borscht and potatoes. Yet, this simple meal was actually the most enjoyable one for me, because at this meal it was customary to relate stories about our *tzaddikim,* stories that fascinated me, some of which I recorded in *Not Just Stories.*

Interceding for His People

Stories are a powerful method of communication. The chassidic master, R' Yisrael of Rizhin said, "When the Baal Shem Tov sought Divine intervention to save the Jews from misfortune, he would seclude himself in the forest, light a fire, and say a special prayer.

"When his successor, my great-grandfather, the Maggid of Mezeritch, wished to intercede for his people, he would go to the same place in the forest and say, 'Master of the Universe! I do not know how to light the fire, but I can still say the prayer,' and with that he evoked Divine mercy.

"Later, R' Moshe Leib of Sassov would go to the place in the forest and say, 'I do not know how to light the fire and I do not know the prayer. Master of the Universe! Have compassion upon us by the merits of the *tzaddikim* who prayed to You here.' "

R' Yisrael would put his head in his hands and say, "Master of the Universe! I do not know how to light the fire, I do not know the prayer, and I cannot even find the place in the forest. All I know is the story about how these *tzaddikim* interceded for their people, and this must be sufficient."

King David and the Prophet Eliyahu

The *Melaveh Malkah* is referred to as "the feast of King David." The reason for this is based on the Midrash stating that David asked G-d to reveal to him the day he would die. G-d said that this is never revealed to a person, but that he would die on Shabbos. Therefore, when Shabbos was over and David was still alive, he made a feast to celebrate his reprieve for at least one more week of life.

The *zemiros* (songs) of the *Melaveh Malkah* feature the prophet Eliyahu. The Talmud says that Eliyahu, who will announce the Ultimate Redemption, will not do so on Erev Shabbos or on Erev Yom Tov, so that the celebration of Shabbos and Yom Tov should not be disturbed. Therefore, when Shabbos passes, we sing about Eliyahu, inviting him to bring us the good tidings of the Redemption.

According to the Midrash, David's life was one of uninterrupted suffering, yet, in his moments of anguish, David could say, "Return to me the joy of Your salvation" (*Psalms* 51:14), never abandoning hope for happiness. Eliyahu is not only the personification of immortality, but is also the harbinger of the Ultimate Redemption. Countless times in Jewish history, Eliyahu has appeared in human form to comfort the suffering.

King David, the prophet Eliyahu, and stories of *tzaddikim*. *Melaveh malkah* is indeed a potent antidepressant.

Chassidic Stories

Stories are the vehicle that can move metaphor and images into experience. Stories can communicate what is generally invisible and inexpressible. Of all the devices available to us, stories are the surest way of touching the human spirit. And *Melaveh Malkah* was rich in stories.

Shabbos is an oasis in a barren desert, and it brings the refreshing water of spirituality into a life often immersed in the arid physicality of the workweek. Little wonder that facing the stresses of the workweek may bring on the "post-Shabbos" blues. I believe that our sages instituted *Melaveh Malkah* as a remedy for the post-Shabbos blues.

The Gaon of Vilna was extremely diligent in observing *Melaveh Malkah*. It is related that the Gaon's wife fasted frequently, and that the Gaon said to her, "All your fasts do not add up to the merit of a single *Melaveh Malkah*."

Among chassidim, it is customary to relate a story about the Baal Shem Tov during *Melaveh Malkah*. I heard many such stories. The following is one of my favorites.

It was once revealed to the Baal Shem Tov in a dream that there was a person who had perfected the trait of *bitachon* (trust in G-d). The Baal Shem Tov traveled to this person's locale, and the latter received his honored guest very cordially.

In the course of their conversation, the Baal Shem Tov learned that this man had bought the rights to a flour mill from the local *poritz* (feudal lord), and that the rental fee was 3,000 *rheinisch* (local currency). "Do you make periodic payments?" the Baal Shem Tov asked. The man answered, "No, I pay in a lump sum. The due date for my payment is just several days away."

"Have you saved the money for the payment?" the Baal Shem Tov asked. "I understand that the *poritz* does not act kindly to anyone who is late with the rent."

"No," the man answered calmly. "I haven't saved a cent. I don't own anything valuable that I can borrow against, and I don't anticipate any income in the next few days."

"Then how do you expect to pay the *poritz* on the due date?" the Baal Shem Tov asked.

"Hashem has taken care of me all these years," the man replied. "He will not forsake me now."

During the next few days, the Baal Shem Tov noted that the man's disposition was cheerful. He did not appear to be the least bit worried.

Two days before the due date, a messenger from the *poritz* delivered a notice of the payment due. The man said to the messenger, "Why are you bothering me now? The payment is not due for two days yet."

On the due date, the messenger returned, demanding the rental fee. The man responded, "Yes, today the payment is due, but that does not mean that it is due early in the day. I still have all day."

The messenger said angrily, "You had better have the money before the day is over. Failure to pay will result in your being thrown into the dungeon." The man did not appear to be perturbed in the least.

The Baal Shem Tov asked, "How do you plan to raise the money before the day is over?"

The man responded, "That is not my worry. Hashem takes care of that." The man continued his usual daily routine, studying Talmud, reciting *Tehillim*, and *davening* with a joyous demeanor.

In the afternoon, three men arrived. One of them said, "We are grain merchants, and we wish to buy this year's harvest of the *poritz's* fields. We understand that the *poritz* strikes a hard bargain. We are total strangers to him, and since you have dealings with him, perhaps you can bargain with him to give us a reasonable price. We are willing to pay up to this sum for the deal."

The man said, "That sum is excessive. I think I can get you a better deal, but I charge 3,000 *rheinisch* to act as a jobber."

"Three thousand *rheinisch*?" the merchant said. "That is far too great a fee. Five hundred *rheinisch* is more than enough."

"I'm sorry," the man said. "You can find another jobber. Three thousand *rheinisch* is my fee, nothing less."

The merchants left angrily, but the man was not upset. The *poritz's* messenger came again, angrily demanding payment. "Why are you so anxious?" the man said. "The *poritz* will have his money before sundown."

Shortly before sundown, the messenger returned. "Your time is up now, " he said. "Where is the money?"

The man took his walking stick and replied, "I will give you your money now." He walked out the door, with the Baal Shem Tov following him, curiously.

As he left the house, the three merchants returned. They had found that the price of grain was on the rise, and that even if they paid the 3,000 *rheinisch,* they would still reap a huge profit. "Come with me," he told them.

The merchants accompanied him to the *poritz.* He negotiated a very profitable deal for them, to everyone's satisfaction. They paid him the 3,000 *rheinisch,* which he then presented to the *poritz.*

The Baal Shem Tov said, "I was well rewarded for my trip. I learned what it means to have *bitachon.*"

Matzoh Brei

For some families matzoh brei is a standard for breakfast on Pesach. If you don't brok, its worthwhile to indulge in this on a winter morning or for melaveh malkah. The proportions do not have to be exact and the matzoh brei can be made as small latkes, as a kugel the size of the frying pan, or scrambled. It's great in any shape or form.

1. Break the matzoh into a large bowl. Pour the boiling water over the pieces. Briefly soak, then pour off the water. Squeeze the excess moisture from the softened matzoh until it is nearly dry.
2. Beat the eggs into a bowl. Add the matzoh. Add seasoning. For a traditional taste, add salt and pepper. For a sweeter version, add the salt and sugar and, if you prefer, the cinnamon and vanilla.
3. Coat a 6″ frying pan lightly with oil, butter or margarine **and heat**. When the oil is hot, fry the mixture according to your liking (as latkes, a kugel, or scrambled).
4. Brown on one side, turn, then fry the second side until golden.

YIELD: 2-4 servings

Ingredients:

3 matzohs
3 cups boiling water
2 eggs
salt and pepper
  or salt and sugar
cinnamon (optional)
vanilla sugar (optional)

2-3 Tablespoons oil, butter, or
  margarine, for frying

Potato Soup

This soup was traditionally served in our home after a fast day. It's fast and easy and I frequently whip it up Motza'ei Shabbos. It is both filling and light on the digestive system. Thinking back to my childhood days, I realize that I could almost tell what day it was by the ambrosial fragrances issuing from the kitchen.

1. Place diced onion, celery, and carrot into a 4-quart pot. Add a dollop of oil and let the vegetables sweat over low heat for 10 minutes until they are soft and aromatic.
2. Add potatoes, water, garlic, parsnip, salt, and pepper.
3. Bring to a boil, then lower to a slow but steady simmer. (I cook it uncovered because the pot I use doesn't have a lid — but either way is ok.)
4. Cook for 10-12 minutes. Potatoes should just be getting soft but not falling apart.
5. To thicken the soup, either add square noodle flakes and cook for an additional 10 minutes until noodles are done, or — the traditional way — add an *einbrenne* (see following page).
6. Remove garlic and parsnip and discard. Serve soup piping hot.

YIELD: 6-8 servings

Ingredients:

1 medium onion, diced
2 stalks celery, diced
1 medium carrot, cut into large dice
3-4 potatoes cut into cubes
5-6 cups water
2 garlic cloves, peeled
½ parsnip, peeled
1 Tablespoon kosher salt
¾-1 teaspoon pepper or to taste
4 oz. square noodle flakes or einbrenne (see following page)

Einbrenne

Ingredients:

1 Tablespoon all-purpose flour
1 Tablespoon fat — butter, margarine, or schmaltz
½-1 cup liquid (soup, water, or gravy)

An einbrenne or roux is a mixture of flour and fat that is used to thicken a soup or sauce. The fat may be butter, margarine, or schmaltz. I usually use margarine even though butter or schmaltz definitely add a more robust flavor.

Using a proportion of 1 Tablespoon fat to 1 Tablespoon flour will thicken a ½ cup of liquid to a sauce and a cup of liquid to soup consistency. If there's thickener in the recipe — such as barley in split pea soup — but you still prefer it a little thicker, use less.

An einbrenne can be any color from very pale (for use in potato soup and light sauces) to very dark, almost like brown sugar (to thicken a meat gravy). When you want a dark einbrenne you have to take care. The pale flour suddenly turns dark — if it burns even the least bit, throw it out and start over or you'll have a bitter taste in your food.

Melt the fat in a heavy frying pan or pot. When it is melted and hot, stir in the flour all at once. It should be smooth, like a thick batter. If it's thin and watery add more flour; if dry and lumpy or crumbly add a bit more fat. Cook over low heat, stirring constantly, until you get the color you want (3-7 minutes).

The liquid to be thickened must be simmering or gently boiling when the *einbrenne* is added or lumps will form. To avoid lumps, pour some of the liquid to be thickened into the *einbrenne* and beat until smooth, then add the blended mixture to the pot to thicken the rest. My mother, who was a pro, could dump the *einbrenne* straight into the simmering liquid and stir until the roux dissolved.

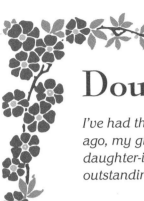

Doughless Potato Knishes

I've had this recipe for a long time, but I rarely make it. Several years ago, my grandson who lives in Eretz Yisrael became bar-mitzvah and my daughter-in-law Raizy made this for the open-house seudah. It was an outstanding hit, enjoyed by all.

1. Preheat oven to 375°.
2. Sauté the diced onions in oil until golden.
3. In a large bowl, thoroughly combine all the ingredients. Put mixture into a 9"x13" pan. Brush with egg wash. Sprinkle sesame seeds on top.
4. Bake for 1 hour.

YIELD: 1 9"x13" pan

Ingredients:

4 onions, diced
½ cup oil
8 potatoes (about 4-4½ lbs.), diced, cooked, and mashed
4 eggs
2½ cups flour
1½ sticks margarine, softened
salt to taste
pepper to taste

1 egg, well beaten, for wash
sesame seeds

Baked Carp

Carp was widely available in Europe. Even in America the fish was sold live. Every fish store had a live fish tank and the balabuste would point to the fish she preferred (I still can't figure out how my mother knew the difference between one fish and another — I think it had something to do with the brightness of the eyes). The fishmonger would use a net to scoop the designated fish out of the tank and place it on his cutting board. Then he would bash the carp's head with a wooden mallet and proceed to fillet or slice it. It sounds cruel, but in reality is not different than hooking a fish in the mouth with a fishhook. The freshness of the fish had a distinct impact on the taste. This recipe comes from my friend, Ruth Mandelcorn.

1. Preheat oven to 350°.
2. Combine the paprika, garlic powder, and pepper in a small mixing bowl. Add just enough water to make a smooth paste.
3. Rub this paste very well into the carp slices. Transfer them to a well-greased pan, placing the fish slices on their sides.
4. Bake uncovered for 20 minutes. Then carefully turn the fish over. Continue baking for an additional 25-30 minutes.

YIELD: 4 servings

Ingredients:

2 Tablespoons paprika
2 teaspoons garlic powder
½ teaspoon pepper
4 slices carp (with bone — not filleted)

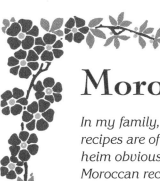

Moroccan Fish

In my family, the alte heim was Mittle Europe and thus nearly all the recipes are of Austro-Hungarian, Polish, or Russian derivation. The alte heim obviously was different for different folks and this is a traditional Moroccan recipe provided by Gail Bessler Twerski's daughter-in-law, Michal.

1. Place 4 cups of water in a large poaching pan or deep roasting pan.
2. Add sliced carrots, peppers, and garlic. Add parve chicken stock mix, salt, and 1 Tablespoon paprika.
3. Bring mixture to a boil. Reduce heat and simmer for 20-30 minutes or until carrots are soft.
4. Place the salmon slices on the simmering sauce.
5. Combine ¼ cup oil with 1 Tablespoon paprika and let paprika settle to the bottom of the cup.
6. Pour seasoned oil on the fish slices and garnish with cilantro.
7. Simmer for approximately 40 minutes, uncovered.
8. Baste fish occasionally with seasoned sauce.
9. If necessary, add ¼ cup of water at a time to ensure that there is adequate sauce.

YIELD: 6 servings

Ingredients:

2 lbs. salmon fillet, cut into 6 5-oz. servings
4 cups water
3 large carrots, cut into circles or sticks
1 red sweet pepper, sliced
1 green or red hot pepper, sliced
2 cloves garlic, chopped
1 handful of fresh chopped cilantro
2 Tablespoons sweet paprika (hot paprika optional for 1 of the Tablespoons)
1 teaspoon salt
1 Tablespoon chicken stock mix (parve)
¼ cup oil

Marble Cake

This cake is a rich marble pound cake. It was always a favorite of my boys and their friends, and, to tell the truth — it's one of my favorites, too. The cake can be made in a 9"x13" pan or a 12-cup bundt pan — but it tastes the best when baked in a 10" tube pan.

1. Preheat oven to 350°. Grease and flour a 10" tube pan.
2. Place the marbling ingredients in a small saucepan and stir over low heat until smooth. Set aside.
3. Prepare the batter. Cream the margarine, shortening, sugar, and vanilla until sugar is incorporated. Add eggs, one at a time, beating after each addition.
4. Combine the flour, baking powder, and salt. Add to the batter, alternating with the liquid, beginning and ending with dry ingredients.
5. Pour batter into prepared tube pan.
6. Top with the marbling mixture. Marbleize by swirling through the batter with a knife or thin spatula.
7. Bake for 1 hour. Remove from oven and cool in pan on a rack.

YIELD: 12-16 servings

Ingredients:

Marbling Mixture:
6 Tablespoons cocoa
2 Tablespoons oil
2 Tablespoons shortening
3 Tablespoons water
½ cup sugar

Batter:
½ cup (1 stick) margarine
½ cup shortening
1½ cups sugar
1 teaspoon vanilla
4 eggs
3 cups flour
1 Tablespoon baking powder
pinch of salt
1 cup non-dairy creamer
  or orange juice

Reciting Tashlich along the banks of the Luga River

Rosh Hashanah

A Truly Happy New Year

The difference between the Jewish New Year and the secular New Year is striking. The Jewish New Year is celebrated through solemn prayer, through arousal to spirituality by the sound of the shofar, and through *teshuvah*. The secular New Year is celebrated by drinking to intoxication and revelry.

I had often wondered, what is the reason for the heavy drinking on New Year's eve? In my work with alcoholics, I found that heavy use of alcohol is often a means to escape. Alcohol can make people forget their misery. But if people are truly happy, as their declaring "Happy New Year!" would seem to indicate, why would they be trying to escape from a happy feeling?

Our lives are often routine. We go through our usual activities day after day without really thinking about what we are achieving in life. The end of a calendar year, however, may be a moment of reckoning. "What! The end of the year already? Where did the year go? I realize that I am one year older, which means that, like it or not, I have used up another year of my allotted stay on earth. So what have I accomplished in the past year? Am I any wiser than I was a year ago? No. Am I better off financially than I was a year ago? No way! I'm deeper in debt than before. And what are the prospects that the coming year is going to be much different? None, really." This realization is depressing. There is no way one can say, "Happy New Year" when the transition to the new year causes sadness. So people drink to escape this sadness, and when totally numbed by alcohol, they shout "Happy New Year" at the top of their voices.

Rosh Hashanah is radically different. It is preceded by *teshuvah* in the month of Elul. We look back on our mistakes and resolve not to repeat them. We are confident that our *teshuvah* has merited Divine forgiveness, and we can enter the new year with a clean slate. Having recognized our shortcomings and resolved to improve upon them, we can look forward to a better year, and as the Jerusalem Talmud says, we dress festively and have a festive meal, secure in the knowledge that G-d will give us a favorable judgment (*Rosh Hashanah* 1). We have no need to escape into alcohol. Rather, we happily greet each other, exchanging the wish, "May you be inscribed for a good year in the Book of Life."

Do We Know for What to Pray?

Before Rosh Hashanah, the *tzaddik* of Sanz would relate the following parable.

A prince committed an offense for which he was punished by being exiled to a distant part of the empire. Not having learned any skills, he had no way of supporting himself other than by tending a herd of sheep. He found no respite from the torrid sun. The other shepherds built themselves thatched huts, but every time he tried to build a hut, it collapsed.

One day he heard that there was going to be a huge parade, because the king was visiting that part of the empire. The practice was that people would write requests on slips of paper, and as the king's coach passed, they would throw their petitions to the king. Any petitions that landed in the coach were read by the king, and the requests were granted.

The prince joined the crowd, and wrote his request: he wanted to have a hut to protect him from the sun. This petition chanced to land in the coach; the king read it, recognized his son's handwriting, and burst into tears. "How sad that my son no longer remembers that he is a prince! Instead of asking that he be permitted to return to the palace, he has resigned himself to being a shepherd and cannot aspire to anything more than a hut!"

The *tzaddik* wept along with the king as he related this parable. "Rosh Hashanah is approaching. These are days that are propitious for prayer. But we have forgotten that we are princes, and that our fervent prayer should be for G-d to return us to Jerusalem and restore the Temple. Instead, we have resigned ourselves to being in exile, and pray only for *parnassah* and other earthly needs. How painful it must be for G-d to see that His children have forgotten who they are and what they should be."

Let us not ask for the equivalent of a thatched hut in exile. Let us pray to be returned to the Divine palace.

Chazzanic Aspirations

Some people have a strong desire to serve as a *chazzan*. One such individual was a wealthy member of the community, and because offending him might cause him to withdraw his support from the *kehillah*, his request was granted. However, when he insisted that he wanted to be the *chazzan* for Rosh Hashanah, the community could not bear it. In desperation, they turned to the *tzaddik,* R' Meir of Premishlan, for help.

It was customary that before Rosh Hashanah, the *chazzanim* from the neighboring communities would come to the *tzaddik* for his blessing. When this wealthy man came, R' Meir said, "We find three references to *tefillah* in *Tehillim*: *Tefillah l'Moshe, Tefillah L'David,* and *Tefillah L'Ani* (of a poor person). Perhaps Moshe, having a speech defect, might not have been fluent as a *chazzan*, but then, he was the greatest *tzaddik*, the father of all the prophets. King David was the 'sweet minstrel of Israel,' who composed the prayers of *Tehillim*. Finally, there is the prayer of the poor person, whose brokenheartedness because of his wretched poverty makes his prayer sincere.

"Now, you know you are not in the class of Moshe nor of King David. The only qualification you can have as a *chazzan* is to be a *tefillah l'ani*, to have the brokenheartedness of a poor person. I cannot intercede that Hashem make you as a great a *tzaddik* as Moshe, nor as sweet a minstrel as David. However, I can pray that you lose all your wealth and become an *ani*."

"No! No!" the man protested. "Please, I no longer have any desire to serve as *chazzan*."

A True Chazzan

But then there is a story of a man who did *not* want to be a *chazzan*.

During a severe drought, the rabbis declared a fast day and ordained special prayers for rain. One night the local rabbi had a dream in which he was told that the prayers would not be answered unless they were led by the proprietor of a small grocery store in town, who happened to be the simplest of all people, very pious but completely unlearned.

The rabbi called the proprietor and told him of his dream, and that he must lead the special prayer services. "But why me?" the man asked. "I know very little about prayer. There are so many scholars who are far more deserving than I am."

When the rabbi insisted that he must lead the prayers, the proprietor went home, and returned with the balance scale that he used in his store. He set the scale on the *bimah* and said, "Master of the Universe! If I have ever given a customer dishonest weight, let a heavenly fire consume me now. But if all my transactions have been with the utmost honesty, then please accept Your children's prayer for rain." Within moments, the sky was covered with clouds that delivered abundant rain.

The rabbi said, "There is no greater virtue than absolute honesty. It is so easy to be tempted to increase one's earnings by giving dishonest weights. This man's impeccable honesty opened the gates of heaven for our prayers."

The Greatest Virtue

One year, prior to Rosh Hashanah, R' Levi Yitzchak of Berditchev was in agony because he sensed that Satan was bringing harsh accusations against Israel for violating the Torah. Unable to rest, he paced the streets of Berditchev, accompanied by his *shammes* (aide). Passing by one hut, he said to the *shammes*, "I feel a *kedushah* (holiness) here. I must see what it is."

In the hut sat a young woman, tearfully reciting the pre-Rosh Hashanah prayers. When she saw the *tzaddik*, she said, "I know you have come to reprimand me for my sin, but I have tried to do *teshuvah* to the best of my ability."

R' Levi Yitzchak said, "No my child. There is great *kedushah* here. Tell me what happened."

The young woman related, "My parents lived in a nearby village, and they rented a flour mill from the local *poritz*. I was 17 years old when my parents both died in an epidemic. I went to the *poritz*, asking him to allow me to keep the flour mill. I was very attractive, and the *poritz* took a liking to me, and began to speak improperly to me. I was frightened, and seeing my fear, he said, 'Do not be afraid. I shall not harm you. Just allow me to touch one of your golden locks of hair.' With that he reached out and touched my hair. I broke loose from him and ran off.

"All that night I was in agony that I had allowed that vile man to touch me, and that it was my long, beautiful hair that had enticed him. I took a scissors and cut my hair. I left the village and moved here, where I worked as a maid. I married a fine man, and just last year he died. I feel that he died because of my sin."

"And what did you do with the locks of hair you cut off?" the *tzaddik* asked.

"I threw them away, all except one, which I take out from time to time to remind me of my sin, and to accept Hashem's judgment as just."

R' Levi Yitzchak wept at her words, and blessed her with a *shanah tovah* (a good year).

Rosh Hashanah, before the blowing of the shofar, R' Levi

Yitzchak said, "Master of the Universe! We sound the shofar, the horn of a ram, to enlist the merit of the offering of the ram that the Patriarch Abraham brought when he willingly obeyed Your command to bring his beloved son Yitzchak as an offering. I have another merit to offer for Israel. When Satan places his accusations on the balance scale, please place the lock of hair of this virtuous young woman on the other side of the scale, and it will outweigh all his incriminations."

Once-a-Year Worshipers

On Rosh Hashanah, the synagogues are usually far more crowded than all year round. The once-a-year congregants pray fervently, asking for forgiveness and for G –d's blessings for the coming year.

This bothered the Maggid of Dubnow a bit. He ascended to the pulpit and said, "Let me tell you a story.

"A merchant lost his store in a fire, and was totally shattered because he had taken the merchandise on consignment and he would be deeply in arrears, without any prospects of being able to pay his debt. He shared his tale of woe with a friend, who said to him, 'Go to your supplier and tell him what happened. I'm sure he will make some accommodation so that you can get back on your feet.'

"The merchant followed this advice, but as he came to the supplier's office, he broke down in tears and could not get himself to enter. He had never asked for charity and had never defaulted on a payment. How could he now face his supplier?

"Hearing the crying, the supplier went out and brought the merchant into his office. When the merchant told him of his tragedy, the supplier comforted him. 'Look,' he said, 'we have been doing business for many years, and you were always on time with your payments. I am going to cancel this debt, and I will give you a new supply of merchandise on credit.'

"The merchant was overjoyed. On the way home, he stopped at an inn, and told people of his good fortune. One of the guests who overheard the story went to the supplier's office, stood outside the door and cried aloud. When the supplier asked him what his trouble was, he said that his business had failed, and he wanted the supplier to give him $10,000.

" 'Ten thousand dollars?' the supplier said. 'Are you out of your mind? I can give you a few dollars for *tzedakah*, but that's about all.'

" 'Well, how come you canceled a $10,000 debt for the other man, and in addition gave him more merchandise on credit?' he asked. 'Why can't you do the same for me?'

"The supplier said, 'You fool! That man has been a customer of mine for many years, and I made much profit doing business with him. Now that he is in need, I'm glad to help him, and I'm sure I will continue to profit doing business with him. But you, I never saw you before and I never profited anything from you. Why should I give you so much money?' "

The Maggid continued, "People who come to synagogue every day and regularly fulfill G-d's mitzvos, if they happen to have sinned and ask G-d's forgiveness and His blessings for the new year, He is glad to give these to them. But those of you who never come to the synagogue all year and do not follow His wishes, with what chutzpah do you come to ask Him to cancel your debts and give you grace for the next year?"

Books of Life and Death

The Talmud says that the reason we do not recite the *Hallel* on Rosh Hashanah is because it is an awesome day on which "the books of life and death lie open before G-d" and it is inappropriate to sing hymns of praise.

On Rosh Chodesh Rabbi Shlomo Kluger once visited a member of the community who was ill. This was a person who indulged in the study of philosophy. Rabbi Kluger found books on non-Jewish philosophy lying on the table, alongside Torah volumes.

"Did you recite *Hallel* today?" Rabbi Kluger asked.

"Of course," the man said. "It is Rosh Chodesh."

"Perhaps you should not have said *Hallel*," Rabbi Kluger said. "You have the books of dead philosophy lying alongside the Torah books of life, and when the books of life and death are open, one does not say *Hallel*."

Tricking Satan

When R' Heschel of Cracow was a child, he helped himself to some goodies on Rosh Hashanah before the morning services. His father reprimanded him, "Don't you know that it is improper to eat before you hear the shofar?"

The young Heschel responded, "Yes, I know, but I have a reason.

"Every day of Elul, the month preceding Rosh Hashanah, we blow the shofar daily. However, on the day before Rosh Hashanah, we do not blow the shofar. This is in order to confuse Satan, so that he should not know which day is Rosh Hashanah and will not bring charges against the Jews.

"I, too, wished to confuse Satan. He knows that we don't eat on Rosh Hashanah morning before the shofar. When he sees me eating, he will think, 'Oh, today must not be Rosh Hashanah.' In that way, I will have tricked Satan."

Sincere Kavannah

R' Levi Yitzchak of Berditchev announced that he was looking for someone to blow the shofar, and that he would interview candidates to see whether they knew the proper Kabbalistic *kavannos* (thoughts) that are proper for the mitzvah of shofar.

After interviewing some candidates who were well versed in Kabbalah, a simple, unlearned man presented himself. R' Levi Yitzchak was surprised. "Do you know the proper *kavannos*?" he asked.

"No," the man replied, "the only thing I can think of when I blow the shofar is, 'Master of the Universe! I have several daughters to marry off, but I do not have money for a dowry for them, and I cannot do *shidduchim*. Please, Master of the Universe, I will blow the shofar to fulfill Your wish. Please grant me my wish, to have enough money to marry off my daughters.' "

R' Levi Yitzchak was impressed. "That is the most sincere, heartfelt *kavannah*," he said. "You will blow the shofar for me."

A Plea for Remembrance

Various reasons are given for the significance of the shofar. One is that when the Jews received the Torah at Sinai, "the sound of the shofar was very mighty" (*Exodus* 19:19). The sounding of the shofar on Rosh Hashanah is thus to commemorate the event at Sinai.

R' Levi Yitzchak of Berditchev, who always pleaded the cause of Israel before G-d, would relate this story before the blowing of the shofar:

A king once went fox hunting, accompanied by his retinue. In pursuit of the fox, the king became separated from his men, and could not find his way out of the forest. As darkness fell, he was afraid of the wild animals in the forest. He saw from afar a dim light, and heading toward the light, he found the hut of a woodsman. The woodsman invited him into his hut, gave him some food and a place to sleep, and told him that in the morning he would show him the way out of the forest. In the morning, he gave the king fresh clothes and guided him back to the city.

The king was very grateful, and rewarded the woodsman by giving him a post in the palace. He gave him the proper garments for a member of the royal court.

As time went by, there was a conspiracy against the king, and unfortunately, the former woodsman was implicated. When apprehended, all the conspirators, including the woodsman, were sentenced to death.

Before the execution, the conspirators were granted one last request. The woodsman asked to be allowed to don his woodsman's clothes and appear before the king. Seeing the woodsman in his old clothes, the king remembered his kindness in helping him when he was lost, and granted him a pardon.

R' Levi Yitzchak said, "So it is with us. G-d took the Torah to all the nations of the world, and they all rejected Him. At Sinai, we were the only ones who accepted Him as our King. We blow the shofar to remind G-d of Sinai, and, like the woodsman, to ask Him for mercy."

An Unfair Advantage

On Rosh Hashanah, R' Noach of Lechovitz would plead, "Master of the Universe! You assigned us the task of fulfilling Your mitzvos. But You created Satan and assigned him the task of obstructing and discouraging us from fulfilling Your mitzvos. We are supposed to resist Satan.

"But we are not on equal footing. Satan has nothing to divert him from fulfilling his assignment. He does not have to earn a living to support a wife and children, he is not subject to the hardships in the world, and most of all, he does not have

a Satan to obstruct him. He can use all his energies to seduce us to sin. But we are at a distinct disadvantage. Much of our energy goes into working to support a family. We are constantly confronted with a wide assortment of anxieties, and we have this powerful Satan who tricks and deceives us. If we have sinned, it is because we are relatively frail, and we cannot stand up against the overwhelming force of Satan. That is why we deserve to be forgiven."

Shofar or Cholent?

When Rosh Hashanah occurs on Shabbos, we do not blow the shofar. The Talmud explains the reason for this: A person who does not know how to blow shofar may carry the shofar to someone who can teach him, and thereby violate the Torah prohibition against carrying objects in the public domain on Shabbos; the sages therefore forbade the blowing of the shofar on Shabbos.

Some commentaries ask why a Torah mitzvah is canceled because of a remotely possible complication, and they say that the sages had additional reasons for their action, but did not reveal all of them.

Chassidim suggest one possible reason. At first glance, it is a witticism, but upon further analysis, it may hold some truth.

We know that G-d designates angels to carry out certain missions. It is also axiomatic that an angel cannot have two simultaneous missions.

Chassidim say that the angel assigned to look after the shofar service also has the assignment of looking after the Shabbos *cholent*. If Rosh Hashanah occurs on Shabbos, one of the two assignments must be dropped. Therefore, the angel attends to the *cholent* and cannot attend to the shofar.

It would appear absurd that the *cholent* should take priority over a mitzvah. However, this is not as far-fetched as it seems.

The sect of Kara'ites, who accept only the Written Torah and reject the Oral Law, was very powerful in ancient times. Because the Kara'ites take the Torah literally, they do not allow fire in their homes on Shabbos, and sit in darkness. Similarly, they do not permit any hot food, even if it is placed on the stove before Shabbos. The halachah, therefore, states that anyone who refuses to eat hot food (heated according to halachah) on Shabbos is suspected of being a Kara'ite.

Eating the hot *cholent* on Shabbos is an expression of our conviction that the Oral Law is indeed the will of G-d. Therefore, *cholent* is not dispensed with on the Shabbos of Rosh Hashanah in order to disprove the contention of the Kara'ites. Inasmuch as the Oral Law is supreme, the sages have the authority to annul the mitzvah of shofar on Shabbos, thus allowing the angel to attend to the *cholent*!

Even Sins Can Be Relative

On Rosh Hashanah afternoon there is the *tashlich* ritual, where certain prayers are recited near a lake, river, or other body of water. The popular perception is that one throws one's sins into the water. This is hardly the case. Sins are disposed of by sincere *teshuvah*, not by throwing them into the water. The *tashlich* ritual is to emphasize to us that if we do sincere *teshuvah*, then G-d will totally eradicate all traces of our sins, as the prophet says, "He will again be merciful to us; He will suppress our iniquities. And will cast into the depths of the sea all their sins (And all the sins of Your nation, the House of Israel, cast away to a place where they will neither be remembered, considered or brought to mind — ever)" (*Micah* 7:19). We are to have a firm conviction of G-d's forgiveness, and separate ourselves completely from the errors of the past, not allowing ourselves to be burdened with guilt.

But the popular concept prevails, if only in wit.

R' Naftali of Ropschitz was on his way to *tashlich* when he met his master, the Seer of Lublin, on his way back. "Where are you going?" the Seer asked.

R' Naftali responded, "I am going to retrieve the sins that the master just threw away."

The Seer felt that his *kavannah* in prayer and mitzvos was defective, and these were his "sins." R' Naftali felt that he was still aspiring to the level of *kedushah* that the Seer had rejected as being inadequate.

Sold Into Servitude

One Rosh Hashanah, in the prayer *Keil Orech Din*, just before the phrase, "He acquires His servants according to judgment," R' Levi Yitzchak of Berditchev paused for a long while, then said, in a cheerful tone, "He acquires His servants according to judgment." After the *davening*, the chassidim asked the reason for the long pause. R' Levi Yitzchak explained:

"I saw what was happening up in heaven. On this Day of Judgment, Satan was bringing before the Heavenly tribunal a wagonload of sins that Jews had done. I was terribly frightened about the judgment this might bring about. I said to Satan, 'Is that all the sins you were able to find? Why, there are many more. Go find them.' Satan was overjoyed, and went to find them. I quickly took the wagonload of sins and emptied them into the depths of the sea from which they would never be recovered.

"When Satan returned, he had found only a few minor transgressions, and was very angry that someone had stolen his wagonload of sins. When it was discovered that I was the thief, Satan took me before the Heavenly tribunal, which ruled that I must pay for the theft. I said that I had nothing with which to pay. The tribunal declared that according to the Torah, a thief who cannot pay must be sold into servitude.

"A call then went out, 'Who wants to buy Levi Yitzchak as a slave?' Hashem said, 'I will buy him.' That is what is meant by 'He acquires His servants according to judgment.' Only when this matter was concluded could I continue."

(This story is sometimes attributed to R' Mendel of Rimanov.)

The Ten Days of Penitence — The Divine Attributes Are for Us

In the prayers on the Ten Days of Penitence we frequently cite the Thirteen Divine Attributes, which state that G-d is compassionate and merciful and forgives our sins. These were revealed to Moses when he pleaded that G-d forgive the Israelites' sin of worshiping the Golden Calf (*Exodus* 34:6-7). Moses then said, "Please, G-d, be with Israel, because they are a stiff-necked people" (ibid. 34:9).

But when G-d expressed His wrath at Israel, He said to Moses, "They are a stiff-necked people" (ibid. 32:9) and threatened to withdraw His presence from them. Why would Moses invoke the trait of stiff-neckedness in pleading on their behalf, as if this were a reason why G-d *should* be with them?

The Maggid of Dubnow explained with a parable:

At the end of a day's work, peddlers assembled to discuss

their fortunes. One peddler complained bitterly that he had not made a single sale all day.

"What were you selling?" his comrades asked. "Wooden cutlery," he replied.

"And where were you peddling?" they questioned. "In the most affluent neighborhood," he answered.

The other peddlers howled with laughter. "You fool!" they said. "Wealthy people don't buy wooden cutlery! They buy gold and silver. You'll never be able to sell your merchandise to affluent people. Go peddle in the poorest neighborhoods. They need your wares."

The Maggid of Dubnow explained that so it was with Moses. When G-d revealed His attributes of mercy and forgiveness, Moses said, "Dear G-d, just what can You do with those attributes in heaven? The heavenly angels do not sin! They do not need mercy or forgiveness. There are no customers for Your wares in heaven. Please, G-d, make Your presence with Israel, because they are a stiff-necked people. With Israel You can put Your attributes of mercy and forgiveness to use."

Are We Like Abraham?

n the *Selichos* prayers we say, "May the One Who answered the prayers of the Patriarch Abraham answer our prayers." The Maggid of Dubnow asked, "Is it not chutzpah to compare ourselves to the Patriarch, whose devotion to G-d was unparalleled?" The Maggid reinforced his question with a parable:

"A wealthy man married off his daughter, and a local merchant gave a wedding gift worth 50 rubles. When a poor man married off his daughter, the merchant gave a gift worth 3 rubles. The poor man reprimanded him. 'Why do you discriminate and favor the rich over the poor?' he asked.

"The merchant answered, 'It is not a matter of favoring the rich,' he explained. 'You must understand that the wealthy man is my best customer, buying things not only for his family, but for his servants as well. He buys many of his business supplies from me. Why, half of my earnings are from him.

"'But what do I earn from you? You occasionally buy a small item, and you haggle over the price so that I hardly earn 2 kopeks from you. That is why the wealthy man deserves a larger gift.'"

The Maggid continued, "So it is with the Patriarch Abraham, whose fulfillment of G-d's wishes was perfect. He gave so much of himself to G-d that he deserved to have G-d answer his prayers. But we, who give so little of ourselves to G-d, how can we demand that He respond to us like he did to Abraham?"

The Maggid continued, "But I can justify our prayer with another parable:

"There was a very wealthy man who was a boor, but he sent his son to a yeshivah, and the son excelled in his studies, becoming an outstanding Torah scholar. When the community was in need of a rabbi, this son applied for the position. The elders agreed that he was well qualified, but, they said, how can we have as our rabbi the son of a boor whom everyone in the community knows to be a vulgar person?

"When the wealthy man got word of this, he pledged a huge amount of money to the community if they would accept his son as their rabbi. Upon receiving the huge gift, they hired the son.

"Fifty years later, the rabbi died. His son, who was also an outstanding Torah scholar, applied to succeed his father. The community elders said that he could get the position only if he made a large donation, as was the case with his father.

"The son said, 'The situation is not the same. My father was the son of a boor, so there had to be monetary compensation. But I am the son of a great Torah scholar, so there is no need for monetary compensation.'"

The Maggid continued, "So it is with us. Abraham had no *yichus* (illustrious genealogy), because his father Terach was an idolater, so he had to have many merits of his own. But we have *yichus*, because we are the children of Abraham; therefore, we deserve to have our prayers answered even if we have few merits."

Surprise! It Wasn't an Apple!

ontrary to what you might have thought, the forbidden fruit in the Garden of Eden was *not* an apple. The apple idea was introduced by the Renaissance painters (Louis Rabinowitz, *The Jerusalem Post International Edition*, "Torah and Flora" column on the apple, February 20-26, 1983).

Well, if it wasn't an apple, what was it? There are four opinions in the Talmud, with each sage giving support to his position.

Rabbi Yehudah says it was grapes, and cites the verse, "Their grapes are grapes of gall, so clusters of bitterness were given them" (*Deuteronomy* 32:32). These were the clusters that brought bitterness into the world.

Rabbi Abba says it was a citron (*esrog*), because Scripture says that Eve saw "that the tree was good for eating" (*Genesis* 3:6); i.e., the tree itself had the taste of its fruit. The only fruit tree that has this quality is the citron.

Rabbi Meir says that it was not a fruit at all, but rather wheat, because it is known that wheat is a brain food (hence Tree of Knowledge). It is referred to as a tree because the wheat stalks were tall as a tree.

Rabbi Yose says it was a fig, and gives a parable. A prince transgressed with one of the maidservants in the palace. The king, his angry father, evicted him from the palace. He sought shelter, but everyone closed the door to him, except the maidservant, who accepted him. Similarly, when Adam and Eve sought to cover themselves, all the trees refused to give their leaves to the sinners, except for the fig tree, which had participated in the sin. Hence, "They sewed together a fig leaf and made themselves aprons" (*Genesis* 3:7).

Interesting, isn't it?

Meat Tzimmes with Knaidel

Carrot-Sweet Potato Tzimmes is a staple for Rosh Hashanah. Everyone loves the knaidel that is cooked in the tzimmes.

Tzimmes:

1. In an 8-quart pot, place the flanken on the diced onions. Simmer over low heat 1-1½ hours, until almost tender. Do not add water. The meat will release its own juices.
2. When meat is nearly done, add the rest of the ingredients and water to cover. Any or all of the optional ingredients can be added at this point. Continue cooking for 1 hour until the vegetables are soft. You can add a knaidel to the tzimmes about 45 minutes before vegetables are finished.
3. Remove the meat, divide into serving size pieces and return to the tzimmes. If the mixture is too liquidy, dissolve 1 Tablespoon flour in ⅓ cup cold water and stir into the tzimmes. Simmer until thickened.

Knaidel:

1. Sift the dry ingredients together. Add oil and water and mix thoroughly. Form this knaidel mixture into a rounded oblong.
2. Put the knaidel into the tzimmes, tucking it next to the meat for the last 45 minutes. Make sure there is enough liquid for the knaidel to absorb and expand. If not, add water in small increments.
3. Cover the pot and let cook for 45 minutes to 1 hour.

YIELD: 10-20 side dish servings

Ingredients:

Tzimmes:
2-2½ lbs. breast flanken (short ribs)
1-2 Spanish onions, in large dice
3 lbs. carrots, in 1" rounds
2 lbs. sweet potatoes, in 1" chunks
¾ cup sugar
salt to taste
water to cover

Optional additions:
1-2 apples, cut into chunks
6 pitted prunes (prunes burn easily, so stir tzimmes frequently)
1 teaspoon cinnamon
1 teaspoon lemon juice

Knaidel:
1 cup flour
½ teaspoon baking powder
pinch of salt
1 Tablespoon sugar
½ cup oil or 1 stick margarine
3 Tablespoons cold water

Breast of Beef

In our house, Rosh Hashanah meals were a combination of the festive and the solemn. The day meals were eaten sometime between 2 and 4 p.m. In the middle of the afternoon we returned home physically and emotionally drained by the seriousness of the prayer services. With the sound of the shofar still echoing in our ears we would listen to the first daytime Kiddush of the New Year and wash for thick slices of round raisin challah smeared with honey. I can still hear my mother cautioning, "Don't eat so much challah, there's a whole meal."

One of my favorite Yom Tov dishes was my mother's breast of beef (brisket). Since my mother spent the day in shul, she would make the meat in advance and quickly reheat the slices in their own gravy on the stovetop. The tasty combination of farfel with mushrooms and the delectable slices of meat in gravy still lingers in my memory.

A caterer taught me how to rewarm thin slices of meat without their falling apart. Place the cold slices of meat into a pan and bring the gravy to a boil in a pot on the stovetop. Pour the hot gravy onto the meat and serve immediately or place in a low (250°) oven until ready to serve.

This recipe can be used for other cuts of meat, such as top of the rib, French roast, or veal shoulder.

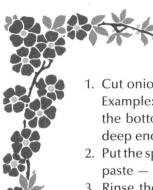

1. Cut onions (the weight of the onions should equal ½ the weight of meat. Example: 8 pounds beef: 4 lbs. onions.) The more the merrier. Place into the bottom of a roasting pan large enough to hold the beef brisket and deep enough (at least 2") to accomodate the gravy it will release.
2. Put the spices into a small bowl and add enough water to make a spreadable paste — not runny, not thick.
3. Rinse the meat under cold running water and place in the roasting pan on top of the onions. Smear all over (top and bottom) with the paste. The potatoes and carrots may be scattered around the roast if desired.
4. Cover the pan tightly with foil and place into a 375° oven for 2-3 hours* until a fork easily pierces the meat but is difficult to remove. Don't overbake or the roast will be dry. Remove from the oven, let the roast rest for 10 minutes for the juices to be absorbed, and then slice thinly across the grain.

*NOTE: The meat can be roasted for only 2 hours, and then removed and sliced thinly across the grain. It is easier to slice when not fully cooked. The slices can be returned to the pan to continue baking until tender.

YIELD: 8-10 servings

Ingredients:

*1 first-cut breast of beef
    (4 lbs. or larger)*
*2 lbs. onions, sliced thin
    or cut into large dice*
2-3 Tablespoons paprika
1 Tablespoon garlic powder
1 Tablespoon seasoned salt
water to make paste

*10 small potatoes, peeled
    (optional)*
*3 carrots, peeled, cut into
    1½" slices (optional)*

Gedempte Honey Chicken

Sury Reinhold works with me at ArtScroll. This recipe came from Mrs. M., her friend's mother. Gedempte is a Yiddish word used for foods that are potted. The chicken cooks slowly in its own juices and is moist and tasty. This amount is sufficient for 4 quarters of chicken. It can be doubled, tripled, or halved. Any way you do it, you can't go wrong.

1. Slice onions to cover the bottom of a pot that will accommodate the chicken quarters in one layer.
2. Sprinkle on some paprika and garlic powder.
3. Place the chicken quarters skin-side down in the pot.
4. Sprinkle additional paprika, garlic powder, and half the honey over the chicken.
5. Cover the pot. Cook over medium heat for 5-10 minutes, and then lower the heat. There's no need to add water; the chicken will release its own juices.
6. After 45 minutes (don't let it cook too long; when the chicken is too soft it's harder to turn) turn over the chicken so that it is skin-side up.
7. Add more honey and let cook for another 45 minutes to 1 hour.

YIELD: 4 servings

Ingredients:

2 onions, sliced
2-4 Tablespoons paprika, to taste
2-3 Tablespoons garlic powder, to taste
4 quarters chicken
½ cup honey or less, to taste

Honey Cake – Lekach

My mother made honey cake for Rosh Hashanah, Simchas Torah, and Purim, when it was one of her shalach manos delicacies. On Purim she dotted the top of the batter with almond halves. Her honey cake was high and fluffy but also had a rich, dense flavor. Somewhere down the line, I lost my recipe, but over the years I've experimented with literally close to 50 different combinations and this is the one I use and the one I like best. The recipe comes from my best friend/cousin Barbara Gold Schaum.

1. Preheat oven to 350°. Line a 9"x13" pan (do not use a standard disposable — it's too small) with foil so that the foil makes a 2" collar around the pan. The batter will rise in the baking and will need the extra room.
2. In a mixing bowl, beat eggs, sugar, honey, oil, and schnapps until smooth.
3. Pour the strong coffee into a mixing bowl or a 1-quart measuring cup.
4. Add the baking soda to the coffee. It will bubble up so make sure the coffee is in a large bowl or cup.
5. In a separate bowl, combine flour, baking powder, and cinnamon.
6. Add the coffee mixture to the batter, alternating with the dry ingredients, beginning and ending with the dry ingredients. Mix until incorporated.
7. Bake for 1-1¼ hours until toothpick inserted in the middle tests dry. Do not overbake.

YIELD: 1 9"x13" pan

Ingredients:

4 eggs
1 cup sugar
2 cups honey
2 Tablespoons oil
2 oz. schnapps
1 cup boiling water in which
    1 Tablespoon instant coffee
    granules have been dissolved
1 Tablespoon baking soda
3⅓ cups flour
2 teaspoons baking powder
½ teaspoon cinnamon

Honey Cookies

These are my cousin Barbara Gold Schaum's honey cookies — they are scrumptious. On the first night of Selichos, while the men were in shul we kept each other company on the phone while these were baking. The color of the cookies depends on the color of the honey. The richer and darker the honey, the darker the cookie.

1. Cream the eggs and sugar until light and lemon colored. Add oil until incorporated and then add the other ingredients.* Mix until thoroughly combined.
2. Refrigerate at least 2 hours — overnight is better.
3. Preheat oven to 375°.
4. Shape into balls the size of walnuts and place 2 inches apart on a parchment paper-lined cookie sheet. The dough is sticky. I flour my palms after every few cookies so it is easier to shape them.
5. Bake 10-15 minutes, until the edge of the cookies are lightly browned.
6. Remove from oven. Allow cookies to cool 3-4 minutes on cookie sheet and then transfer to a rack to finish cooling.

*NOTE: You may need to switch to the dough paddle at this point.

YIELD: 50-60 cookies

Ingredients:

3 eggs
1 cup sugar
½ cup oil
4 cups flour
1 teaspoon cinnamon
1 teaspoon baking powder
1 teaspoon baking soda
1 lb. honey (1⅓-1½ cups)

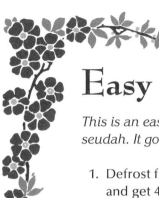

Easy Apple Strudel

This is an easy dessert, ideal for Rosh Hashanah and/or the Friday night seudah. It goes perfectly with a piping hot gleizele tay (glass of tea).

1. Defrost flaky dough until soft. When it's soft you will be able to cut it in 4 and get 4 rolls of strudel. The dough will yield only 2 loaves with thicker crusts if it is not soft enough. Either way is fine.
2. Preheat oven to 350°.
2. On a well-floured board, roll dough into a 15″ by 8″ rectangle.
3. Along the 15″ edge nearest you, smear a 3″ wide thin layer of any jam you prefer (I like blueberry).
4. Sprinkle breadcrumbs lightly over jam, then add chunked apples, sugar/cinnamon mixture, and raisins if desired.
5. Lift the long edge and roll the dough and filling over onto itself to enclose the filling. Place seam side down on a parchment paper-lined jellyroll pan.
6. Bake at 350° (not higher, the apples need to soften) for 35-45 minutes until lightly browned.
7. Slice when ready to serve.

VARIATION: Chumie Lipshitz, who works with me at ArtScroll, told me that her mother, Mrs. Zaidman, makes a very similar strudel, but she uses one can of cherry pie filling in place of the jam and omits the cinnamon.

YIELD: 2-4 rolls, each yielding 8-10 slices

Ingredients:

1 package frozen flaky dough (pink wrapper)
6-12 large Cortland apples, cut into medium chunks (3 apples for each roll)
jam
⅓-½ cup bread or cornflake crumbs, depending on number of rolls
½ cup sugar mixed with 1-2 Tablespoons cinnamon
raisins (optional)

Shopping for fish before Yom Kippur, 1930, in Kalish, Poland

Yom Kippur

 ## Erev Yom Kippur

Just as it is a mitzvah to fast on Yom Kippur, it is also a mitzvah to eat on the day before Yom Kippur. In fact, the Talmud says that if one eats on Erev Yom Kippur, it is considered as though he had fasted both days.

Rabbeinu Yonah explains that having a festive meal on Erev Yom Kippur is an expression of joy that Hashem has given us the extraordinary gift of amnesty whereby our sins are forgiven on Yom Kippur. It is also a statement of our confidence that our sins will be forgiven.

Before *Kol Nidrei*, R'Levi Yitzchak of Berditchev would say, "Master of the Universe! When other peoples have a festive day, they eat and drink to intoxication. You have told Your children to have a festive day today. Look at them! Not a single one of them has drunk to excess. They are all here, sober and alert, standing in awe of Your majesty and humbly asking Your forgiveness. Is there another nation such as Israel?"

Although Erev Yom Kippur was indeed a Yom Tov, it was also a solemn day in my father's home. We went to the *mikveh* before the first meal, and during the meal my father would sing the portion of the *Selichos* prayer for that day, the refrain of which was "Tomorrow will be this wonder." The verses of this prayer are heartrending, and the melody with which they were chanted opened the floodgates of tears. Indeed, the *teshuvah* requisite for forgiveness was attained at this meal.

Forgiveness for G-d

The Midrash says that on Rosh Chodesh, G-d requests that we offer a sin-offering for Him! "I wish to be forgiven for having reduced the size of the moon."

One Yom Kippur eve, the worshipers had gathered for *Kol Nidrei*, but R' Levi Yitzchak of Berditchev was in deep meditation. His expression conveyed profound concern, and the worshipers assumed that the *tzaddik* was aware that in heaven matters were not propitious for forgiveness. Abruptly, the *tzaddik* opened his eyes, scanned the assemblage and said, "Is Berel, the tailor, here?" When it was evident that Berel was absent, R' Levi Yitzchak sent someone to fetch Berel.

"Berel," the *tzaddik* said, "why aren't you in shul for *Kol Nidrei?*"

Berel said, "I have no dialogue with Hashem anymore. I don't agree with His sense of justice."

"What happened, Berel?" the *tzaddik* asked.

"The *poritz* (wealthy non-Jewish landowner) commissioned me to make a *peltz* (fur-lined coat) for him, and he gave me adequate furs to make the *peltz*. I know my work well, and I was able to lay out the fur so that I had three skins left over.

"After I finished sewing the *peltz*, I hollowed out a loaf of bread that I had bought, and stuffed the leftover skins inside. On the way home, I stopped to rest under a tree. Suddenly, I saw a horseman coming toward me. It was one of the *poritz's*

servants. They must have discovered somehow that I had taken three skins for myself. 'The *poritz* wants you back immediately,' he said. I knew I was doomed. Trembling, I mounted the horse, leaving all my tools and the loaf of bread under the tree.

"When I entered the castle, the *poritz* greeted me with, 'Berel! You did not finish the job. There is no band on the coat with which to hang it up.'

"I was so relieved! I borrowed a needle and thread and sewed on a hanger. Joyfully, I made my way back to the tree where I had left everything. But, lo! The bag with the loaf of bread was gone! This was clearly the work of G-d, Who considered my taking the three skins to be theft, and took them away from me. But, Rebbe, it was not theft. I could have cut the furs with less precision and would have needed those three. It was my skill that I was able to salvage those skins, and they legitimately belong to me. I have a large family to feed, and with those skins I could have put food on the table for my children. G-d was not fair, and I want nothing to do with Him.

"I did not wash for meals and I did not say any *berachos*. I did not *daven* (pray) and on Rosh Hashanah I did not hear shofar. You tell me, Rebbe, whether G-d was just."

R' Levi Yitzchak smiled. "But Berel," he said, "it is Yom Kippur, and we must forgive all grudges. Certainly you can discharge your grudge against G-d."

Berel thought for a while, then said, "All right, I will forgive

Him, but only on the condition that He forgives all the sins of all the Jews in the world."

The *tzaddik* lifted his eyes toward heaven and said, "Master of the Universe! I, Your servant, Levi Yitzchak son of Sara Soshe, Rav of Berditchev, rule in favor of Berel. He forgives You, and in turn You must forgive all the sins of all the Jews in the world." And with that, the *tzaddik* joyously began the Yom Kippur service.

An Even Exchange

A disciple of R Elimelech of Lizhensk asked the master for an explanation of the *kaparos* ritual, wherein one seems to be saying that he is shifting his sins onto a chicken, which is then slaughtered. In the *siddur* it says that one should say, "This instead of that," i.e., that the chicken is exchanged or substituted for the person. Just how does such an exchange work?

R' Elimelech told the disciple to go to a certain inn and observe the innkeeper, who would teach him the principle of exchange.

The disciple did as he was told, but could not understand how the innkeeper, who was a simple, unlearned man could teach him anything. Then, on the evening before Yom Kippur, he saw the innkeeper take two ledgers. He opened the first, and

began reading a list of the things he had done that were wrong, occasionally sighing with remorse. When he finished the list, he took the second ledger and began reading off the adversities that he had experienced that year: a barrel of wine had spoiled; a storm had torn off part of his roof; one of his cows had died; a person who had incurred a huge bill had departed without paying; he had slipped and broken a leg.

The innkeeper then closed both ledgers, turned his eyes toward heaven and said, "Master of the Universe! I know that in the past year I did many wrong things. But You were not exactly kind to me, either. But now that Yom Kippur is upon us, let us make an even exchange: I will forgive You, and You will forgive me."

When the disciple reported this strange soliloquy to R' Elimelech, the latter said, "Some people attribute adversities to accidents, 'natural acts.' This man believed that whatever occurred was an act of G-d. His belief in Divine Providence earned him forgiveness."

Begging for Cake

T here is a custom that on Erev Yom Kippur people "beg" for cake. My mother used to bake huge honey cakes, and people would come to my father and say, "May

I please have a piece of cake?" My father would give them a piece of honey cake and wish them a sweet year.

The reason for this custom is that in the event it might have been decreed on Rosh Hashanah that one must be a beggar this year, the decree would be fulfilled by begging for cake. The person could then go on to have a prosperous year.

Kaparos

The ritual of *kaparos*, although widely practiced, is not universally accepted. Rabbi Joseph Caro, author of the *Shulchan Aruch*, disapproves of the practice. However, *Rama,* whose rulings are accepted by Ashkenazic Jews, encourages the practice.

In the Talmud (*Shabbos* 81b) Rashi cites a custom wherein three weeks before Rosh Hashanah, beans were seeded in a flowerpot, one for each child, and they sprouted. On Erev Rosh Hashanah, the child would circle the pot over his head seven times, saying, "This is in exchange for this," and the flowerpots would then be thrown into the river.

This appears to be a synthesis of the rituals of *kaparos* and *tashlich.* As was pointed out earlier, we divest ourselves of sins only by doing *teshuvah*, not by casting them into the river. The latter represents the Divine promise that if a person has done sincere *teshuvah*, his sins will be cast into the depths of the sea, never to be retrieved.

A Sincere Penitence

It is never too late for *teshuvah.* No one is too far gone.

R' Leib, the son of Sarah, as he is known in chassidic lore, would travel among the villages to redeem imprisoned Jews who had been cast into dungeons by the *poritzim* for failure to remit their rent on time. On one such trip, R' Leib found himself stranded in a tiny village for Yom Kippur. The villagers told him that there were exactly ten Jews living there, two of whom had left and had not returned for Yom Kippur. R' Leib was, therefore, the ninth Jew, and they had no *minyan.*

"I never *davened* on Yom Kippur without a *minyan*," he said. "Is there not another Jew anywhere in the area?"

The villagers said that the local *poritz* was born a Jew, but had converted to Christianity. As a young man, he had worked for the *poritz,* whose daughter had wanted to marry him. Since the daughter was the *poritz's* only child, he would allow the marriage only if the Jew converted, and would then be the heir to all the *poritz* possessed. The young man could not withstand the temptation and converted. For the past forty years, he has been a devout Christian.

R' Leib said, "A Jew is always a Jew. I must go fetch the *poritz*." The villagers tried to dissuade him, warning him that the *poritz* would turn his dogs on him, but R' Leib was adamant.

Somehow, R' Leib gained access to the palace, and when the *poritz* saw the saintly countenance of R' Leib, he was stunned into silence.

R' Leib said, "I am known as Leib, the son of Sarah. My father was a *melamed*, who had hired himself out as a teacher for a rural innkeeper. My mother, the innkeeper's daughter, was a beautiful young woman, and when the local *poritz* saw her, he said, 'I am going to take this woman to be my wife! I will return tomorrow with a priest to perform the marriage. Nothing will stop me,' and then with a fiendish laugh, he said, 'unless she is married to someone else.'

"There was no arguing with the *poritz*, who had the power of life or death over his vassals. The innkeeper was distraught, and his daughter said, 'I will kill myself before I let that monster touch me.

" 'I know what I will do. I will marry R' Yosef, the *melamed*. Then the priest will not allow the *poritz* to marry me.'

"R' Yosef said, 'Child, what are you saying. You are 17, and I am an old man of 75. You must marry a young man.'

"The young woman said, 'There is no young man around here. You, R' Yosef, are my only hope.' They gathered a *minyan*, and she married R' Yosef.

"I was born of that marriage," R' Leib said. "My father died before I was Bar Mitzvah. Before he passed away, he said, 'Leib, your mission will be to travel among the villages and save Jews from the wicked *poritzim*. Your mother made the supreme sacrifice in marrying me, and she deserves to have her name perpetuated. You should call yourself Leib, the son of Sarah.' "

R' Leib fearlessly confronted the *poritz*. "My mother sacrificed her life to avoid being violated. You did not withstand temptation, and you forsook the faith of your ancestors. Your sin was grave, but there is always forgiveness before G-d.

"Tonight is Yom Kippur. You are the tenth for a *minyan*. You can join us and pray to G-d for forgiveness."

The *poritz* remained silent for a bit, then agreed to accompany R' Leib to the shul.

You can imagine the shock of the villagers when R' Leib entered the shul accompanied by the *poritz*. R' Leib began chanting *Kol Nidrei*, and the *poritz's* eyes welled up with tears as he recalled the Yom Kippurs of his childhood. Soon, the *poritz* joined in the prayers, and his crying was heartrending.

The *poritz* did not leave the shul. He stood on his feet all Yom Kippur night and the following day, praying and crying bitterly. At the close of *Ne'ilah*, he shouted *Shema Yisrael* at the top of his voice, followed by declaring seven times, "Hashem is the G-d." He then fell lifeless to the floor.

R' Leib said to the villagers, "The Talmud says that there is nothing that stands in the way of *teshuvah*. Like Elazar ben Dordia of the Talmud, who led a dissolute life but died in *teshuvah*, the *poritz* redeemed himself and will enter Gan Eden."

A Precocious Child

When R' Avraham of Sochachov, author of *Avnei Nezer*, was a child of 8, his father sent him home from shul on Yom Kippur to eat. "Don't forget," he said, "that Yom Kippur is a Yom Tov, and those who are permitted to eat must make *Kiddush.*"

The young Avraham said, "No, I don't think so. As a minor, I am not obligated to perform the mitzvos. Minors observe mitzvos as training, so that when they become Bar Mitzvah, they will be familiar with the mitzvos. But when I become Bar Mitzvah, I will not be eating on Yom Kippur, so there is no purpose in my saying *Kiddush* for training!"

Every Person Has His Place

A man who lived in a distant village traveled to Mezhibozh to spend Yom Kippur with the Baal Shem Tov. He traveled all night, and in the early morning of Erev Yom Kippur, he was very close to Mezhibozh. He was weary and also wanted to let his horse rest. There was plenty of time to get to Mezhibozh, so he concluded that it was safe to nap a bit.

When he awoke, the sun was setting, and he was unable to travel. He was broken-hearted that not only would he not be with the Baal Shem Tov, but he would even be without a *minyan* on Yom Kippur. All that night and all the next day he cried during his *davening.*

When Yom Kippur was over, he traveled to Mezhibozh, and the Baal Shem Tov greeted him warmly. "You should know," he said, "that there are sparks of *kedushah* dispersed throughout the world, waiting and longing to be rejoined with their source in Heaven. Your sincere and heartfelt prayers elevated the sparks of *kedushah* that were in the field. It was *hashgachah* (Divine Providence) that kept you in the field over Yom Kippur."

Quenching a Severe Thirst

In the *beis midrash* of the *tzaddik* of Sanz, a man fainted on Yom Kippur. When he was revived, he said he was dying of thirst. The local *dayan* ruled that he could be given teaspoonfuls of water at intervals which would not violate the Torah prohibition on drinking. However, the man said that this was not enough. The *dayan* consulted the *tzaddik* on what to do.

This man was known to be a wealthy miser who never gave adequate *tzedakah*. The *tzaddik* said to whisper to him that he could have water by the tablespoon, but that for each tablespoon he would have to give a sum for *tzedakah* the next day.

The man promptly opened his eyes. His thirst was gone.

Roasted Garlic Potatoes

1. Place potatoes in salted water to cover and bring to a boil. Continue boiling for **two** minutes. Drain thoroughly and cool.
2. Preheat oven to 400°.
3. Smear a thin layer of schmaltz and oil on the bottom of a pan in which the potatoes will fit in a single layer. Place potatoes and crushed garlic cloves into the pan.
4. Roast uncovered for 45 minutes or until potatoes are golden brown and tender. If the garlic cloves begin to turn dark brown remove them. Shake pan or turn potatoes several times during roasting. If the pan seems dry, add a little more fat or oil.
5. Sprinkle potatoes with salt and pepper and stir to distribute seasoning evenly.

NOTE: If you prefer not to have to wash a pot you may skip step 1. Instead, after step 3, roast potatoes in a covered pan for one hour and continue to step 4.

NOTE: If you are roasting meat or chicken at the same time, you can baste the potatoes with the juices.

YIELD: 4 servings

Ingredients:

6 large potatoes, peeled and cut into large chunks
salted water for boiling
1 Tablespoon schmaltz
1 Tablespoon vegetable oil
6 large garlic cloves, peeled and lightly crushed
salt to taste
black pepper to taste

Kreplach

My mother started her kreplach dough on a lukshen breitel (wooden noodle board) by placing the flour in a circle and forming a well. I do this in a bowl or a pot, it's less messy. The dough is great to work with and stretches like magic to encase the filling. Although I think the dough is tastier the thinner it is, it's still great if it's thicker. Her one-egg dough recipe yields 225-250 kreplach. Making this amount is time-consuming. Use the dough all at once and freeze the finished product, or use ⅓ of the dough and freeze the rest for later use.

1. Put the flour into a bowl. Form a well. Add the egg to the well, add the salt, and slowly add the water, mixing steadily until all the liquid is incorporated and the dough can be kneaded. This dough is sticky.
2. Divide the dough into 3 pieces. Place 2 of the pieces on parchment paper that has been well floured. Sprinkle them with additional flour.
3. On a **well**-floured board, lightly knead the third piece of dough and roll out very thin into a 15"x20" rectangle. Cut into 1½" squares. (I use a parve pizza cutter.)
4. Place 1-2 teaspoons of filling on each square. Lift a square, fold it in half diagonally to form a triangle, and, with well-floured fingers, seal the edges together. Bring the two corners at the fold together and pinch in place. Set the finished krepel on a well-floured surface (the dough is sticky) while you shape the rest.
5. Meanwhile, fill an 8-quart pot halfway with water and bring to a boil. Add 2 Tablespoons kosher salt. Carefully add the kreplach (20-25 at a time) one

Ingredients:

Dough:
3½ cups all-purpose flour
1½ Tablespoons kosher salt
1 egg
1½ cups warm water
margarine or schmaltz to prevent sticking

Fillings can be found on the following page.

by one. Bring the water back to a boil, then lower heat to a steady simmer and cook for 6 minutes. Don't overcook. (Recipes using uncooked fillings require a longer cooking time).

6. While the kreplach are cooking, melt margarine or schmaltz (**not** oil) in a 10" frying pan. Set aside.
7. Turn off the heat under the kreplach and immediately pour in 1 cup cold (room-temperature) water to stop the cooking process.
8. Using a slotted spoon carefully remove the kreplach to a strainer. Drain and turn into the prepared frying pan. The kreplach must be "*baschmaltzed*" (greased) or they will stick to each other.
9. Repeat steps 3-8 until all the dough and filling have been used.
10. Serve as an appetizer or soup accompaniment. Refrigerate in a container for up to two days or freeze kreplach on a parchment-lined cookie sheet. Do not allow them to touch. When frozen, transfer kreplach to a plastic bag and seal.

Meat Filling:

Place the diced onions and meat into a small pot. Cover and cook 1½ hours over low heat until soft. Grind the meat with the other ingredients. Add seasoning to taste. If the mixture seems dry, grind in some of the cooking onions. (Boiled or roasted chicken [no more than ¼-⅓ of total mixture] can be ground in.)

Mrs. Zaidman's Chicken Filling:

Combine ground chicken and egg in a pot. Stir over low heat for 2-3 minutes. Remove from heat. Soak challah in water and squeeze dry. Add challah, liver, and spices. Mix to combine. If desired, add 1-2 Tablespoons of matzoh meal.

YIELD: Both fillings are for ⅓ of the dough; each third yields 75 kreplach.

Ingredients:

Meat Filling:
⅘ lb. fillet steak or beef chuck
1 large Spanish onion, diced
1¼ cups sautéed onion
1 Tablespoon kosher salt
pinch of pepper
pinch of garlic powder

Chicken Filling:
½ lb. ground raw chicken
1 lb. Spanish onion, sautéed
   (yields ¾ cup fried onions)
2 koshered chicken livers,
   mashed
1 egg, beaten
small piece of challah
   (about 2 slices)
salt to taste
pepper to taste
onion powder to taste
sugar to taste
matzoh meal or matzoh ball
   mix (optional)

Cherry Compote

Ingredients:

4 pints fresh sour cherries
6 qts. water
11-15 cups of sugar to taste

Mrs. Reinhold is a distant cousin of mine and a superb cook. She gave me this recipe, cautioning, "Don't mind the mess, it's worth it." To demonstrate its worthiness she very generously sent me a huge container. The proof is in the compote; this is definitely worth any mess. Since fresh sour cherries have a short season, and are available only in late summer, stock up then and freeze them if you plan on making this during the year.

1. Rinse the cherries, drain, stem, and check (in good lighting). If not using right away, freeze the cherries in doubled plastic bags.
2. Fill an 8-10 quart pot ⅔ of the way with water and bring to a boil.
3. Add the cherries. (There's no need to defrost the cherries.) Place over medium heat and cook for 1½ hours.
4. After 1½ hours just pour in the sugar. Begin with ¾ of a bag, mixing well so that the sugar dissolves. Keep on tasting; the cherries are tart, so you'll just keep on pouring and pouring — and tasting and tasting. (Just don't taste it while it's piping hot). Continue cooking for an additional ¾-1¼ hours.
5. Use immediately or freeze in containers.

YIELD: 4 quarts

Eggless Cookies

When times were difficult financially, even eggs were an ingredient that was too costly for many housewives. This recipe must have been invented under such circumstances. This cookie dough is easy to make and is tasty too.

1. Preheat oven to 350°.
2. Cream the sugar and oil together until smooth.
3. Add 4 cups of flour and the baking powder alternately with the orange juice. Slowly incorporate up to 2 additional cups of flour* as needed until the dough is smooth and no longer sticky.
4. Divide the dough into 3 or 4 pieces.
5. Roll out each piece of dough on a lightly floured board to the thickness preferred. The thinner the dough is rolled, the crispier the cookie will be, but it can't be too thin if you want to make shapes with a cookie cutter. Sprinkle the surface of the dough with the sugar/cinnamon mixture and gently press into the dough. Cut into diamonds or use a cookie cutter to make any shape you prefer.
6. Transfer the cookies to a parchment paper-lined cookie sheet and bake 15-20 minutes until edges are lightly browned.

*NOTE: If you are making the dough in the mixer, remove the beaters and use the dough paddle at this point. The batter will become thick and can break the beaters. Alternatively, add the last 2 cups of flour by hand.

YIELD: 60-80 cookies

Ingredients:

1 cup sugar
1 cup oil
1 cup orange juice
4-6 cups flour
2 teaspoons baking powder

¾ cup sugar mixed with
1 teaspoon cinnamon

In search of "a perfect esrog" in Warsaw

Succos

Memories of Succos

Succos (Feast of Tabernacles) is referred to as "the season of joy," and it was just that for me.

When I was a child, there were no prefabricated *succahs* nor roof-coverings. Shortly before Succos, Chuna, a member of my father's shul, would come with a helper and remove the stored lumber from the garage for construction of the *succah*. I would get the chance to use hammer and nails and all the wonderful tools.

One memory stands out in my mind. I had taken a long piece of lumber and hammered a nail into it for the fun of it. Chuna pulled out the nail and rebuked me, saying, "Someone might try to saw that piece of wood, and when his saw is damaged on the nail, he might curse the one who put the nail there. Never do anything which might cause someone to curse you." Chuna's reprimand has stayed with me, and I am grateful to him to this day.

The greatest fun was going with Hersh on his horse and wagon to get willow branches for the roof of the *succah*. Hersh let me hold the reins! "Giddiyup!" I exclaimed. I helped Hersh tie up the branches into bundles and load them onto the wagon. Today, in my reveries, I can go back to those scenes, and sometimes even smell the freshly cut willows.

Today, ready-made *succah* decorations can be purchased. Not too much fun there. In those days, we had to make our own. Father would do the lettering on cardboard, and we would fill in the colors. We painted the fruits with bronze paint to make them appear golden.

We made decorative birds for the *succah*. Inasmuch as there were no foam balls, the body of the bird consisted of a hollow eggshell. This was fashioned by puncturing a raw egg at both ends and extracting the contents. (This is the origin of the Yiddish expression that something is "as worthless as a blown-out egg.")

The bird's wings were fashioned out of pleated colored paper and affixed to the eggshell with sealing wax. The bird's head was molded out of beeswax. But be careful! This was a very delicate process. Just a bit too much pressure and the fragile eggshell was crushed, necessitating repetition of the whole process.

There were always many guests in our *succah*, itinerant rabbis and townspeople who had no *succah* of their own. There was much singing and dancing, and the telling of many, many stories.

I recall Father saying that halachah requires that the *succah* must be a temporary structure. He said that the *succah*, as a temporary dwelling, represents our temporary sojourn on earth, the seven days of Succos corresponding to the seven decades of the average lifespan, following which one returns to one's permanent and eternal home.

I thought it a bit strange that the festival that emphasizes man's brief lifespan should be the most joyous of all festivals. To the contrary, this would appear to be a rather depressing thought. Why, then, the singing, dancing and celebration of human mortality?

As I grew older I realized the wisdom of this. If all there is to man's existence is the few decades one spends on this planet and then one disintegrates into nothingness, *that* is a depressing thought. The awareness that we are here to prepare for an eternal existence, *that* is something to celebrate with joy.

To Merit Gan Eden

In the olden days, when travel and shipping were fraught with danger, it occasionally happened that very few *esrogim* (citrons) arrived in Europe. One year, there was not a single *esrog* in all of Berditchev. R' Levi Yitzchak was terribly distraught that he would not be able to fulfill the mitzvah of the Four Species. He asked all his followers to be on the lookout for someone coming to the Berditchev market who might have an *esrog*.

Two days before Succos, R' Levi Yitzchak was told that a merchant traveling through Berditchev had the Four Species. R' Levi Yitzchak summoned him, and pleaded with him to remain in Berditchev for Succos. "Think of it!" he said. "You will give hundreds of Jews the opportunity to fulfill this precious mitzvah. What a great *zechus* (merit) you will have! I will promise you long life and great prosperity." However, the merchant refused, saying that he had been away from home on a long business trip, and that he wanted to be with his family for the festival. No amount of cajoling could change his mind.

In desperation, R' Levi Yitzchak said, "If you remain here for Succos, I promise you a place near me in Gan Eden (Paradise)." Now, this man was no fool. He could recognize a bargain. He agreed to remain in Berditchev on the condition that he share Gan Eden with the Rebbe.

R' Levi Yitzchak then sent messengers all through Berditchev, ordering everyone to absolutely not permit the merchant to enter their *succah*. On Succos night, when the merchant sought to eat in a *succah*, he found all doors closed to him. People explained that by order of the Rebbe, they were not permitted to allow him into the *succah*.

Enraged, the merchant confronted R' Levi Yitzchak. "Is this how you repay a favor? I sacrificed being with my family on Yom Tov, and you refuse me the mitzvah of *succah*!" But R' Levi Yitzchak stood his ground. "Only on one condition can you enter the *succah*. You must release me from my promise that you will share Gan Eden with me."

The merchant was in a quandary. He had sacrificed being with his family only because of the Rebbe's promise to share Gan Eden with him, and now he was to be a loser both ways. He was not with his family, nor would he share Gan Eden with the Rebbe. After due consideration, he said, "I release you from your promise. At this moment, fulfilling the mitzvah of *succah* is more important to me than Gan Eden."

R' Levi Yitzchak welcomed the merchant into his *succah* and embraced him. "Now you will indeed share Gan Eden with me," he said.

R' Levi Yitzchak continued, "Gan Eden cannot be acquired so easily. You did not have sufficient merits to warrant Gan Eden. However, now that you had the *mesiras nefesh* (self-sacrifice) to give up Gan Eden in order to fulfill the mitzvah of *succah*, you have indeed earned it, and you will be close to me in Gan Eden."

A Berachah on a Horse?

R' Mordechai of Neshchiz lived a very frugal existence, rarely having enough money for more than bread for his family. Yet, he managed to save a few kopeks every week, in the hope that when Succos came, he would be able to acquire an *esrog*.

A few days before Succos, R' Mordechai took the bag of coins and headed for the marketplace, where he hoped to buy an *esrog*. Along the way, he met a man sitting at the side of the road, wringing his hands and crying bitterly. On inquiring what the problem was, the man said, "I make my living as a deliveryman. This morning, my horse dropped in his tracks and died. Now I have no way of supporting my family."

R' Mordechai pushed his bag of coins into the man's hands. "Take this money," he said. "Maybe that will enable you to buy a horse."

The man thanked R' Mordechai profusely and ran off to buy a horse. R' Mordechai turned his eyes toward heaven. "Master of the Universe!" he said. "This Succos, people will be reciting the proper *berachah* on an *esrog*, but I, Mordechai, can only make a *berachah* on a horse!"

R' Mordechai's action was in accordance with a ruling given by the Aderet (R' Eliyahu Dovid Rabinowitz - Tumim) in Jerusalem that an act of *chesed* can preempt a mitzvah. A young woman died, leaving a child of 8. The woman's grieving parents asked that the child be with them for the Seder to assuage their grief a bit. The father said that the child should be with him, so that he could fulfill the mitzvah, "You shall tell it (the miracles of the Exodus) to your children." The Aderet ruled that the *chesed* to the parents overrode the mitzvah.

Choosing the Perfect Esrog

t one of the *esrog* markets, HaGaon R' Polonsky was observed by an acquaintance selecting an *esrog*. Using a magnifying glass, he examined a number of *esrogim* and set them aside, until, after two hours of selection, he found an *esrog* with which he was satisfied. He paid for it and went off happily.

On Succos morning, the acquaintance was surprised to see R' Polonsky come to shul empty-handed, without an *esrog*. He made the *berachah* on the communal *esrog* and did not have an *esrog* for *Hallel*. The acquaintance could not contain his curiosity, and asked R' Polonsky, "I saw you carefully choose an *esrog*. Why are you using the communal *esrog*?"

R' Polonsky answered, "I can tell you why, but you must promise me not to reveal this story during my lifetime.

"My neighbor is a very angry person, and I have heard him shout at his children abusively. I have spoken to him about it, but to no avail.

"Early this morning, I heard a young boy crying on the porch next to mine. I asked the neighbor's son why he was crying. He told me that he had been curious to see his father's *esrog*. When he removed it from its case, it fell to the floor and the *pitum* (tip) broke off. He said, 'I know my father will kill me when he finds out.'

"I told the child, 'Here, take my *esrog* and put it in your father's case. He will probably not know the difference.' So, I was left without an *esrog* for myself."

All the effort that R' Polonsky had invested to have a perfect *esrog* was set aside to spare a child from being punished. R' Polonsky indeed had a beautiful *esrog*, similar to the *esrog* of

R' Mordechai of Neshchiz. They both made a *berachah* on a communal *esrog*, beautified by acts of *chesed*.

The Gaon's Simchah

One year, their was a dearth of *esrogim*, and there were none available in Vilna. The Vilna Gaon was extremely worried that he would not be able to fulfill the mitzvah of the Four Species, and sent his students to search through Vilna. If anyone had an *esrog*, the students were to give whatever price was asked.

They did find a wealthy man who had managed to acquire an *esrog*. However, he was not interested in selling it at any price. He did not need the money. When the students pleaded with him, he said, "All right, I will sell it to you. My price is that the reward the Gaon will get for this mitzvah belongs to me."

Having been instructed to offer "any price," the students agreed. When they brought the *esrog* to the Gaon, he was overjoyed. They were hesitant to tell him that they had given away the reward for the mitzvah as the price the man had demanded. Reluctantly, they told the Gaon. The Gaon's joy on hearing this exceeded that of the acquisition of the *esrog*. He explained: "The Talmud states that we should fulfill the mitzvos with no intent to get reward. That is so difficult to do when you know that there is a reward. But now that the reward has been given away to this man, I will be able to fulfill the mitzvah as the Talmud says, with no aspiration for the reward."

Priorities May Vary

R' Michoel Ber Weissmandl spent one Succos in Yemen, where *esrogim* grow wild. Erev Succos morning, a man came into shul with a huge sack, and emptied out a hundred or more *esrogim* onto the table. Each of the worshipers took an *esrog* and put a coin in a *tzedakah* box as payment.

R' Weissmandl was bothered by this. He was accustomed to people spending hours examining *esrogim*, looking for one without a blemish, and here the people took an *esrog* in a haphazard way, without concern for the quality of the *esrog*.

The following morning, just before *davening*, service, a man approached the *amud* (pulpit) to serve as *chazzan*. Another man came over and pushed him away, exclaiming, "Yesterday he said a lie, and today he wants to be the *chazzan*!"

R' Weissmandl said, "We each have our priorities. We insist on a perfect *esrog*, but we are not as meticulous that the *chazzan* be without a blemish. These people may not be so particular about an *esrog*, but they want the *chazzan* to be perfect!"

Beautifying the Mitzvos

It is a tradition to beautify mitzvos, showing how dear they are to us. When I visit a Jewish museum, I am fascinated by the silver ornamentation of Torah crowns and breastplates, Shabbos candelabras and Chanukah menorahs, *Kiddush* cups and spice boxes; by the laboriously handwritten and artistically decorated Haggadahs and Megillahs; by the beautiful *kesubahs* (marriage contracts), and by all the varied Judaica. Only an intense love for the mitzvos could have produced these.

Succos provides opportunities for beautifying mitzvos. Some *succahs* are elaborately decorated. Silver *esrog* boxes come in a variety of charming styles. And as for the *esrog* itself? Many people are not satisfied with an *esrog* that just meets the halachic criteria. They may go to great expense to acquire an *esrog* that has the ideal configuration of ridges and bumps, and that is totally free of the slightest blemish.

Although these are all praiseworthy practices, some people had other ideas. The *succah* of the *tzaddik* of Sanz was simple, without any decorations. The *tzaddik* said, "The money I would have spent on *succah* decorations, I gave to the poor. Their having provisions for Yom Tov is my *succah* decoration."

This was in keeping with the Sanzer *tzaddik's* unparalleled *tzedakah*. One Erev Succos the *tzaddik* came into the *beis midrash* and said to the scholars, "I am in a dilemma. Tonight, the *Ushpizin* (the seven shepherds of Israel: Abraham, Isaac, Jacob, Moses, Aaron, Joseph and David) will be in the *succah*. How can I face them when I am so full of sins?"

The scholars remained speechless. What were they to say to a *tzaddik* whose mind was never diverted from Torah and *yiras Shamayim* for even a second?

The *tzaddik* then said, "I know! I will disguise myself so that they will not recognize me.

"But what kind of a disguise can I use? Ah! I know. We say, '*Levusho tzedakah*, His garment is *tzedakah*.' If *tzedakah* is a garment, then I can wear it to disguise myself! Please go fetch the *gabbai tzedakah* (the community official for *tzedakah*)."

Minutes before Yom Tov, the *tzaddik* sent someone to a wealthy man in town to ask him to lend him money. The wealthy man knew how lavishly the *tzaddik* gave *tzedakah*, but he could not understand to what use the *tzaddik* could put the money so late in the day, when all the stores were closed. Curious, he personally delivered the money to the *tzaddik* and asked him how this money could possibly be used for Yom Tov so late in the day.

The *tzaddik* explained, "It is not enough to have food and drink for Yom Tov. The Torah says that one must have *simchah* for Yom Tov. I know of a man who is deeply in debt, and all Yom Tov he will be worrying about the creditors who will pressure him after Yom Tov. How can he have *simchah* on Yom Tov? But if

I give him money now, when he cannot spend it before Yom Tov, he will know that after Yom Tov he will have something to give his creditors, and he can be free of worry on Yom Tov."

One can beautify with decorations, and one can beautify with *tzedakah*.

The Wonderful Guest

My father occasionally said the *Kaddish* Friday night following the chapter of *Tehillim* at the end of *Kabbalas Shabbos*. This a family tradition, based on the following story.

R' Avraham Yehoshua Heschel, whose name I am proud to bear, is known as the *tzaddik* of Apt. He lived in dire poverty, and one Succos, he did not have money to acquire even bread and candles for Yom Tov, let alone an *esrog* and *lulav*. He told his wife that she should not accept any *tzedakah*. "If Hashem wishes me to be without provisions for Yom Tov, that is fine with me." He left early to shul to learn.

After the *tzaddik* left, a man came to the home and said to the rebbetzin, "I am a merchant on my way home from a business trip, but because of a number of delays, I cannot make it home in time for Yom Tov. I have a large sum of money with me, and I don't feel safe anywhere. I would feel safe in the Rav's home, if you can have me."

The rebbetzin said, "I would love to be able to help you, but we have nothing at all to serve you."

The man said, "That is no problem. If I can stay here, I will get everything necessary." He then set off to the market, and returned with wine, challahs, candles, abundant food, and an *esrog* and *lulav*.

When the *tzaddik* returned from shul and saw that there was light in the *succah*, he was upset, assuming that the rebbetzin had not been able to withstand a barren Yom Tov. When he entered the *succah*, he saw the table lavishly set, and when the rebbetzin told him of the guest, the *tzaddik* was ecstatic that he would have a *simchas* Yom Tov without recourse to *tzedakah*. He greeted the guest warmly, and when the latter showed him the *esrog* and *lulav*, the *tzaddik's* joy was boundless. He embraced the guest, thanking him profusely.

After they had the *hamotzi*, the guest seated himself next to the *tzaddik*. The *tzaddik* then said to him, "Could you please move down a bit." When the guest complied, the *tzaddik* said, "A bit further, please," and kept pushing the guest until he was at the extreme end of the table.

After the meal, the guest said, "Rebbe, you really do not owe me anything. Everything I bought was really for myself, because I needed a place to be on Yom Tov. But why did you object to my sitting near you? If there were others in the *succah*, I could understand that they are more deserving than me. But with no one else in the *succah*, why did it bother you if I sat closer to you?"

The *tzaddik* embraced the guest. "You are very dear to me," he said. "But how can you say there was no one else in the *succah*? The *Ushpizin* were there with us! I had to make room for them."

Upon hearing that he shared the *succah* with the *Ushpizin*, the guest was elated. The following morning he promptly seated himself at the far end of the table.

The next day, the guest said to the *tzaddik*, "If indeed it has been my good fortune to be in the *succah* with the *Ushpizin*, I would like to see them."

The *tzaddik* said, "No, my dear friend, do not ask for that. If you were to see the *Ushpizin*, you could not remain in this world."

On Chol HaMoed, the man said to the *tzaddik*, "I am past 60. How many years do I have to live anyway? It is worth dying earlier if I could see the *Ushpizin*." The *tzaddik* was unable to discourage the guest, and on Hoshana Rabbah, he enabled him to see the *Ushpizin*.

The next day, the guest took sick. He said to the *tzaddik*, "Rebbe, I do not regret for one moment forfeiting my life to see the *Ushpizin*. However, I am childless, and there is no one who will say *Kaddish* for me and keep my *yahrzeit*."

"I will do that for you," the *tzaddik* promised.

The guest continued, "And afterward …?" meaning, who would keep the *yahrzeit* after the *tzaddik* passes on?

The *tzaddik* said, "I will leave instructions for my descendants, that they should say the *Kaddish* Friday night before Maariv for you." The guest died the following day.

And so it has remained a tradition among the descendants of the *tzaddik* of Apt to recite the Friday night *Kaddish* for the guest who provided the *tzaddik* with *simchas* Yom Tov.

How Clever Are Jews — Really?

The sages cite the verse (*Leviticus* 23:40) commanding that on the first day (of Succos) we are to take the *esrog, lulav, hadass and aravah*. The sages ask: Why does the Torah refer to this as "the first day"? It is, after all, the *fifteenth* day of Tishrei. The sages answer: because it is the first day for an accounting of sins (*Tanchuma, Emor* Ch. 22). All the commentaries raise the question: Why is the first day of Succos the first day for an accounting of sins? Assuming that all the sins of the previous year were forgiven on Yom Kippur, then the day after Yom Kippur should begin a new account.

R' Shlomo of Radomsk (*Tiferes Shlomo*) offers this explanation.

On Yom Kippur, Satan brings before the Heavenly Tribunal the many sins that Jews committed. The angel Michael, the defender of Jews, says, "The Jews are not guilty of sinning. They would never knowingly commit a sin. It's just that Satan deluded them into thinking that these acts are not sins. The Jews are innocent because Satan has duped them." Satan laughs. "A likely story," he says. "Everyone knows how clever Jews are.

They can't be duped. They knew full well what they were doing. They should be accountable. Here are the sins they did."

The Angel Michael says, "Not so. They may be clever, but they can still be duped. They are innocent."

The Heavenly Tribunal says, "Neither of you have proven your points. We must delay the accounting of sins until we can clarify whether Jews can or cannot be duped."

On the first day of Succos, people come to shul with their *esrogim*. One person says, "I paid $200 for this *esrog*. I was assured it was pure, not a *murkav* (hybrid)." Another person says, "I paid $300 for this *esrog*. It comes from an orchard that was guaranteed not to be *murkav*." And so continues the conversation in the shul.

The Angel Michael comes before the Heavenly Tribunal triumphantly. "Look down there," he says. "Just look at how many Jews allowed themselves to be duped."

The Heavenly Tribunal says, "You have proven your point. We can now take an accounting as to whether or not the Jews really sinned."

Effective Prayer

I n Frankfurt, there was a *chazzan* who did not measure up to the highest standards of observance. The rabbi, R' Abish, restrained himself from dismissing him from his position only because he had compassion for the *chazzan's* family, who would be left without a source of income.

On the last day of Succos, Shemini Atzeres, it is traditional to pray for rain. No sooner did the *chazzan* finish reciting the prayers, than it began to rain. Beaming with pride, the *chazzan* said to R' Abish, "Now you can see the truth, how dear I am to G-d. It was by virtue of my prayers that it began to rain."

R' Abish said, "You are in error. It is because of your kind that there was not only rain, but a flood, with forty consecutive days of rain!"

Spiritual People

A chassid of R' Menachem Mendel of Lubavitch (*Tzemach Tzedek*) visited Eretz Yisrael, and on his return, told the Rebbe that he had been disappointed because he had expected to find highly spiritual people there.

"And how do you know that you are a *mayvin* (expert) as to who is a spiritual person? Let me tell you a story."

In a village in Eretz Yisrael, there lived a very simple but sincerely pious man. He was totally devoid of any Torah knowledge and could not understand anything in the *Shulchan Aruch*. Once a month he would come into town, and the Rav would write out the schedule of the month for him: what *parashah* to review for Shabbos, and the daily prayers for the month, for Rosh Chodesh, etc.

One time, there was a serious drought, and the Rav decreed a fast day to pray for rain. The villager happened to come into town that day, and went to the Rav's home. The rebbetzin told him that the Rav was in shul, because this was a fast day and a full day of *tefillah*.

The man went to shul and complained to the Rav that he had not put this fast day on his schedule for the month. The Rav explained that he had not known in advance that there would be a fast say. This was not a regular fast day, but one decreed because of the need for rain.

The villager was bewildered. "And if there is no rain, why do you have to fast? Why, when I need rain, I simply go into the field, turn my eyes toward heaven and say, 'Father in heaven! The land is dry. I need rain,' and then it rains."

The Rav realized with whom he was dealing. "Can you do that for us?" he asked.

"Certainly," the man said. He and the Rav went out to the fields. He lifted his eyes toward heaven and said, "Father in heaven! The land is dry. Your children need rain." Within moments the sky was covered with dark clouds, and abundant rain showered on the fields.

"*Nu*," the Tzemach Tzedek said, "are you a *mayvin* on who is spiritual?"

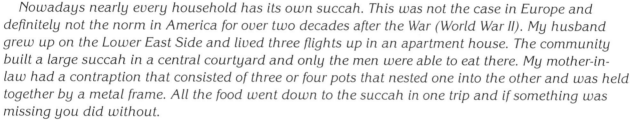

My Memories of Succos

Nowadays nearly every household has its own succah. This was not the case in Europe and definitely not the norm in America for over two decades after the War (World War II). My husband grew up on the Lower East Side and lived three flights up in an apartment house. The community built a large succah in a central courtyard and only the men were able to eat there. My mother-in-law had a contraption that consisted of three or four pots that nested one into the other and was held together by a metal frame. All the food went down to the succah in one trip and if something was missing you did without.

I also grew up in an apartment house and our landlord did not give permission to build a succah. However, a building around the corner had a community succah, large enough for entire families to enjoy. All of us helped in its construction. We went to the water's edge to cut the s'chach to cover the succah (there's nothing like soup with s'chach floating in it) and we made the decorations. The walls of the succah consisted of old doors joined together — different colors, different sizes, but one communal effort that joined to build what I thought was the most beautiful succah imaginable.

We brought all our things to the succah in a shopping cart. Remember, there was no disposable anything. All the dishes, glasses, silverware, napkins, tablecloths, salt shakers, honey dishes, and the many pots of delectable foods were all transported with a sense of adventure and a spirit of joy.

There was no eruv so Shabbos posed its own unique set of problems. We ate in the succah of the local yeshivah and that meant numerous trips back and forth (four city blocks and three avenue blocks) on Erev Shabbos to get everything there (there also was no car). My mother set her cholent on a

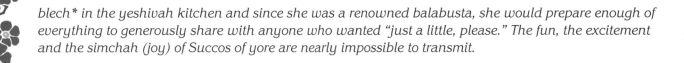

blech* in the yeshivah kitchen and since she was a renowned balabusta, she would prepare enough of everything to generously share with anyone who wanted "just a little, please." The fun, the excitement and the simchah (joy) of Succos of yore are nearly impossible to transmit.

---

*piece of tin placed over an open flame on the Sabbath

Chopped Beef Liver

Have you ever noticed that when you see chopped liver at a simchah or buy it at the take-out counter, there are never any noticeable pieces of egg. My mother asked a caterer for his secret. Scramble the raw eggs into the sautéeing onions. This lightens the dense liver taste without being obvious or unsightly. This dish freezes well. Taste and adjust seasonings before serving. We've placed this recipe under Succos but its perfect any time of the year — including Pesach.

1. Sauté the onions in oil until golden. Add the uncooked eggs and mix thoroughly over medium heat until scrambled. Add liver cubes and mix thoroughly.
2. Put the mixture through a meat grinder twice.
3. Season with salt, pepper, and, if desired, add schmaltz and/or gribenes.

YIELD: 1 lb. liver yields 2-2½ lbs. chopped liver

Ingredients:

1¼ -1½ lbs. raw onions for every lb. of liver (example: 2 lbs. of liver to 4-5 lbs. onions)

oil for sauteéing

4-5 uncooked eggs per pound of liver

koshered beef liver, cut into 1½" cubes

salt to taste

pepper to taste

schmaltz, see page 263 (optional)

gribenes, see page 263 (optional)

Meat Roll

In my family we make this several times a year. The recipe came from my daughter-in-law Reizi in Lakewood. It is made completely by hand and does not use or need a mixer. It's ideal in the succah, for Purim or as a first course at sheva berachos. We serve it with mushroom sauce (see facing page).

1. Prepare dough: In a bowl, place all the ingredients and mix to combine. Knead until a smooth dough forms. Divide into 2 equal parts. Set aside.
2. Prepare filling: Combine all filling ingredients and mix until smooth.
3. Preheat oven to 325°.
4. Roll out one piece of dough into a 9" by 15" wide rectangle. Spread with ½ the chopped meat mixture and roll up jelly-roll style. Seal the ends so the roll stays juicy. Repeat with second piece of dough and remaining filling.
5. Place seam-side down on a parchment paper-lined cookie sheet.* If desired, brush rolls with beaten egg and sprinkle with sesame seeds.
6. Bake for 45 minutes to 1 hour.
7. Cool slightly and, using a sharp knife, slice into portions.

*NOTE: The rolls may be frozen at this point. Remove from freezer (do not defrost) and place on a lined cookie sheet. Cover and bake in a preheated 300° oven for 1 hour, then uncover and continue baking until baked through.

YIELD: 2 rolls, each yielding 10-14 servings.

Ingredients:

Dough:
½ cup oil
3 eggs
¼ cup sugar
2½ cups flour
¼ teaspoon salt

Filling:
2½-3 lbs. ground meat
3 eggs
⅔ cup bread crumbs or matzo meal
1 grated onion
salt to taste
garlic powder to taste
⅓ cup ketchup (optional)
2 Tablespoons deli mustard (optional)

1 egg, well beaten, for egg wash (optional)
sesame seeds (optional)

Mushroom Sauce

This recipe is fast and easy and makes a rich, creamy mushroom sauce that can be served over blintzes, knishes, meat roll, and meat. It's a keeper and you will find yourselves using it many ways. The sauce can be frozen.

1. Sauté the onions until they look waxy but are not yet browned.
2. Add mushrooms and simmer over medium/low heat for 20-30 minutes until the mushrooms are soft.
3. Add seasonings to taste.
4. Dissolve cornstarch in water and add to mushrooms. Cook for 5 minutes. If the sauce is too thick, add additional water.

YIELD: 2 lbs.

Ingredients:

2 large onions, cut in strips
oil for sautéing
20 oz. mushrooms, sliced or diced or 2 (16-oz.) cans, well-drained — save liquid
1-2 Tablespoons paprika, or to taste
2 teaspoons garlic powder, or to taste
1 Tablespoon salt or 2 Tablespoons soy sauce
⅓ cup cornstarch (or potato starch) dissolved in 2 cups water (or water plus the liquid from the canned mushrooms to equal 2 cups)

Sweetbreads

Sweetbreads are delicious served as an appetizer in a baked pastry shell or over rice.

1. Cook sweetbreads in boiling water for 20-30 minutes until they test soft when a fork is inserted.
2. Meanwhile, sauté the diced onion in oil until golden. Add the diced celery and mushrooms and sauté until tender. Set aside.
3. When the sweetbreads are done, pour off the cooking liquid and run cold water over them until they are cool enough to handle. Pop the sweetbreads out of the membrane into a bowl and discard the membrane.
4. Combine sweetbreads with onion-mushroom mixture and heat through. Sweetbreads are salty, so taste to see if salt is needed. Add the other seasonings if desired. If there is a lot of liquid, thicken it by mixing 1 Tablespoon flour into ¼ cup of water to form a paste and add to the mixture. Simmer for 5 minutes.

YIELD: 10-12 servings

Ingredients:

1½ lbs. sweetbreads
1 Spanish onion, diced
oil for sautéing
3 stalks celery, diced
1-2 (8-oz.) can(s) of mushrooms
   or, if desired, ¾ lb. fresh
   mushrooms, sliced
dash of pepper (optional)
dash of garlic (optional)
dash of paprika (optional)
1 Tablespoon flour mixed into
   ¼ cup water — to thicken, if
   necessary

Stuffed Breast of Veal

Stuffed breast of veal is an impressive and scrumptuous Yom Tov main dish. I use a whole breast of veal because it holds the stuffing better.

1. Take 2 large deep disposable roasting pans. Put one into the other. Line the pan with diced onions. Place the veal on the onions. Set aside.
2. Make stuffing. Place oil, potatoes, and onions in bowl of food processor fitted with the S-blade. Process until smooth. Transfer to a large bowl and add the rest of the ingredients. Mix until thoroughly combined.
3. Insert loosely into the pocket. (Do not pack the stuffing — it expands.) Close the opening by sewing or with skewers. If there is extra stuffing it can be baked in the pan or frozen to be used as a cholent kugel.
4. Combine paprika, garlic powder, and salt in a bowl. Add a small amount of water and mix into a paste. Rub paste all over the breast of veal.
5. Cover pan and roast at 350° for 2-3 hours, until a fork inserts easily. Let sit 20 minutes before slicing. Cut 1/2"-3/4" slices, slicing until the bones. Then slice horizontally to remove slices from bones.

NOTE: Veal can be sliced and frozen. When ready to use, do not defrost. Reheat the veal in its gravy, covered, for 1-1½ hours at 350°.

YIELD: 12-16 main dish servings

Ingredients:

Veal:
4-5 Spanish onions, cut into large dice
1 whole 7-9 lb. breast of veal, in which a pocket has been cut
5 Tablespoons paprika
2-3 Tablespoons garlic powder
2 Tablespoons seasoned salt or kosher salt

Stuffing:
¾-1 cup oil
9 potatoes (about 6-6½ lbs.)
3 small onions
3 cup crushed cornflakes (I prefer to crush my own cornflakes rather than using purchased cornflake crumbs — but measure after crushing)
3 cup flour
4½-6 Tablespoons paprika
3 Tablespoons kosher salt
pinch of pepper
garlic powder, to taste (optional)

Plum Kuchen

I have always loved anything made with plums, and this recipe satisfies any cravings. This German recipe comes from Mrs. Judy Neuberger. It's a delicious and attractive dessert.

1. Preheat oven to 350°.
2. Combine the shortening, sugar, egg, and flour and press into the bottom and sides of a 9″ round pie plate.
3. Wash the plums. Cut plums in half, lengthwise, on the natural seam, and pit. Cut each, lengthwise, ¾ of the way through, starting from rounded edge. Do not cut all the way through. The plum halves should resemble a heart shape — two petals held together at a point.
4. Arrange the plum halves in the pie plate — cut end up, flesh side facing center (skin side facing crust) — first around the outer edge and then fill the center (starburst fashion).* There is no need to press the plum halves into the dough — lay them out on a slight angle so that each circle of plums rests on the previous layer.
5. Sprinkle the top of the pie with sugar.
6. Bake 30-45 minutes until golden. Serve room temperature. Freezes well.

*NOTE: Spread apart the two petals of each plum as you lay them out on the pie plate. This will result in a beautiful pie resembling a flower in bloom with all its petals fully open.

YIELD: 7-8 servings

Ingredients:

¼ cup shortening
½ cup sugar
1 egg
1½ cups flour
12-14 Hungarian plums
   (these have a dark purple skin and are oval in shape)
sugar for sprinkling

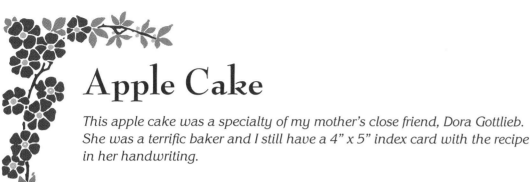

Apple Cake

This apple cake was a specialty of my mother's close friend, Dora Gottlieb. She was a terrific baker and I still have a 4" x 5" index card with the recipe in her handwriting.

1. Preheat oven to 350°.
2. Grease and flour a 9"x13" baking pan.
3. Beat eggs and sugar until sugar is incorporated. Add oil and beat well.
4. In a separate bowl, combine the dry ingredients and add to the egg mixture until a smooth batter forms.
5. Fold apples into the batter. Mix well. Pour into the prepared pan. Sprinkle with sugar/cinnamon mixture.
6. Bake 45 minutes to 1 hour, until a toothpick inserted in the center comes out dry.

YIELD: 1 9"x13" pan

Ingredients:

3 eggs
1½ cups sugar
1 cup oil
2 cups flour
1 teaspoon baking soda
½ teaspoon cinnamon
½ teaspoon salt
4-5 apples, peeled, cored and
   sliced or chunked

2 Tablespoons sugar mixed with
   ¼ teaspoon cinnamon

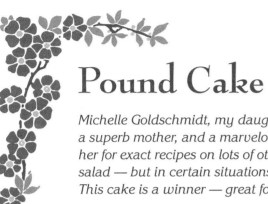

Pound Cake

Michelle Goldschmidt, my daughter-in-law Reizi's mother, is a dear friend, a superb mother, and a marvelous cook. I wish I had the nerve to pester her for exact recipes on lots of other goodies — most notably her hot potato salad — but in certain situations I try to be on my best behavior. This cake is a winner — great for the succah or a kiddush.

Ingredients:

1½ cups sugar
¾ cup shortening
3 eggs
2 teaspoons vanilla
2½ cups flour
4 teaspoons baking powder
½ teaspoon salt
1 cup cold water

1. Preheat oven to 350°.
2. Grease and flour a 9"x13" pan.
3. Cream sugar and shortening until well blended.
4. Add eggs one at a time, beating after each addition. Add vanilla. Then add the dry ingredients alternating with the water, beginning and ending with the dry ingredients.
5. Pour into prepared pan. Bake 45 minutes to 1 hour.

YIELD: 1 9"x13" pan

Sandwich Cake

Sara Rivka Spira is a member of the ArtScroll family. She volunteered her mother's recipe. It is her family's favorite and will quickly become your family's favorite, too.

Dough:
Combine all the dough ingredients and mix well. Divide dough into two equal parts. On a well-floured surface, roll out one piece of the dough and place into a 10"x16" pan.

Filling:
1. With a mixer, beat 10 egg whites on high speed until soft peaks form. Slowly add sugar until incorporated and stiff peaks form.
2. With the mixer on low speed, add the egg yolks and the remaining ingredients until combined.
3. Pour mixture over the dough in the pan.
4. Roll out the second piece of dough. Place on top of the filling. Prick the surface with a fork.
5. Bake for 1 hour at 350°. Let cool. Sprinkle with confectioners' sugar and cut into 2" squares.

YIELD: 25-35 squares

Ingredients:

Dough:
3 egg yolks
   (save the whites for filling)
½ cup sugar
1 packet vanilla sugar
2 sticks margarine
3 cups flour
1 teaspoon baking powder
pinch salt
½ cup seltzer

Filling:
7 eggs, separated + 3 egg whites
   (see above)
1½ cups sugar
4 teaspoons fresh lemon juice
¾ lb. ground walnuts
1 heaping Tablespoon cocoa

confectioners' sugar, for
   sprinkling

Rugelach I – Eggless

Fresh-baked rugelach are truly a taste of home. Many cookbooks give a cream-cheese based dough, but my mother never baked anything milchig (dairy) other than those delicacies that obviously were cheese-filled. I remember her saying that if you couldn't tell by looking that it's milchig, there's always a chance that someone would eat a milchig rugelah with or after a meat meal. I make the dough by hand in a large bowl using a wooden spoon, but it can be made in a mixer using a dough hook.

1. Proof the yeast until bubbly in warm water with a pinch of sugar.
2. Put all the other rugelach ingredients into a very large bowl. Add the yeast mixture and knead until thoroughly combined.
3. Cover with plastic wrap and let rise until doubled, about one hour. If I'm not pressed for time, I punch the dough down and let it rise again for ½ hour.
4. Divide dough into 8 pieces. Using one piece at a time, roll into a circle on a well-floured board. Lightly smear with oil; cover with ⅛ of desired filling.
5. Cut circle into 8-12 wedges, pizza pie style. Roll each wedge from wide end to narrow, stretching the dough as you roll.
6. Preheat oven to 375°.
7. While oven is heating, transfer rugelach to a parchment paper-lined cookie sheet. Let rise until doubled, about ½ hour. Brush eggwash onto rugelach.
8. Bake for 20-30 minutes until well browned and crisp. Cool on rack.

YIELD: 64-84 rugelach

Ingredients:

Rugelach:
2 oz. fresh yeast
1 cup warm water to proof yeast
pinch of sugar
11-12 cups flour
    (high-gluten or all-purpose)
1 cup water
2 cups orange juice
1½ cups oil
1½ cups sugar
1½ Tablespoons kosher salt

oil for smearing

Filling I:
Combine: 3 cups sugar,
    6 Tablespoons cinnamon,
    raisins as desired (optional)

Filling II:
Combine: 3 cups sugar,
    1 cup cocoa,
    4 Tablespoons cinnamon

Egg Wash: *(optional)*
Combine: 1 egg, lightly beaten,
    1½ teaspoons sugar,
    ⅛ teaspoon vanilla

Rugelach II

Rabbi Twerski's daughter-in-law Ratzi is a balabusta par excellence. Just hearing him rave about her baking skills is enough to make your mouth water. This is her rugelach recipe — they are really super.

1. Proof the yeast in the water with a pinch of sugar until it bubbles.
2. Put all the dough ingredients in the kneading bowl of the mixer. Knead until well blended and a soft dough forms.
3. Put dough in an ungreased bowl. Cover with plastic wrap and let rise until doubled. Punch down.
4. Divide dough into 8 pieces. Roll out each piece into a circle. Smear with oil. Sprinkle with filling.
5. Cut into triangles and roll up from wide end. Transfer to a lightly greased cookie sheet. Let rise again for ½ hour.
6. Preheat oven to 375°.
7. Prepare egg wash. Brush on the rugelach. Bake for 20-25 minutes until lightly browned. Cool on a rack.

YIELD: 64-75 rugelach

Ingredients:

Dough:
2 oz. fresh yeast
1 cup warm water
4 sticks (1 lb.) margarine, softened
6 eggs
1 cup sugar
8 scoops vanilla sugar (about ½ cup)
3 lbs. flour

oil for smearing

Filling:
Combine:
2½ cup sugar
1¼ cup cocoa
½ cup confectioners' sugar

Egg Wash:
1 egg, lightly beaten with 1 teaspoon sugar

Carrying hoshana-bundles in Warsaw

Hoshana Rabbah

We have solemn days, like Rosh Hashanah and Yom Kippur, and festive days, like Passover, Shavuos and Succos. Hoshana Rabbah is unique, because as part of Succos, it is a joyous day, but it also has similarities to Rosh Hashanah and Yom Kippur. The *chazzan* wears a *kittel*, parts of the *davening* are chanted with the melody and even the *tefillos* of the High Holy Days, and in several chassidic sects, the shofar is blown after each *hakafah* (procession around the altar).

As we say in the High Holy Day prayers, the decree is written on Rosh Hashanah and is signed on Yom Kippur. However, it is not sealed until Hoshana Rabbah, which, therefore, takes on the flavor of the High Holy Days. A person can still alter his/her decree with proper *teshuvah*. It is customary to wish one another *g'mar tov* (may your judgment be concluded benevolently) on Hoshana Rabbah.

Hoshana Rabbah is reminiscent of the verse in *Psalms* (2:11), "Serve Hashem with awe, that you may rejoice when there is trembling." The Baal Shem Tov said that in earthly relationships, fear and love are mutually exclusive, but in spiritual relationships the two can coexist. We worship Hashem with both *yirah* and *ahavah*, awe and love. Similarly, we stand in utter awe of the Majesty of the Infinite One, and we rejoice that He has chosen Israel to be His children.

As on Erev Yom Kippur, it is customary to go to the Rebbe and request a piece of cake. I recall people from all segments of the Jewish community, non-observant as well as observant, coming to my father on Hoshana Rabbah for cake. In a brief conversation, my father would ask each person how the members of his family were and about matters they had confided to him during the previous year. Some of these people marveled that although they had not met my father since the previous Hoshana Rabbah, he remembered every detail about them.

Helping Hashem

My great-grandfather, R' Motele of Hornostipol, said that Hoshana Rabbah can be translated three ways: (1) a great salvation; (2) the Great One shall help; and (3) help the Great One. The first two are understandable, but what is meant by "help the Great One"? Hashem does not need anyone's help.

The chassidic writings state that Hashem wants to bestow His infinite kindness on us. "Even more than the calf desires to suckle, the cow wishes to nurse it" (*Pesachim* 112a). However, inasmuch as Hashem operates according to the laws of strict justice, He cannot give us what we do not deserve. Hashem, therefore, needs us to be meritorious so that he can bless us with His bounty. In this way, we can "help Hashem."

True Teshuvah Tested

A chassid was en route to his Rebbe, R' Yitzchak of Vorki, for Hoshana Rabbah, carrying his *lulav, esrog* and his *hoshana* (bundle of five willow twigs). His heart was full of joy, yet he was in great awe because Hoshana Rabbah was the final day of the Heavenly judgment, and his thoughts were focused on *teshuvah*. Suddenly he was accosted by a *poritz* who said to him angrily, "Jew! What is that you are carrying?"

"It is a *lulav* and *esrog*," the chassid answered.

"You lie and are mocking me," the *poritz* said. "It is nothing but a broomstick and a lemon," and with that, he lashed the chassid with his whip.

"No, your lordship," the chassid said, "it is not a broomstick and a lemon. It is a *lulav* and *esrog.*"

The *poritz* raised his whip. "Don't you dare mock me! Admit that it is a broomstick and a lemon!" When the chassid insisted it was a *lulav* and *esrog*, the *poritz* again struck him with his whip.

"And what is that little broom you are carrying?" the *poritz* asked.

"It is not a broom," the chassid replied. "It is a *hoshana*."

"Again you are mocking me, " the *poritz* shouted. "Admit that it is a broom," and delivered another blow with his whip.

"No, your lordship, it is a *hoshana*."

The *poritz's* eyes blazed with anger. "And where do you think you are going?" he questioned.

"I'm going to see my Rebbe," the chassid replied.

"Hah! You are going to see Itcha, aren't you, and you think he is a Rebbe!" the *poritz* again wielded his whip. "Admit it! You are just going to see Itcha."

The chassid protested that he was going to his Rebbe. The *poritz* inflicted additional lashes on the helpless man and left.

When the chassid arrived in Vorki, the Rebbe greeted him warmly. "That *poritz* was none other than Satan," the Rebbe said. "Satan could not tolerate the sincerity of your *teshuvah*, and wanted you to degrade the *lulav, esrog* and *hoshana*, as well as to show disrespect to your Rebbe by calling him by a nickname. Your refusal to yield, in spite of his beating you, stands to your merit, and you will be blessed with a happy and prosperous year."

The Strange Solution

A chassid of R' Naftali of Meletz came to the Rebbe before Rosh Hashanah and poured out his tale of woe. He had leased an inn from the *poritz*, but because the weather was extremely bad, there were few travelers. To make things worse, both of the cows on whom he depended for milk for use in the inn died. In addition, several family members were severely ill. He was simply unable to meet the rental this year. However, the *poritz* would not listen to his troubles. The rent was overdue, and if he did not make payment properly, the *poritz* would send his henchmen to destroy everything the man owned and throw him into the dungeon.

"The *poritz* is an evil man," the chassid said. "He has caused the death of more than one Jew and has rendered families homeless. Everyone hates him, Jews-and non-Jews alike, but he is all-powerful and no one can do anything to escape his wrath."

R' Naftali said, "The *poritz* is not all-powerful. The only One Who is all-powerful is Hashem. Stay here for Yom Tov."

Rosh Hashanah passed, as did Yom Kippur and the first few days of Succos, without R' Naftali addressing the chassid's problem. Finally, on Hoshana Rabbah, after the *hakafos* were completed, R' Naftali called the chassid to him. "Can you show me in what direction your town lies?" he asked.

The chassid looked about and then pointed. "It is that way," he said.

R' Naftali pointed the *lulav* in the direction indicated by the chassid. Then, wielding the *lulav* as though it were a machine-gun, he shook it and made staccato sounds as if he were firing it. He then said to the chassid, "You may go home. The *poritz* will not bother you anymore."

Upon his return home, the chassid found the townsfolk breathing a collective sigh of relief. On Hoshana Rabbah, the evil *poritz* had suddenly keeled over and died.

Sole Survivor

One of the Hoshana Rabbah prayers reads, "Master Who saves, other than You there is no savior. You are powerful and abundantly able to save. I am impoverished, and You can save me."

The *tzaddik* of Sanz said that when a person appeals to another human being for help, the latter may say, "Why is it my responsibility to help you? There are others to whom you can turn." Or, one may say, "I'm sorry, but I'm just unable to help you." Or, one may say, "You are dissimulating. You really don't need anyone's help."

Therefore, we say to Hashem, "You are the One Who saves. There is no one else to whom we can turn, You have the power and ability to help us, and You know the truth, how desperately in need we are. There is no way You can turn us away."

Celebration and Solemnity

n Succos, there was a special service in the Temple — the water libation on the Altar. Inasmuch as on Succos Hashem decrees the amount of rainfall for the coming year, special prayers were offered for abundant rain.

Beginning with the second night of Succos, there was joyous celebration in the Temple, with singing, musical instruments, and dancing. We commemorate this with festive gatherings — *simchas beis hasho'evah* — every night of Succos (from the second night onward).

However, the night before Hoshana Rabbah is solemn. People gather to recite *Tehillim* (*Psalms*) and read the book of *Deuteronomy*. Therefore, some do not celebrate *simchas beis hasho'evah* on the eve of Hoshana Rabbah. The Vilna Gaon, however, did celebrate it. Others reached a compromise, singing and dancing after completing each of the five books of *Tehillim*.

Joy and solemnity are not mutually exclusive on the spiritual plane.

Liver Sauté — Cold or Hot

Liver sauté seems to have been a staple in many homes. I remember my mother occasionally making it with beef liver cut into chunks and adding green peas and mushrooms to the sauce at the last minute. We loved it and enjoyed sopping up the sauce with chunks of challah.

The cold version is often served in place of chopped liver on Shabbos morning. The hot version is delectable served over rice or mashed potatoes.

Liver Sauté — Cold:
1. Sauté 1 diced Spanish onion until golden.
2. Add salt and pepper.
3. Chop each chicken liver into 3-4 pieces and add to the onions. Sauté until heated through.

NOTE: The cold version does not use mushrooms, water, or cornstarch.

Liver Sauté — Hot:
1. Sauté 2 diced Spanish onions until golden.
2. Add mushrooms, salt, and pepper.
3. Add ¼ cup water.
4. Cut the livers in half — sauté in the mixture for 1-2 minutes.
5. Add ¼-⅓ cup warm water into which 1½ teaspoons cornstarch has been dissolved. Stir until liver is warmed through and sauce has thickened.

YIELD: 4 appetizer servings

Ingredients:

For both versions:
1-2 large Spanish onions, diced
salt and pepper to taste
¾ lb. chicken livers, kashered

For hot version:
1 (8-oz.) can mushrooms, drained
½ cup water, divided
1½ teaspoons cornstarch

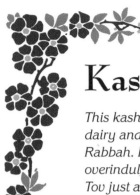

Kasha Varnishkes

This kasha-pasta recipe is a hearty, filling side dish, and can be used for both dairy and meat meals. It has become our traditional side dish for Hoshana Rabbah. By the time we have our Hoshana Rabbah seudah, we have overindulged in meat and chicken main dishes — and with a two-day Yom Tov just around the corner, I want something tasty, attractive, and a little different. So my main dish is breaded veal cutlets with kasha varnishkes. The one disadvantage of this recipe is that you have to wash several pots.

The proportions vary according to your taste. Some like lots of onions. Some, equal amounts of kasha and bow-tie noodles. Some add sautéed mushrooms at the end, etc. Any way you make it — I'll like it. It's that good.

Ingredients:

2 large onions, diced
4 Tablespoons oil
1 cup whole grain kasha
2 Tablespoons oil or margarine
2 cups boiling water or chicken
   soup
salt to taste
½ lb. small bow-tie noodles

1. In a heavy frying pan, sauté onion in oil until golden. Set aside.
2. Place kasha and oil in a 4-quart pot. Toast briefly until the kasha grains are dry and crunchy. Then add the boiling water or chicken soup and salt to taste. (Soup may not need extra salt.) Bring to a boil.
3. Cover pot, lower the heat, and simmer for about 15 minutes. Check if liquid has been absorbed and kasha is tender. If not, cover and steam another 5 minutes.
4. Meanwhile, bring a 4-quart pot of salted water to a boil. Cook varnishkes (bow-tie noodles) according to package directions, *al dente*. Drain.
5. Combine noodles, kasha, and onions. Adjust seasoning.

YIELD: 6-8 servings

Overnight Potato Kugel

When my einiklach (grandchildren) will be visiting on Sunday, I make an extra 9"x13" pan of potato kugel on Friday. On Sunday, about 2 hours before I plan to serve the kugel, I divide it into portion-size pieces (leaving it in the pan and taking care not to cut through the bottom). I then pour about ½-⅔ cup of cold water over the kugel, cover it tightly with foil, and bake it in a 375° oven for 1½-2 hours. (This also works well with frozen kugel). The kugel comes out dark and creamy (like a caterer's kiddush kugel).

My daughter Miriam achieves this same taste right off the bat. My husband loves the flavor of her overnight kugel. Here's her recipe.

1. Preheat oven to 500°. Pour the oil into a 9"x13" pan and heat in the oven.
2. Place eggs in a large mixing bowl.
3. Using a food processor, process the potatoes and onions on the S-blade until almost smooth but not liquidy. Add to the eggs along with salt and pepper.
4. Carefully remove the hot pan from the oven. Pour the hot oil into potato-egg mixture and mix until incorporated.
5. Pour mixture into the pan and bake until the top is brown, about 1 hour. Remove from the oven. Reduce oven temperature to 200°. Cover the kugel with parchment paper, and then cover tightly with foil.
6. Return pan to the oven. Place a pan of water (cold) on the rack underneath the kugel and continue baking at least 4 hours or overnight.

YIELD: 20-24 servings

Ingredients:

¾ cup oil

10 extra large eggs

5 lbs. potatoes, peeled and cut into chunks

1 medium onion, cut into chunks

2 Tablespoons kosher salt

¼ teaspoon pepper, or to taste

Yerushalmi Kugel

I have an interestingly shaped scar on my right forearm because I did not proceed with caution when making a Yerushalmi kugel under pressure. Pressure means all the married kids and their kids coming for Shabbos Chanukah on the shortest Friday* of the year. My original recipe said to use a low flame under the oil-sugar mixture and stir often until it caramelized. But that took at least ½ hour and was extremely tedious and time-consuming. I once read a Yerushalmi kugel recipe in a secular newspaper and the instructions were to heat the oil-sugar over high heat quickly so I adapted my recipe to their instructions and it's fast and easy.

1. Preheat oven to 400°.
2. Fill a 5-quart pot ¾ full of water and bring to a boil.
3. While waiting for the water to boil, put the sugar and oil into an 8-quart pot and place it on the stove.
4. As soon as the water boils, add kosher salt and the thin noodles. Cook for 4-5 minutes and strain in a colander.
5. At the **same** time that you added the noodles to the water, turn the heat up to high under the sugar-oil mixture. Do not worry and do not mix. Let the mixture heat as you cook and drain the noodles.
6. Then place a dry dishtowel **into** the sink — by now the oil and sugar should be quite dark — the trick is to get it as dark as you can without burning it. The oil-sugar mixture is ready when it starts to foam.

Ingredients:

1 lb. thin egg noodles
2 Tablespoons kosher salt
¾ cup sugar
½ cup oil
1 onion, grated fine
3 eggs, beaten together
½ teaspoon salt
½ teaspoon pepper, or to taste
— I use more, much more

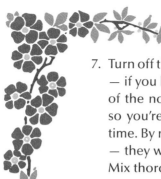

7. Turn off the heat and place the oil-sugar pot into the sink. Now — carefully — if you have long pot-holder gloves they're a plus — spoon one ladleful of the noodles into this mixture — it will bubble up but it's in the sink so you're safe. And then add the rest of the noodles one ladleful at a time. By now the oil will have cooled a bit, so mix the noodles thoroughly — they will turn caramel-colored — then add the rest of the ingredients. Mix thoroughly.

8. Pour mixture into a 9"x13" pan and bake for about 1 hour until dark and crusty.

YIELD: 1 9"x13" pan

*NOTE: I must tell you an anecdote about "short Fridays." When I was first married (45 years ago) I frequented a fruit and vegetable store owned by an Italian. The store was very small and one Friday morning in November was packed with shoppers. In walked an elderly Italian woman. She took one look at the mob scene and said "Tony, what's the occasion — why is the store so crowded?" Without looking up he nonchalantly replied, "It's a short Friday." She gave him an astonished look. "What's a 'short Friday'?" she asked. "Doesn't every day have 24 hours?"

Sponge Cake

I don't remember a week that my mother didn't make a sponge cake. I'm lazy and hesitate to separate eggs and would rather not have 2 bowls to wash, but when I tested this old favorite in my kitchen I couldn't figure out why I gave in to the laziness and dropped this from my repertoire. It's really scrumptious, doubly so when served with a dollop of whipped cream and fresh strawberries.

1. Preheat oven to 350°.
2. Place the yolks in the mixer bowl and beat on medium speed for at least 5 minutes or until light and fluffy. Slowly add sugar until thick and creamy, about 8 minutes in all. Stir in the juice and the vanilla extract. Whisk in the flour. Pour into a large bowl.
3. In a clean mixer bowl with clean, dry beaters beat the egg whites on low until foamy. Add the salt or cream of tartar, turn mixer to high, and beat until stiff peaks form.
4. Fold ½ of the beaten whites into the yolk mixture in the large bowl. When fully incorporated, fold in the rest until thoroughly combined.
5. Pour the batter into an **ungreased** 9" or 10" tube pan. Bake about 45 minutes until the top is golden and springs back when touched.
6. Turn over the tube pan if it has legs, or invert it over the neck of a bottle. Let the cake cool completely before removing from the pan.

YIELD: 10 servings

Ingredients:

8 eggs, separated
1¼ cups sugar
1 cup orange juice
1 teaspoon pure vanilla extract
1½ cups sifted flour
1 teaspoon salt or ¾ teaspoon cream of tartar

Applesauce Cake

This yummy rich cake is moist and not crumbly. I suspect applesauce was used so that the batter would need fewer eggs and less flour and cocoa and therefore was more affordable. I got this recipe while relaxing at the pool in the bungalow colony (oh, were those great summers). It was given to me by Miriam Lasker. We're all deeply indebted to her — it's marvelous.

1. Preheat oven to 350°.
2. Cream the margarine and sugar until sugar is dissolved. Add eggs.
3. Combine flour, baking soda, cocoa, and cinnamon and add to egg mixture alternating with the applesauce, beginning and ending with flour mixture. Chocolate chips can be added to the batter at this point. (It's worth it even if it's not traditional.)
4. Pour into greased and floured 9"x13" pan. Prepare the topping. Combine the chocolate chips, nuts, and sugar and sprinkle on top of cake batter.
5. Bake at 350° for 45 minutes to 1 hour until a toothpick inserted in the center comes out dry.

YIELD: 1 9"x13" pan

Ingredients:

1 stick margarine
1¾ cups sugar
2 eggs
2 cups flour
1½ teaspoons baking soda
3 Tablespoons cocoa
½ teaspoon cinnamon
1 lb. applesauce
1 cup (6-oz.) chocolate chips (optional)

Topping:

1 cup (6-oz.) chocolate chips (optional)
1 cup chopped walnuts or pecans
3 Tablespoons sugar

Boys with flags for Simchas Torah

Shemini Atzeres/Simchas Torah

Simchas Torah marked the close of Succos. The joy of dancing with the Torah knew no bounds. Whoever saw Father dancing with the Torah retains a memory never to be forgotten. Father's dance essentially defined the concept of spiritual joy as explained in chassidic teachings. Father would stand, holding the Torah, his face radiating joy, singing a lively melody, a tune reserved exclusively for Simchas Torah. Family tradition has it that our ancestor, the Maggid of Chernobyl, said that he heard the heavenly angels sing this melody in their adoration of G-d. Father would stand motionless while the singing increased in crescendo, and abruptly break into a dance that was at once serene yet ecstatic.

The message of this dance was that joy is an internal experience, and should find external expression only when it reaches an intensity at which it can no longer be contained.

Then, and only then, may it burst into spontaneous and manifest action. Even then, the expression of joy must be modest and somewhat subdued.

Years later, when I learned the chassidic elaboration on the verse "rejoice with trembling" (*Psalms* 2:11), I was able to understand it. Father's Simchas Torah dance had been a penetrating lesson.

My Brother's Simchah

R' Naftali of Ropschitz would tell of a simple person who once outwitted him. One Simchas Torah, R' Naftali observed a man who was essentially illiterate of Torah singing and dancing with all his heart and soul. "Do you know anything about Torah that you are so elated over it?" R' Naftali asked.

"No," the man said, "I know nothing of Torah. But if my brother were making a *simchah*, wouldn't I celebrate along with him? So, my learned brothers rejoice with the Torah, and I am participating in their *simchah*."

The Happiness of the Torah

On another occasion a rather unlearned man was dancing passionately with the Torah. When he was asked the reason for his elation, he said, "I have reason to be happy with the Torah.

"I had borrowed a large sum of money, but the lender lost the promissory note and there was no proof of the loan. I was, therefore, able to deny that I owed the money. The lender took me to *beis din* (rabbinic court), and the rabbi said that according to the law of the Torah, inasmuch as there was no evidence, I could swear that I did not owe the money and be absolved of the debt. I did just that. The law of the Torah saved me a huge amount of money. That's why I am happy with the Torah."

The rabbi said, "You are very mistaken. Simchas Torah means 'the happiness of the Torah'; that is, that the Torah be happy with you. In this case, you are happy with the Torah, but the Torah is not happy with you, because you distorted it and exploited it to cheat someone of the money due him. You have no right to celebrate Simchas Torah unless the Torah can be happy with you."

My Memories of Simchas Torah

After the morning hakafos in our shul, the men and boys went from home to home to make Kiddush. This evolved into each housewife preparing her specialties for the entire community.

After the seudah on Hoshana Rabbah, my mother would chide me, "Hurry to take a shower. The iceman will be here soon." We never had an icebox but a modern up-to-date refrigerator. However — in anticipation of the many thirsty men and boys who came for "Kiddush" on Simchas Torah — shortly before Shemini Atzeres began the iceman would ring the bell. He made several trips, hauling huge 4' by 4' chunks of ice and setting them into the scrubbed clean bathtub. These ice mounds were covered with burlap to slow the melting. Before we went to bed on Simchas Torah night we would fill the tub with bottles upon bottles of soda and seltzer to be chilled by the ice. It seems so long ago that it feels like it was in another lifetime — but it wasn't — that's how it was then.

My mother didn't go to shul on Simchas Torah night for hakafos. She was busy preparing her famed strudel, rugelach, and lekach. But the pièce de résistance was her halubchas. Yes, we had a refrigerator — a small refrigerator — but a freezer was not something to even dream about. You have to understand that nearly forty men would crowd into our apartment for the Kiddush. My mother stayed up all night long coring and separating five or six large heads of cabbage. She would put up three huge pots of sauce and then add the cabbage rolls to simmer through the night, until our guests arrived. Along with the halubchas she would serve what she jokingly called roast katchke (duck) — except that my mother would roast a large pullet in such a fashion that the skin was crisp and the meat so juicy that it passed as katchke, and kishke — real kishke. The singing and dancing and the simchas Yom Tov (joy of the Holiday) still reverberate in my ears.

Stuffed Cabbage – Halubchas

Ingredients:

Halubchas:

leaves from one large head of cabbage, frozen, defrosted, separated, and checked

(see facing page for sauce and filling)

This recipe takes time but preparing the sauce in which the cabbage rolls cook is very worthwhile. It brings a whole new dimension to the taste of this fantabulous delicacy.

My mother would carefully remove the core from the cabbage head, submerge the head in boiling water, and slowly remove each leaf, pouring more boiling water over the head from time to time. This was tedious and still necessitated removing the tough "spine" from the leaves before they could be rolled.

*I place the head of cabbage into the freezer 2 days to 2 weeks **before** I plan to make the rolls. Carefully remove the cabbage the night (or at least 6 hours) before using. Frozen cabbage is brittle and can shatter into icy slivers. Place the head into a deep bowl (the defrosting cabbage releases quite a bit of liquid). When totally defrosted, the leaves are soft, pliable, translucent, and readily separated — making them very easy to check.*

As my mother repeatedly said, "Use a bigger pot." This precludes a messy stovetop. My mother would cook her sauce and place the rolls into the pot of simmering liquid on the stovetop, but I "cook" them in the oven.

The first time I made halubchas I added sugar, then tomato sauce, over and over but I couldn't get the right taste. In walked my mother, took one sip of the sauce, and said "It's missing salt," and — voila — perfection.

YIELD: Each head of cabbage will differ. For example, when I used 2 heads of cabbage, one head yielded 19 rolls (8 large, 7 medium and 4 small) and the second, 24 rolls (7 large, 7 medium and 10 small).

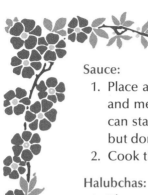

Sauce:

1. Place all of the ingredients in a 10- or 12-quart pot. I add some marrow and meat bones — my husband loves that — but it's not necessary. You can start with less brown sugar and tomato sauce and add to your taste, but don't spare the salt.
2. Cook this sauce at least 2 hours — longer is even better.

Halubchas:

1. Thoroughly combine filling ingredients. Place 3-5 Tablespoons of the mixture, depending on the leaf size, at the core end of each leaf. Roll up and, using your forefinger, tuck the sides in.
2. Preheat oven to 350°. Take one large (10"x16") or two small (9"x13") pans and pour in most of the sauce. If using disposable pans, double them, inserting one into the other, for added strength.
3. Place the rolls seam-side down in the pan and top with remaining sauce.
4. Cover the pan tightly with foil and cook in oven for 2-2½ hours. If the sauce has cooled, obviously more time is needed until the cooking begins.

NOTE: This can be frozen and reheated.

VARIATION: The recipe for the sauce in which the stuffed cabbage simmers is basically the recipe my mother used for cabbage soup. When I make it for my grandkids, I cut several peeled Idaho potatoes into long spears and let them cook in the soup for the last 20 minutes — yum!

VARIATION: Any leftover meat mixture can be formed into meatballs and cooked in the sauce. The raw rice cooks up in spikes and my grandchildren crave "porcupine" meatballs. The taste of halubchas without the work!

Ingredients:

Sauce:

2 Spanish onions, cut into chunks

1 bag Bodek white cabbage, to which you will add all the extra cabbage leaves you aren't using for the rolls

2 big (1 lb.) Cortland apples, sliced (any apple will do)

4-5 Tablespoons kosher salt or more, to taste

6 quarts water

1½-2 lbs. dark brown sugar

2-3 (15-oz.) cans of tomato sauce

meat and marrow bones (optional)

Filling:

3½ lbs. ground beef (I use lean, but **not** extra lean)

1½ cups uncooked long grain rice

1 large apple, grated

1 large Spanish onion, grated

3-4 Tablespoons kosher salt or more, to taste

Kishke and Helzel

What we call kishke today is a far cry from the kishke of the shtetl. Kishke is literally the kishkes (intestines) of a cow. The casing was turned inside out, scraped clean, then turned back and stuffed with a flour-based filling and roasted with the Shabbos chicken. I made this authentic kishke once. The flavor was better than anything you can imagine — but I never did it again.

Much easier and more common was stuffed helzel. Helzel is Yiddish for neck, and the neck skin of any poultry fowl — chicken, duck, goose, or turkey — would be used. It's difficult to obtain an unslit long neck skin, and if it's slit, it requires so much sewing that most of it is thread. If your butcher can give you an unslit neck skin from a bird that's at least 6 lbs., it makes a very tasty treat.

The stuffing my mother used is the one I provided for a cholent kugel (page 73). Here I include another stuffing that you may want to try.

1. Singe the neck skin over a flame after feathers are removed.
2. Turn it inside-out and scrape clean of all meat and sinews, but leave the fat that lines the skin.
3. Turn the skin right-side out and sew up the bottom of the tube.
4. Combine all stuffing ingredients until well mixed. Stuff poultry neck skin loosely. Sew the ends closed.
5. Roast in a 350° oven on its own on a bed of onions, or alongside the poultry.
6. Baste occasionally with pan juices and roast until crisp and golden brown.

YIELD: 4-6 servings

Ingredients:

1 cup flour or ½ cup flour plus ½ cup matzoh meal
¼ cup schmaltz or oil
1 small onion, grated or minced
1 clove garlic, finely minced
½-1½ teaspoon paprika
½ teaspoon salt
¼ teaspoon pepper

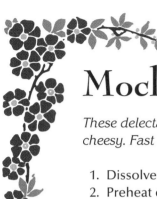

Mock Cheese Rugelach

These delectable parve rugelach actually taste as if they are milchig and cheesy. Fast (no-rise yeast dough) and easy — it's a Mrs. Zaidman specialty.

1. Dissolve yeast in ½ cup warm water.
2. Preheat oven to 350°.
3. Mix all the dough ingredients together until smooth and elastic. Dough should be used immediately and not left to rise.
4. Divide dough into 3 balls. Roll one ball at a time into a 9"-10" circle. Cut into wedges, pie fashion, then roll up each triangle, from widest part toward point, to form rugelach.
5. Line a cookie sheet with parchment paper and transfer rugelach to the sheet.
6. Bake at 350° for 20 minutes or until light brown.
7. While the rugelach are baking, prepare the glaze. Put the water and sugar into a 2-quart pot. Bring to a boil and stir until the sugar dissolves
8. When the sugar has dissolved, add remaining ingredients and stir to combine.
9. Remove rugelach from oven and, using a fork, immediately dip each one into the glaze. Remove from glaze and place on a rack to cool.

YIELD: 24-36 rugelach

Ingredients:

Dough:
2 oz. fresh yeast
½ cup warm water
3 sticks (1½ cups) margarine
1 cup sugar
4 eggs
1 cup orange juice
½ cup seltzer
½ teaspoon salt
8 cups flour (approximately)

Glaze:
1½ cups water
1 cup sugar
1 scant Tablespoon vanilla sugar
1 teaspoon vanilla extract
¼ cup orange juice or lemon juice

Mandlebroit

Mandlebroit is a favorite in almost every culture. The Italians call it biscotti, which means "twice-baked." Everyone loves this dry cookie and it's especially delicious with a cup of coffee or tea. We had a neighbor who would dunk his slice into his glass of tea.

1. Preheat oven to 350°.
2. Sift flour, baking powder, and salt together.
3. Beat the eggs with sugar until thick and lemon-colored. Add oil,* extracts, and zest. Beat until combined. Add nuts and stir in the sifted flour to form a soft and workable but not sticky dough. If need be, add up to ½ cup flour. Divide dough. This batter can be made into 2, 3, or 4 logs depending on the desired length and thickness.
4. With floured hands, shape logs and place on parchment paper-lined cookie sheet, leaving 3 inches between each log.
5. Bake for 30-45 minutes until lightly browned. Using a serrated knife, cut the logs into ½" slices.
6. If desired, return slices to the cookie sheet (do not grease) and place back into oven. Bake 5 minutes on each side until toasted.
7. When thoroughly cool, store in an air-tight container.

*VARIATION: My mother often reduced the oil to ½ cup and added the juice of one orange along with 1 Tablespoon of orange zest.

YIELD: 60-80 slices

Ingredients:

3½ cups flour
1 Tablespoon baking powder
1 teaspoon kosher salt
4 eggs
1¼-1⅓ cups sugar
¾ cup vegetable oil*
½ teaspoon almond extract
½-1 teaspoon vanilla extract
1 Tablespoon grated lemon zest
1½ -2 cups coarsely chopped
    nuts (almonds or walnuts)
½-1 cup raisins (optional)

Babke – with a Twist

A slice of babke is delicious and filling and ideal to quell hunger pangs on Simchas Torah when the main seudah is served well past midday.

1. Sift flour into the kneading bowl of mixer. Make a well in the mound of flour. Crumble yeast into the well. Pour some of the water mixed with juice over this. Add the sugar. Let this ferment for 5 minutes. Add the margarine, eggs, and vanilla sugar along with the rest of the water or juice.
2. Knead with the dough hook for 1 minute. Add the salt. Knead for an additional 10 minutes.
3. Divide dough into 5 balls, cover, and let rise for 1 hour, covered.
4. Meanwhile, combine filling ingredients.
5. Divide each ball in half. Roll out dough in a rectangle, smear lightly with oil, cover with ⅓ of the filling, and roll up jelly-roll fashion. Do the same with the second half. Then twist the two rolls together to form babke. Place into 12″x6″ loaf pan. Repeat with the remaining balls of dough.
6. Let the babkes rise for ½ hour.
7. Preheat oven to 350°.
8. Brush tops of babke with egg wash.
9. Combine streussel ingredients to form crumbs and sprinkle on top of each babke.
10. Bake for 45 minutes to 1 hour, until golden on top.

YIELD: 5 babkes; each babke yields 8-10 slices

Ingredients:

Dough:
5 lbs. flour
4 oz. fresh yeast
3¾ cups warm water
¼ cup orange juice
2 cups sugar
8 sticks margarine, softened
8 eggs
2 packets vanilla sugar
2 teaspoon kosher salt

Filling:
1 cup cocoa
2 cups sugar
1½ teaspoons cinnamon
1 Tablespoon vanilla sugar
1 Tablespoon instant coffee granules

oil for smearing
1-2 eggs, well beaten, for wash

Streussel:
1 stick margarine
1¼ cups flour
½ cup sugar
½-1 teaspoon cinnamon

Kiddush Levanah/Sanctification of the New Moon, being recited following Yom Kippur

Rosh Chodesh

The Jewish calendar is based on the phases of the moon. A month consists of approximately 29½ days. The year consists of 354 days. This results in a complication. Eventually the months would not correspond with the seasons, and Passover, which is called *Chag HaAviv* (the Spring Festival), would occur in the fall instead of in the spring. To bring the lunar calendar in alignment with the solar calendar, the Sages intercalated seven leap years within a 19-year cycle. In a leap year, an additional month (Adar II) is added.

The lunar calendar is symbolic of Jewish history. In contrast to the sun, whose light is constant, the light of the moon is phasic. Although it loses its brightness, it soon renews its glow. The mighty empires — Egyptian, Hittite, Greek, Roman — shone brightly during their zenith, but once they faded away, they never returned to their glory. Jewish history has been replete with periods of utter darkness, but light has always followed.

The Hebrew word for "month" is *chodesh*, which is similar to *chadash*, "new." Renewal is characteristic of the Jewish nation.

Rosh Chodesh is a quasi-holiday. As on some festivals, we recite a portion of the *Hallel*, and eulogizing is prohibited. Although work is permitted, it is traditional that women avoid some types of work, such as knitting and sewing. This distinction is given to the women because, according to the Midrash, the women refused to give their gold jewelry for the fashioning of the Golden Calf.

The *Shulchan Aruch* recommends that Rosh Chodesh be celebrated with a festive meal. If Rosh Chodesh occurs on Shabbos, it is customary to make an extra kugel in its honor.

Kosher or Tereifah

In Hornostipol, the rabbis from neighboring communities assembled at the table of my great-grandfather, R' Mordechai Dov, the Rebbe of Hornostipol, for the Rosh Chodesh meal. One time, it was discovered that there was a break in the thigh bone of the chicken served for the occasion. This raised the question of whether the chicken was kosher. If it was *tereifah*, all the food and the utensils that had come in contact with it were *tereifah*. Although the assembled rabbis ruled that the chicken was kosher, the Rebbe insisted that it be shown to the local rabbi, "Yankel the Rav," for his opinion.

When the messenger returned with the ruling that Yankel said it was *tereifah*, the Rebbe ordered that all the food be discarded and all the utensils *kashered*. The rabbis in attendance were furious, because Yankel had erred in his ruling. They let Yankel know in no uncertain terms that they considered him to be ignorant in halachah.

His head hanging down in shame, Yankel came to the Rebbe, apologizing for his error. The Rebbe said to him, "Yankel, it is not unheard of that a Rav may err in halachah. That would have been forgivable. But, Yankel, where was your common sense? If I had thought it to be *tereifah*, would I have asked for your opinion? You should have understood that I considered it to be kosher, but that it was improper for me to render a favorable ruling for myself, since I had a personal interest in it being ruled kosher. Good judgment would have told you it was kosher."

Onion Kugel

This kugel is very tasty. I'm usually too pressured for time to fry so many onions but whenever I do, it's worth it. The recipe was given to me by my neighbor's son. He is a close friend of my youngest son and taught me how to make it at my son's behest.

1. Make the dough: Thoroughly combine the ingredients and knead to form a dough. Set aside.
2. Make the filling: Sauté the diced onions in oil until brown and crispy. Add salt to taste and, if desired, pepper to taste.
3. Preheat oven to 350°.
4. On a lightly floured surface, roll the dough very thin into a rectangle. Cover the surface of the dough with the onions. Roll up jelly roll fashion and curl the roll (seam-side down) into a 9″ round pan. Bake for 30-45 minutes or until nicely browned.

YIELD: 8 servings

Ingredients:

Dough:
1⅓ sticks margarine
⅜ cup seltzer
1 Tablespoon salt
1-2 cups flour

Filling:
4-5 lbs. onions, diced
oil for sauteéing
salt to taste
pepper to taste (optional)

Potatonik

Potatonik is a Polish meichel. It's actually a potato bread — almost equal parts potatoes to flour that rises due to the yeast. It's a treat to many, while some can't understand why you played around with a perfectly-good potato kugel. If the crusts are your favorite part — this can be made in several smaller pans.

1. Using the S-blade of a food processor, pulse the potatoes and onion until there are no lumps but the mixture is not liquefied.
2. Place the mixture in a 10-quart pot or bowl and thoroughly combine with the flour and proofed yeast. Cover with plastic wrap and let rise 2-3 hours until slightly more than doubled in volume.
3. Preheat oven to 400°.
4. Lightly grease a 9"x13" baking pan. Add oil, eggs, kosher salt, and pepper to the potato mixture and mix thoroughly. The risen mixture will fall when it is mixed. (I taste the mixture — you may like it more salty or peppery).
5. Pour into the prepared pan and let rest for 10-12 minutes. The batter will rise slightly in the pan.
6. Place in preheated oven on a low shelf for about one hour until browned and crusty.

YIELD: 1 9"x13" pan

Ingredients:

3 lbs. Idaho potatoes, cubed
1 medium onion, diced
2-2¼ cups flour
1½ oz. fresh yeast dissolved
   in ⅓-½ cup warm water
½ cup oil
2 eggs
1½ Tablespoons kosher salt,
   or to taste
1½ teaspoons pepper,
   or to taste

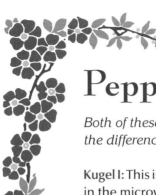

Peppery Lukshen Kugel

Both of these kugels are tops. I think using different width noodles makes the difference in the taste.

Kugel I: This is Rabbi Twerski's specialty. He heats a small amount of the raw batter in the microwave for 40 seconds. He then tastes and adjusts the seasonings.

1. Preheat oven to 375°. Grease the bottom of 9"x13" baking pan with oil.
2. Boil noodles in salted water for 8 minutes and drain. Allow to cool.
3. Combine eggs, onion powder, oil, salt, and pepper. Add noodles and mix.
4. Place pan in oven to heat the oil. Dust with corn meal.
5. Pour mixture into pan. Bake 1 hour or until the top noodles are brown.

Kugel II:
1. Preheat oven to 375°.
2. Cook noodles in boiling salted water for 4 minutes. Drain.
3. Beat eggs. Add oil, noodles, and grated potato.
4. Add salt and pepper to taste. There may be enough salt from the cooking water but don't stint on the pepper.
5. Pour into a 9"x13" pan and bake ¾-1 hour until top is light brown and crunchy.

NOTE: This is a fairly low and crisp kugel. If you prefer a high, 2"-thick kugel, just double the ingredients and pour into the same size pan.

YIELD: 1 9"x13" pan

Ingredients:

Kugel I:
2 Tablespoons oil, for greasing the pan

16 oz. medium or wide noodles
4 eggs
½ Tablespoon onion powder
2 Tablespoons oil
2 Tablespoons kosher salt
½-1 teaspoon white pepper

2-3 Tablespoons corn meal, for dusting

Kugel II:
12 oz. thin noodles
4 eggs
⅓-½ cup oil
1 medium Idaho potato, grated
1-2 Tablespoons kosher salt, if needed
1-2 teaspoons pepper, or to taste

Distributing Chanukah gelt

Chanukah

The festival of Succos is not the only occasion on which the fun of homemade adornments has been diminished.

Before Chanukah, my father would buy a cake of beeswax. He would cut it into small pieces, which he would then soften in a pan of hot water, and flatten into 8-inch pieces. He would then insert a length of string to serve as a wick, and roll the wax until it formed a candle. He would make nine candles, eight to serve as the *shammes*, and an extra one to be used in the search for *chametz* before Pesach. The beeswax had a sweet smell, and I would be given some unused chips with which to play. The wicks for the menorah would be made of cotton.

Today, Chanukah lights come packaged: oil, wicks, and ready-made *shammasim*. Too bad that technology is depriving children of fun.

My mother related that when she was 5, she saw her grandfather, the first Rebbe of Bobov, light the Chanukah menorah. After kindling the lights, he would sit before them, meditating for half an hour. My mother asked him, "Zeide, what are you thinking about?" He answered, "I'm praying that you should have good children." [The Talmud (*Shabbos* 23b) says that the reward for Shabbos and Chanukah lights is having children who are Torah scholars.]

As a child of 5, my mother was told that she would have the responsibility of raising Torah scholars.

My father had the practice of reciting several psalms seven times after he kindled the Chanukah lights. He would hold me on his lap, and I internalized the melody of these psalms.

It was indeed a miracle that one vial of oil lasted eight days. It is likewise miraculous that the memories of my father's Chanukah have lasted more than seventy years.

The Shammes

The *shammes* is the candle used to kindle all the Chanukah lights. Although it gives light to others, its own light does not diminish. This should serve as a teaching that when we give of ourselves to others, whether by giving *tzedakah* or doing an act of *chesed,* our strength and possessions are not diminished.

In many menorahs, the *shammes* stands above the lights. The miracle of the lights was indeed very great, but giving of oneself to others stands even higher than a miracle.

Chanukah Dreidel vs. Purim Gragger (Noisemaker)

Many practices in Judaism have symbolic meaning. On Chanukah, we play *dreidel*. We spin the *dreidel*, and whichever of the four Hebrew letters appears on top indicates the spinner's luck. *Shin* stands for *shtel* (put), "pay into the pot"; *gimmel* stands for *ganz* (all), "take the whole pot"; *hei* stands for *halb* (half), "take half the pot"; and *nun* stands for *naut* or *nisht,* "pass."

On Purim, we use the *gragger* to drum out the name of the evil Haman.

But note the subtle difference. On Purim the handle of the *gragger* is underneath, and when you spin it, the top of the *gragger* rotates. The action below cause the rotation above. On Chanukah, it is just the reverse. You spin the *dreidel* from on top, causing the bottom to rotate.

The salvation of the Jews on Purim was brought about by their *teshuvah,* their fasting and intense prayers, resulting in Divine forgiveness. It was an action from "below" that elicited a Divine response from "above." There is no indication that there was such *teshuvah* on Chanukah. Rather, it was Divine inspiration that motivated the Hashmonaim to battle the Syrian Greeks. The stimulus from "above" caused the action "below."

Hence, the *dreidel* and the *gragger* represent the character of the salvation.

Chanukah Gelt

It is axiomatic that any Jewish custom that is widely practiced has meaning, if only symbolic. What is the meaning of Chanukah *gelt*?

According to Kabbalah, there are several stages in the judgment one receives for the year. The first judgment is made on Rosh Hashanah (written), then on Yom Kippur (signed), then on Hoshana Rabbah (sealed), and then on the eighth day of Chanukah, "Zos Chanukah" (delivery of the verdict). Until the verdict is delivered, it is subject to modification.

We ask Hashem to bless us with *parnassah*. He is our Father and we are His children. In giving our children Chanukah *gelt*, we symbolize the beneficence of a father to his children, and pray that Hashem will bless us with His bounty.

Only to Look at Them

Halachah dictates that one may not use the Chanukah lights as a source of illumination. They are solely for commemoration of the miracle. But this commemoration is in itself exceedingly useful.

Lazer was an immigrant from Russia in the early 1900s. Like many of his co-immigrants, Lazer had a horse and wagon, and collected scrap metal and rags. Lazer was an unlearned man, but very pious.

When Lazer took sick, I visited him in the hospital. He was depressed, having received a dire prognosis from his doctor. Chemotherapy was then in its infancy.

That night would be Chanukah. The hospital forbade lighting candles because of a fire hazard, and said that he could use an electric menorah. Lazer was not satisfied. Electric bulbs were just not Chanukah candles. I entered a plea on his behalf, assuring the hospital administrator that Lazer's wife would sit with him for the 30 minutes that the candles burned, and I won a dispensation. Lazer was thrilled.

The next day, Lazer spirits were high. He said, "The vial of oil they found in the Temple could burn naturally for only one night, but it burned for eight days and nights. The doctors say I have only one year to live. That is, according to the laws of nature. But who cares about the laws of nature? One year can turn into eight years, maybe even more."

Lazer stupefied the doctors. They were certain that their diagnosis was correct, and they could not explain why Lazer survived *ten* years without any treatment.

Lazer knew why. Perhaps conventional radiation could not help him, but the radiant light of the Chanukah candles was much more powerful.

Before Cholesterol

Potato *latkes* are a Chanukah staple. In Israel, there is a widespread custom to eat *sufganiyot*, doughnuts. Perhaps these customs began because oil is used in the preparation of these foods, thus being another reminder of the miracle of the oil.

Potato *latkes* are like potato chips and peanuts. You can't have just one.

One woman felt bad that when the family visited on Chanukah, she ran short of *latkes*. "This time," she said, "I'm going to continue making *latkes* until the last person leaves." It was a good try, but no matter how many *latkes* she made, they were soon gone, and she ended up short anyway.

The Ladies Auxiliary of my father's shul had special events. One such event was a Chanukah party. The *latkes* were not potato *latkes*, but buckwheat *latkes* fried in *schmaltz*. This was before medicine invented cholesterol.

I would take advantage of these meetings to ask the ladies for candy and gum, which they never refused to give me. My mother disapproved of my being a *schnorrer* at such an early age, and forbade me to ask for candy or gum. So I took a *siddur* and showed the ladies the Hebrew word "*gam.*" I did not ask for it, so technically I did not violate my mother's instruction.

Chanukah was also the time of the year when geese were available, and my mother would make *schmaltz* for Pesach from goose fat. This was somewhat of a feat, because the house was all *chometz'dig*. Mother scrubbed the dining-room table and covered it with several layers of butcher paper, *Pesach'dige* utensils were brought up, and the stove was made kosher for Pesach. The problem was that in contrast to Pesach, when everything is *Pesach'dig*, here only a circumscribed area was *Pesach'dig*. If someone touched anything outside of this area, he was considered contaminated and had to scrub.

Many years later, in medical school, I was taught about surgical sterility. In the operating room, only a certain area is sterile. If one touches anything outside the sterile area, one is contaminated and must scrub again. I had no difficulty adjusting to the operating room routine. It was just like making *Pesach'dige schmaltz* on Chanukah.

Chanukah Festivities

Chanukah and Purim are both post-Biblical holidays, established by the sages, and Mordechai and Esther respectively. However, whereas there is a mitzvah to have a festive meal on Purim, there is no such requirement on Chanukah. The reason given is that since Purim is celebrated as our salvation from physical annihilation, we celebrate it with physical festivity. On Chanukah, on the other hand, there was no threat of physical annihilation. Rather, the Syrian-Greeks wished to impose Hellenistic culture on the Jews and force them to reject the Torah. Chanukah thus commemorates a spiritual salvation, and it is, therefore, commemorated primarily with special prayers and the candle-lighting.

Nevertheless, the *Shulchan Aruch* suggests that we do have a festive meal on Chanukah, and also that we serve dairy foods (*Orach Chaim* 670). The reason for this is because one of the Greek generals ordered every bride to submit to him. Judith, the daughter of Yochanan, the High Priest, fed sharp cheese and wine to the evil general, and when he fell asleep, she killed him. His soldiers then fled. To commemorate the courage of Judith, we eat dairy foods on Chanukah.

During the Chanukah week, we read the portion of the Torah that describes the dedication of the Altar (*chanukas hamizbe'ach*) in the Sanctuary in the desert (*Numbers* 7). That dedication lasted twelve days, with the *Nasi* (leader) of each of the twelve tribes bringing an offering. We read the offering of each day for seven days, and on the eighth day of Chanukah we read the offerings of days 8-12, which are summarized with the verse, *Zos chanukas hamizbe'ach* (this is the dedication of the Altar). The last day of Chanukah is, therefore, referred to as "Zos Chanukah."

It is customary among chassidim to have a festive meal on the last day of Chanukah, at which there are Torah discourses and songs of praise to G-d. It is of interest that among Turkish Jews, there is a festive meal on the last day of Chanukah, called *merenda*. Relatives and friends gather, each one bringing something for the meal.

One possible reason for a special festivity on the last day of Chanukah is that we celebrate the completion of another mitzvah. Just as we celebrate the completion of a volume of Talmud, we celebrate the completion of the Chanukah mitzvah.

The Teachings of Chanukah

When we kindle the Chanukah candles, we recite the *berachah*, "Blessed are You, G-d, King of the Universe, Who has sanctified us with His commandments and instructed us to kindle the lights of Chanukah."

Inasmuch as the Divine commandments of the Torah were given at Sinai, how can we say that G-d commanded us to kindle the Chanukah lights, being that the miracle of Chanukah did not occur until centuries later?

The Talmud explains that the Torah commands us to heed the teachings and instructions of the Torah authorities throughout the ages. "You shall not deviate from the word that they will tell you" (*Deuteronomy* 17:11). Thus, since by following the Rabbinic instructions we are obeying the Divine commandment, and inasmuch as the Rabbis decreed that we are to observe Chanukah, we may refer to the latter as fulfilling the Divine wish. This teaches us that by following the dictates of the Torah sages, we are fulfilling the will of G-d.

When the Maccabees reclaimed and cleansed the Temple of pagan items, they found only enough pure oil to last one day, and it would be a week before they could prepare a new batch of pure oil. Their disappointment at not being able to kindle the Menorah for a full week was certainly profound. No doubt there were scholars who pointed out that under such circumstances, the use of defiled oil for the Menorah was permissible.

The Maccabees insisted on using the pure oil for the one day, and were not concerned what would happen afterward. They believed that they must do what is most proper today, and leave the future to G-d. This attitude merited a Divine miracle. The Maccabees were true teachers of the principle, "*A mentch tut un G-tt tut oif*, A person does his utmost, and Hashem does the rest."

Our practice is to light one candle on the first night of Chanukah, two on the second night, etc. Why not light eight candles every night?

The progressive increase in the number of candles symbolizes spiritual growth. We should never be stagnant, but allow Torah illumination to increase every day. Furthermore, we must progress gradually in spirituality, and not try to grasp it all at once. Eight lights the first night would be too much and too soon.

In the *Amidah* prayer on Chanukah, we refer to the triumph of the Hashmonaim, saying, "For Yourself You made a great and holy Name in Your world, and for Your people You worked a great victory and liberation."

In expressing our gratitude for the miracles of Chanukah, we give first mention and priority to the greater glory of G-d, and only then speak of our own victory. If we will place the honor of G-d above our personal needs, we will avoid the pitfalls that may result from striving primarily for personal gratification.

In the prayer that may be recited prior to kindling the Chanukah lights, we pray that our children and descendants be spiritual people, loving and living by the word of G-d.

Values are transmitted by example rather than by preaching. Children are apt to esteem that which they see their parents hold dear. When parents are willing to sacrifice for the principles they espouse, the children are likely to adopt these values in their own lives.

Lighting the Chanukah menorah should not be a mere ritual, but a dedication to the ideals of the Maccabees. If we demonstrate in our lives that we are willing to stand up for our principles and accept self-sacrifice for our faith, we teach our children the supreme value of spirituality.

(from *Living Each Day*)

Keep This Chanukah Gelt Secret

ne Chanukah, Rabbi Gershon Henoch Leiner of Radzin suffered a severe toothache. He was able to get a prompt appointment with the dentist, who told him that the tooth could not be saved and must be extracted. The dentist then extracted the painful tooth.

When Rabbi Leiner asked the dentist what his fee was, the dentist replied, "Rabbi, today is Chanukah. You don't owe me anything. Consider this my Chanukah *gelt* to you."

Rabbi Leiner thanked the dentist and said, "You must do me one favor. Please keep this secret."

"What do you mean?" the dentist asked.

"You see," Rabbi Leiner said, "it is customary that on Chanukah, members of the Jewish community bring Chanukah *gelt* to the rabbi. If they were to find out that pulling out my tooth constitutes Chanukah *gelt*, why, they would all line up to knock my teeth out to discharge their Chanukah *gelt* obligation!"

The Pecan Rolls Really Were Delicious

Sara Baila was a tiny woman who would visit my mother, and always brought some pecan rolls she had baked. These were delicious, and I looked forward to her coming.

Sara Baila would say to me, "Those pecan rolls I brought last time were no good, right?" I would say, "Why do you say that? They were delicious." She would say, "Oh, no. I know you threw them into the garbage." I would say, "No way! We ate them right up." Sara Baila would gloat with pride. This dialogue repeated itself many times.

At age 8, I didn't realize that this was Sara Baila's way of eliciting praise. One time, I decided I would not play her game, so when she made her remark that the pecan rolls were no good, I said, "That's right. They were terrible." "So you threw them into the garbage, didn't you?" she asked. I answered, "Right into the garbage." Eight-year-old kids can be so cruel.

Then I overheard Sara Baila telling my mother that she never knew her mother, who had died in childbirth. When she was 9 years old, they took her for the first time to the cemetery to her mother's grave. She related how she had thrown her arms around the monument and shouted, "I want my mother! I want my mother!" My heart melted, and I cried. I felt that I was the world's worst criminal, denying her the praise she sought. I apologized to her and told her I was only kidding, that her pecan rolls were delicious as ever, and that I hoped she would bring more.

I had learned my lesson, but Sara Baila didn't. After the next batch, she again asserted that they were no good and asked whether I had thrown them into the garbage. I didn't understand anything about reverse psychology and how desperate she was for praise she had never received. But I couldn't say anything negative to a person whose only mother was a cold slab of granite. I went back to the old dialogue. "They were delicious! Please bring more!" and Sara Baila just beamed with pride.

Sweet Latkes: Absolute Trust in G-d

euben was my special friend. I was 8, he was in his 70s, but he was still my special friend. I suspect that I was his special friend, too.

Sabbath services began at 9 a.m., but Reuben would come to the synagogue at 7 a.m., because he wished to recite the entire book of *Tehillim* before davening. Our living quarters were above the synagogue, so I knew when he came. I would cuddle up to him and listen to him chant the Psalms. When he would read the verse, "For I am poor and destitute," I would say, "Reuben, you're not poor. You have a lot of money." I had seen him take out his coin purse to put a few coins in the charity box, and at age 8, a few coins was a lot of money. Reuben would say, "King David had much, much more money than me, but he said he was poor. Money does not make a person rich."

At age 8, I did not know what Reuben was talking about. In my forty years of psychiatric practice, I found out. I have seen people whose wealth actually made them poor. "The truly wealthy person is not the one who has the most, but the one who needs the least."

Like many other Eastern Europeans, Reuben came to America as a youngster, all of 17. His father had been killed when Reuben was 9, and at 10 he had to drop out of *cheder* to help his mother earn a living. His mother was a seamstress, but there were not enough customers in their village to supply her with work. Reuben would go to the nearby villages, often on foot, sometimes lucky enough to hitch a ride on a horse-and-buggy. He would go from door to door asking people if they needed any clothing repaired. His mother was expert at turning over collars to make an old shirt wearable, or altering a hand-me-down to fit a younger child. This way she earned enough kopeks to feed her three children.

Reuben rarely complained of anything, but he did bewail his dropping out of school at age 10. "If only I could have had an education," he said, "I could have amounted to something." This may have slightly lessened my resentment at having to spend two hours after school with a Hebrew tutor while the other kids were having fun.

Realizing that Reuben had no future in the *shtetl*, his mother sent him off to America, the land of opportunity. Just how she managed to do this was a mystery. Arriving at the shores of the United States, Reuben discovered that "there is gold rolling in the streets of America" was a myth. Alone in New York, illiterate of English, he found work in a sweatshop. After a year he made his way west and settled in Milwaukee. There he plied his old trade, apprenticing himself to a tailor and knocking on doors to solicit work for him. Eventually he acquired a pushcart and proudly became an entrepreneur.

Reuben married a young woman, an immigrant like himself, and they had a large family: four boys and four girls. I would see the family picture in Reuben's living room. Tragically, his wife and six of his eight children died. Reuben was blind in the left eye, and wore a thick lens over his right eye. "I became blind from crying," he said. One son died on his wedding day. I once visited the cemetery with Reuben. The monument over this young man's grave was a tree trunk, cut off before it grew branches. It never bore any fruit.

One might think that the harsh suffering Reuben had experienced would have embittered him, but Reuben was not a bitter nor an angry person. Perhaps he identified with the suffering of the persecuted psalmist, who, though saying (*Psalms* 6:7), "I am weary with groaning, I soak my bed with tears," goes on to say (ibid. 100:2), "Serve G-d with joy."

Every Tuesday night, Reuben would take me to his home where he served me delicious potato *latkes*. He grated the potatoes on a hand-grater, telling me stories about life in the Old Country. Never, in the past sixty years, has anyone been able to match Reuben's potato *latkes*. Was this due to his culinary expertise, or was it perhaps because I was 8 years old?

At age 8, children are very sensitive. Had Reuben been embittered, his *latkes* could never have been so tasty. Reuben was often the reader in the synagogue, chanting the prayers of gratitude. He submitted to the Divine judgment and he was not angry with G-d. His *latkes* testified to this.

Whole Wheat Rolls

These whole wheat rolls are the best of both worlds — both tasty and healthy. The recipe comes from Hendel Twerski, Rabbi Twerski's daughter-in-law.

1. Put the flour into the bowl of a mixer fitted with a dough hook. Make a well in the flour. Pour in 2 cups warm water. Sprinkle in yeast. Add 1 Tablespoon sugar. Wait until it bubbles, about 10 minutes.
2. Add the other ingredients, one at a time, leaving salt for last. Mix for 10 minutes or longer until a smooth dough forms.
3. Let rise for 1 hour. Punch down the dough and reknead. Let rise again for 45 minutes.
4. Divide dough into 30 pieces. Shape into rolls and place on 2-3 parchment paper-lined cookie sheets. Let the shaped rolls rise for 45 minutes. Meanwhile, preheat the oven to 350°.
5. Bake for ½ hour until the rolls sound hollow when you knock on the bottom.

NOTE: These rolls are made from 5 lbs. of flour and *challah* must be taken.

YIELD: 30 rolls

Ingredients:

5 lbs. whole wheat stoneground flour
5 cups warm water
3 Tablespoons dry yeast
1 Tablespoon sugar
½ cup oil
¾ cup honey or sugar
2 eggs
1½ teaspoons baking powder
2 Tablespoons table salt

Split Pea Soup

Every — well, almost every — meal in the shtetl was served with soup as a first and often the main course. Soup was economical and filling and thus the thrifty housewife could satisfy her family's gnawing hunger and go easy on the more costly proteins.

My mother and numerous other balabustas continued this practice in America. I remember coming home in the evening to the savory aroma of any one of a number of delectable soups. I tended to prefer whichever soup my mother was serving at the moment. Nevertheless, split pea soup was and still is my hands-down favorite; it is rich, hearty, and heavenly.

1. Place all the ingredients (except butter) in an 8-quart pot. Bring to a boil.
2. Lower heat and simmer for 2 hours. If the carrot is whole, remove it along with the parsnip and the parsley root. Blend or mash them and return to the pot.
3. If desired, add the butter and simmer an additional 5 minutes.

VARIATION: For a hearty meat meal in a bowl, in step one add 1½ lbs. flanken (short ribs) and do not add the barley. In step two, after 1½ hours add ½ cup square noodle flakes and let cook for the final ½ hour. If the soup is too thick, add boiling water in ½-cup increments until it reaches the desired consistency. Eliminate step 3.

YIELD: 10-12 hefty servings

Ingredients:

¾ cup green split peas
½ cup yellow split peas
2-4 Tablespoons barley
6 quarts water
2 celery stalks, diced
2 carrots, whole or diced
1 parsnip
1 parsley root
1 Tablespoon kosher salt
½ teaspoon pepper
1 teaspoon garlic powder
2 Tablespoons butter or
 margarine (optional)

Barley and Mushroom Soup

I refer to this as barley and mushroom soup because there is more barley than mushrooms, but many people know this as mushroom-barley soup. This soup by any name is still delicious.

1. Using a large frying pan, sauté the onions in oil until golden brown. Set aside.
2. Place barley and water in a 6-quart pot and bring to a boil. Lower the heat and cook for 30 minutes. Add sautéed onions, carrot, and celery. The amount of mushrooms is flexible, according to your taste. If you are using fresh mushrooms, clean and slice them and add them at this point. I sometimes add 1-2 mushroom soup cube(s). Continue cooking on low heat for an additional 30-45 minutes.
3. If using canned mushrooms, drain the mushrooms and add to the soup at this point. Season and taste. If too thick, add water in ½-cup increments. Cook 10 minutes longer.

YIELD: 10-12 servings

Ingredients:

3-5 medium onions, diced
¼ cup oil
1 cup barley
10 cups water, or more as
   needed
1 carrot, diced
1 stalk celery, diced
1-1½ lbs. fresh mushrooms
   or 1-2 (16-oz.) can(s)
   mushroom stems and pieces
salt to taste
pepper to taste
½ teaspoon onion powder
1-2 teaspoons paprika
1-2 mushroom soup cubes
   (optional)

Rice Pudding

My husband's cousin, Barbara Gold Schaum, was my closest friend. She was also an honest critic and a big fan. And most of all a superb cook and baker in her own right. Several of my recipes are hers and this is one of them. This cuts nicely and has a rich custardy flavor. It's great for a milchig side dish when you've had your fill of pasta and potatoes.

1. Preheat oven to 350°.
2. Put the rice, water, salt, and margarine or oil in a 3-quart saucepan. Bring to a boil, then lower the heat, cover the pot, and let the rice simmer for 17-20 minutes or until all the water is absorbed and the rice is fluffy. Let cool slightly.
3. In a bowl, beat the eggs, add milk, sugar, and vanilla and mix thoroughly until sugar has dissolved. Add the cooked rice and stir to combine.
4. Pour the mixture into a 9"x13" pan and cover tightly with foil. Bake for 1½ hours.

YIELD: 1 9"x13" pan

Ingredients:

1 cup long-grain rice
2 cups water
1 teaspoon kosher salt
1 Tablespoon margarine or oil
4 eggs
1 quart (4 cups) milk
½-1 cup sugar
1 teaspoon vanilla

Cheese Latkes

Sweet and crunchy — a combination that is hard to beat. Cottage cheese latkes are a Chanukah specialty and can be used as a quick, kid-friendly super supper. For a special treat, these can be served with sour cream or jam on the side.

1. In a bowl, combine all the ingredients in the order given, beating with a fork after each addition. If the mixture seems very loose, add a small amount of flour. The mixture can be used immediately or refrigerated at this point.
2. Pour a thin layer of oil into a large frying pan and set it on the stove over medium heat.
3. When the oil is heated but not sizzling, drop the batter in by heaping tablespoons. Fry 2-3 minutes on one side until golden. Carefully turn latke to second side and fry 1-2 minutes. Drain on paper toweling.

YIELD: about 30 3" latkes

Ingredients:

1 lb. cottage cheese or pot cheese

6 eggs

¼-¾ cup sugar, according to taste

pinch of salt

½ teaspoon vanilla and/or cinnamon

1 cup flour, or more as needed

oil for frying

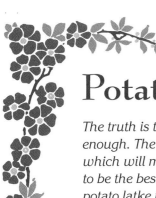

Potato Latkes

The truth is that I don't measure. I just know whatever I make is never enough. The recipe of just about any potato kugel you like best is the one which will make the best latkes. However, I once got this recipe that claims to be the best potato latkes ever. I'm positive it's so — but then how can any potato latke not be the best? One thing I know for sure — this one is delicious.

1. Grate potatoes and onion by hand or in food processor by pulsing the S-blade. Do not use a blender; the batter will be too liquidy.
2. Add the eggs and mix thoroughly. Then add the rest of the ingredients and stir.
3. Pour a thin layer of oil into a large frying pan and set on the stove over medium heat.
4. Drop mixture by heaping tablespoonfuls into heated oil. Fry 2-3 minutes on one side until brown and crispy. Carefully turn latke to second side and fry 1-2 minutes. Drain on paper toweling.

YIELD: 12-16 latkes

Ingredients:

4 potatoes
1 onion
2 eggs
¼-⅓ cup flour
salt to taste
pepper to taste

oil for frying

Fish Croquettes

I think the first time I made a dairy supper after I was married I served these. They're still a family favorite. I originally made them from cod, but since there recently has been a problem with insect infestation in cod I just asked the fishmonger to suggest a fish that's similar. He recommended Nile perch. The original recipe called for cooking the fish in one pot and the potatoes in another and then combine. I cook them together.

1. Cook fish and potatoes in about 2 cups of water until the fish flakes easily and the potatoes are tender.
2. Drain well and mash thoroughly. Add the remaining ingredients and mix well until mixture is light and fluffy.
3. Refrigerate for 2 hours or overnight.
4. Shape into patties and fry in hot oil until browned. Drain on paper toweling.

VARIATION: I sometimes dip the shaped patties into matzoh meal for a crispier crust.

YIELD: 6-8 servings

Ingredients:

*1 lb. cod or Nile perch fillets
   (see introduction)
2-3 potatoes (1-1½ lbs.), cubed
2 cups water
2 eggs, slightly beaten
2 Tablespoons butter
¼ cup milk**
*⅛ teaspoon pepper
1 teaspoon paprika*

oil for frying

*Note: Many people do not use milk with fish. Non-dairy creamer or soy milk can be substituted.

Goulash with Knuckaloch

We tend to think of Chanukah as a milchig holiday. I for one could never get away with eight nights of dairy meals. I've always wanted to know how to make authentic, tasty goulash. It's really a meal in one pot and very filling on a cold wintry night. Mrs. Zaidman to the rescue. Quick, easy, delicious.

1. Place diced vegetables into a 5- or 6-quart pot. Add meat. Add water to cover the vegetables. Season with lots of garlic powder and a little pepper.
2. Cover the pot and cook over low heat for 2½ hours. Add boiling water sparingly if needed.
3. Prepare the knuckaloch: Bring a 4-quart pot ⅔ full of salted water to a boil.
4. Beat the eggs well. Add flour to thicken. Add the rest of the ingredients and mix thoroughly. The end result should be a loose but not runny batter.
5. Dip a teaspoon into the boiling water and then, using the heated spoon, scoop up ¼-½ teaspoon of batter and quickly drop into the boiling water. If you act quickly, your spoon will remain hot and the knuckaloch will slip off the spoon easily.
6. Simmer, covered, for 15 minutes over low heat, taking care that the pot doesn't boil over.
7. Drain and combine with goulash. Simmer 5 minutes for flavors to mellow.

NOTE: When making knuckaloch for soup, drop small amounts of batter from the edge of the teaspoon directly into the soup. Simmer for 10-15 minutes.

YIELD: 4-6 servings

Ingredients:

Goulash:
1 large onion, diced
1 large carrot, diced
2 stalks celery, diced
1 large kalichel or other stew meat (3-4 lbs.)
water
1 Tablespoon garlic powder
¼ teaspoon pepper

Knuckaloch/Egg Drops:
3 eggs
6 Tablespoons flour
2 Tablespoons oil, melted margarine, or melted schmaltz, cooled
1 teaspoon water
salt to taste
pepper to taste (optional)

Tomato Salad

This salad or its variation is one of my Shabbos salads. We enjoy it so much and it is so easy that I frequently make it during the week for supper. Its especially refreshing with the hearty meals served on Chanukah.

1. Place the tomatoes and scallions in a bowl.
2. Combine marinade ingredients in a second bowl and pour over the vegetables. Mix well to coat.
3. Serve immediately or refrigerate for up to 2 days.

VARIATION: For a crispy/crunchy salad you may add 3 kirbies, ½ green pepper, ½ red pepper, and 1 stalk celery. Dice all the vegetables and mix into the salad.

YIELD: 4-6 servings

Ingredients:

6 large, hard ripe tomatoes, diced
½ bunch scallions, chopped

Marinade:
juice of 1 lemon
1 Tablespoon oil
1 Tablespoon sugar
1 Tablespoon kosher salt
½-¾ teaspoon pepper

Old-Fashioned Cheese Cake

Toby Goldzweig introduced me to this recipe. It's one of her mother Henny Brander's staples. One taste and you'll know why I consider it to be top notch.

1. Prepare dough: Cream sugar and margarine. Add 1½ eggs. Beat well. Add flour and baking powder to form dough.
2. Prepare a 12"x16" pan — do **not** grease. Roll the dough into a 16"x20" rectangle to fit the bottom and up the sides of the pan.
3. Roll the dough rectangle around the rolling pin and transfer to the prepared pan by unrolling it into the pan. Press dough into pan, being careful not to tear it.
4. Preheat oven to 350°.
5. Spread cherry pie filling over dough.
6. Prepare filling: Cream eggs and sugar until thick. Add the rest of the ingredients one at a time, mixing until each is incorporated and the filling is smooth.
7. Pour the filling into the pan over the pie filling. Bake for 1-1½ hours until set.

YIELD: 30 servings

Ingredients:

Dough:
6 Tablespoons margarine
6 Tablespoons sugar
1½* eggs
1½ cups flour, or more as needed
1 teaspoon baking powder

1 can cherry pie filling

Filling:
4½* eggs
1 cup sugar
3¼ lbs. farmer cheese
3 lbs. whipped cream cheese
¾ cup flour
1 Tablespoon lemon juice
1 Tablespoon vanilla
1⅛ cups milk

*You will need a total of 6 eggs for this recipe. Lightly beat one egg until the yolk and white are well mixed. Use half of this in the dough with one whole egg and the rest in the filling with the other 4 whole eggs.

Shabbos Shirah

🌸 It's for the Birds

The Shabbos that we read *Parashas Beshalach* (*Exodus* 13:17-17:16) is known as *Shabbos Shirah*, the Shabbos of Song. This portion of the Torah contains the Song of Triumph of Moses and the Israelites after the miraculous splitting of the Reed Sea. This portion also relates the miracle of the manna.

Moses told the Israelites that on Shabbos manna would not descend. During the week, if anyone took more than the allotted portion for that day, it would decay. However, on Friday, when they gathered one measure of manna, they found that although they had done the same as every day, when they measured, it had miraculously doubled and remained fresh through Shabbos. We commemorate this miracle by having *lechem mishneh*, two loaves of challah at each Shabbos meal.

There were two Israelites, Dasan and Aviram, who tried to disprove Moses' statement that there would be no manna on Shabbos. Early Shabbos morning, they scattered manna in the field, intending to show that manna had indeed descended on Shabbos. A flock of birds ate the manna, thus foiling their nefarious plot. As a reward, we give the birds *kasha* on this Shabbos.

There is some disagreement about this practice, because on Shabbos we are permitted to feed only those animals that are dependent on us for their food. Therefore, many put out the *kasha* on Friday. However, there are halachic authorities who approve of this practice (*Minhag Yisrael Torah*, vol. 2, p. 24).

One of my childhood thrills was to throw *kasha* to the birds on *Shabbos Shirah* (in our enclosed yard, of course).

Kasha

Kasha is buckwheat groats. It is a staple of the Russian (and Polish) diet. For Shabbos Shirah, my mother would place cooked kasha in jar lids before Shabbos and put it out for the birds. She always made extra kasha to use for the Shabbos seudah. My granddaughter Shaina Leah has her birthday at this time of year and is always excited since she loves kasha.

I use only whole-grain kasha. Medium or fine kasha cooks up too much like cereal for my liking.

I sauté onions and mushrooms and combine this with the kasha for a really tasty and Shabbosdik side dish.

1. Melt the schmaltz or margarine in a small (2-3-quart) heavy-bottomed pot. Add the kasha and toast over a medium flame. Stir often so that the kasha grains are separate, taking care not to burn them.
2. Lower the flame and carefully add the boiling water or chicken soup. Add the salt (if using soup, it may be salty enough) only if needed.
3. Cover the pot tightly and simmer over very low heat about 15-20 minutes, until the liquid is absorbed.
4. If desired, add the sautéed onions and/or the mushrooms. Fluff the kasha with a fork and serve.

YIELD: 4-6 servings

Ingredients:

2 Tablespoons schmaltz
or margarine
1 cup whole grain kasha
2 cups boiling water
or chicken soup
½-1 teaspoon table salt, if
needed
1 large onion, sautéed
(optional)
1 can (4-8 oz.) mushrooms
(optional)

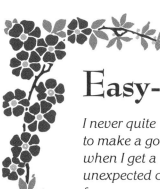

Easy-As-Pie Apple/Fruit Cake

I never quite understood the expression "easy-as-pie." It's not that easy to make a good pie — but this cake is a breeze. It's the one I fall back on when I get a call just hours before Shabbos informing me that I'm getting unexpected company for the seudah or for dessert. I got the basic recipe from my good friend Hindy Diskind Katz — who just happens to be my daughter Rachael's mother-in-law. For the fastest and easiest method, use a can of any pie filling — cherry or blueberry are especially good — but for a traditional taste, any apples you have at hand work just fine.

1. Preheat the oven to 425°.
2. Place eggs and sugar in a mixing bowl, and using a fork, beat until combined. Add oil and beat. Add flour and baking powder; mix until smooth.
3. Pour ⅓" to ½" of the batter into a greased and floured 9"x13" pan.
4. Place filling on the batter, then pour on the rest of the batter by tilting the bowl and moving it back and forth over the filling. It does not matter if the filling is not completely covered. It will seal during the baking.
5. Sprinkle top with cinnamon-sugar mixture.
6. Bake at 425° on middle rack of oven for 10 minutes. Lower oven temperature to 375° and bake until done, approximately 20-25 minutes.

YIELD: 1 9"x13" pan

Ingredients:

Batter:
4 eggs
1 cup sugar
1 cup oil
2 cups flour
1 rounded teaspoon baking powder

Filling:
3 apples, shredded on thick shredder and mixed with 4 Tablespoons sugar and 1 teaspoon cinnamon
or
1 can of pie filling

Topping:
Combine: 4 Tablespoons sugar with 1 teaspoon cinnamon

Fruit peddlers in the marketplace of Kazimierz, Poland

Tu B'Shevat

Tu B'Shevat (15th of Shevat) is the "Rosh Hashanah" for trees. It is traditional to serve fruits on Tu B'Shevat, especially those with which the Torah praises the Land of Israel; i.e., grapes, figs, dates and pomegranates.

The Very Best Fruit

Chassidim flock to their Rebbe on Tu B'Shevat. Once the throng by R' Izik of Zidachov was so great that there was not enough fruit to go around. R' Izik arose and said, "You seek fruit? I will tell you where to find good fruit — in the first mishnah of *Pe'ah*, which states: 'These are the mitzvos whose *fruits* are eaten in this world.' Do these mitzvos, and you will have the best fruits!"

Fish in Place of Fruit

There is a tradition that on Tu B'Shevat one should pray for a good *esrog* on Succos.

R' Mendel of Kotzk conveyed his blessings cryptically. One Tu B'Shevat, his chassid, Hirsch Leib, visited him. To Hirsch Leib's surprise, instead of serving fruit, R' Mendel served him fish roe (in Yiddish, roe is "*roigen*"), saying to him, "Hirsch Leib, *ess roigen* (eat the roe)." The chassidim did not grasp that "*ess roigen*" is phonetically similar to "*esrogen.*"

That year, because of wartime, it was virtually impossible to obtain an *esrog*. Hirsch Leib was able to procure an *esrog* and brought it to the Rebbe. Only then did the chassidim understand what the Rebbe had intended with "*ess roigen.*"

Esrog Jelly

This is my daughter Rachael's recipe. She has been making it for years and doling it out to all the family members. This is made shortly after Succos before the esrogim dry out. There is a tradition to eat this on Tu B'Shevat as a segulah (propitious) for health and success, especially for expectant women. This is also a segulah that one will have a kosher esrog in the coming year.

Ingredients:

2-3 esrogim
4 lbs. pears or quinces, or a
   mixture of both
2 lemons
3½-3¾ cups sugar, to taste
water to cover

1. Soak *esrogim* for seven days in water to cover, changing the water each day.
2. At the end of the week, slice the *esrogim* very thin and remove the pits (leave the rind on the *esrogim*).
3. Put the *esrogim* in a saucepan and cover with boiling water. Bring to a boil and then spill out the water.
4. Repeat this 6 more times. (The soaking and the boiling remove the bitterness.)
5. Meanwhile peel the lemons, slice thinly, and remove all pits. Peel the pears and/or quinces and slice. Remove the pits.
6. Place all the ingredients into a 4-quart heavy-bottomed saucepan and barely cover with water. Stir briefly until the sugar dissolves. Let simmer for 3-4 hours, stirring often, taking care that it doesn't burn.
7. Separate into portions. Place in bags or containers and freeze for use on Tu B'Shevat.

YIELD: 1 quart

Fruit-filled Mandlebroit

This mandlebroit is very rich and very delicious. I got the recipe from Irma Kramer in the bungalow colony one summer while sitting under the tree and chatting. I'm sure she doesn't remember, but after trying this I went into her bungalow and copied all her recipes.

1. Preheat oven to 350°.
2. Purée the lemon and the orange in the food processor until smooth.
3. In the mixer, combine all the ingredients except the flour. Change the beaters for the paddle or put in a bowl with the dough hook (the beaters can break when the flour is added) and incorporate the flour into the mixture.
4. Refrigerate the dough for 2 hours or overnight.
5. Divide the dough into 5 parts.
6. Roll each piece into a 9"x15" rectangle. Smear each rectangle with ⅕ of the jam (I love raspberry or blueberry; my husband prefers apricot). Combine the dried fruits, raisins, and nuts and sprinkle ⅕ of the mixture over the jam. Dust ⅕ of the sugar/cinnamon mixture over it all.
7. Roll up jelly-roll style and place on a lightly greased or parchment paper-lined cookie sheet. Repeat with remaining dough and filling.
8. Bake for 50 minutes until lightly browned.
9. Remove from oven and cool. Cut on the diagonal into ¾" slices.

NOTE: This freezes beautifully.

YIELD: 60-70 slices

Ingredients:

Dough:
6 eggs
1 lemon, quartered and pitted
1 orange, quartered and pitted
1 cup plus 1 Tablespoon oil
1½ cups sugar
5 Tablespoons baking powder
1 Tablespoon vanilla
7 cups flour

Filling:
32 oz. jam
1 lb. diced dried fruit
8 oz. raisins
¾ cup chopped walnuts or
  pecans
1¼ cups sugar mixed with
  2 Tablespoons cinnamon

Apricot Jam Squares

*These cookie-like squares are attractive and delicious. My machateneste/
close friend Miriam Rubnitz gave me this recipe. My youngest son is
learning in Eretz Yisrael and he says he and his friends are thrilled
whenever these are included in a "care" package.*

1. Preheat oven to 350°.
2. Beat the margarine and sugar together until sugar is incorporated. Add
   eggs, vanilla, and finally the flour and baking powder. Mix to thoroughly
   combine into a dough forms.
3. Separate a piece of dough, about ⅕ of the whole, and place it in the
   freezer.
4. Press remaining dough onto an ungreased cookie sheet.
5. Smear the dough with all the apricot jam.
6. Remove dough from freezer and grate on the wide holes of a grater directly
   over the jam. All the jam will not be covered but will look like confetti has
   fallen on it.
7. Bake until the edges are brown and the grated dough is golden.
8. Cool on a rack and cut into squares or diamonds.

YIELD: 30-40 square or diamond-shaped cookies

Ingredients:

Dough:
2½ sticks of margarine (1¼ cup)
1 cup sugar
2 eggs
¾ teaspoon vanilla
4 cups flour
1 teaspoon baking powder

Filling:
1 lb. jar of apricot jam

Brownies

The recipe is the invention of my good friend, Hindy Sirkis. These brownies are dark and chewy, and does not contain any margarine. There is no margarine in the recipe. Traditionally cocoa or melted baking chocolate is used for brownies. However, she uses use chocolate chips. The addition of almonds makes them ideal for Tu B'Shevat.

1. Preheat oven to 350°.
2. Melt chocolate chips in the microwave for one minute. Add oil and mix. Continue melting in microwave and stirring until well combined. It's easier to burn chocolate chips than chocolate chips combined with oil.
3. While the oil/chocolate mixture is still hot, add the sugar and mix well. When sugar is dissolved, add remaining ingredients one at a time and mix briefly until incorporated into batter.
4. Line a small rimmed cookie sheet (approximately 10″x15″) with parchment paper. Pour batter into rimmed cookie sheet. Bake for 20 minutes and remove from oven. Cool on rack. Cut into squares.

YIELD: 30 brownies

Ingredients:

16 oz. chocolate chips
7 oz. oil
2 cups sugar
4 eggs
½ teaspoon salt
1½ cups flour
1½ cups chopped almonds
   or nut of your choice

Purim players in Leczyca, Poland, in the late 1800's

Purim

The Purim Delicacies

Kreplach, *nuant*, and of course, hamantaschen.

Why are hamantaschen three-cornered? Some say it is because Haman wore a triangular-shaped hat. Well, who said so? There are no photographs of Haman. Furthermore, why is it a haman-tasch? *Tasch* is Yiddish for "pocket," not for hat.

The real reason is that the original hamantaschen were filled with poppy seeds, not with jam. The Yiddish for poppy seed is "moon," and because the "moon" was contained in a "pocket" of dough, it was called a "moon-tasch." This sounded similar to "hamantasch," and so the latter name stuck.

But why poppy seed in a pocket? And why *kreplach*, which, too, are meat contained in a pocket of dough?

These foods are symbolic of the miracle of Purim. The miracles of the Exodus were clearly supernatural. The Hand of G-d was patently visible in the splitting of the Reed Sea, the Ten Plagues, the manna, and the Clouds of Glory that accompanied the Israelites during the forty years in the desert.

But there was nothing supernatural on Purim, just a series of seemingly natural events. A drunken king flies into a rage and has the queen executed. She is replaced by Esther, a Jewess who keeps her ethnic identity a secret. An anti-Semitic prime minister plots to exterminate the Jews. The queen's uncle, Mordechai, foils a palace intrigue to assassinate the king, saving the king's life. The king orders Haman, who wishes to kill Mordechai, to bestow honors on him. The queen reveals she is a Jewess, and pleads for her people. Haman is executed, and Mordechai becomes prime minister. The Jews are saved.

No miracle, right? Wrong! The series of "natural" events were orchestrated by G-d. Purim was no less a miracle than the Exodus, but the Hand of G-d was *concealed.*

We believe that there are many "miracles" which we mistake as natural phenomena because the Hand of G-d is concealed. To symbolize this, we have hamantaschen and *kreplach,* where the sweets and the meat are *concealed.*

What on earth is *"nuant"*? It is a gooey praline made of nuts and honey. It tastes good, but it sticks to your fingers. What is the significance of *nuant* on Purim? I haven't the faintest idea. If anyone knows, please enlighten me.

I heard that some people eat turkey on Purim. Why? Because in Hebrew "turkey" is *tarnegol Hodu,* which means "chicken of India." Apparently, this is the origin of the name: When turkey, which is indigenous to America, was first seen by Columbus' sailors, who had assumed they had reached India (and erroneously called Native-Americans "Indians"), they called it "chicken of India," which became in Hebrew *tarnegol Hodu.* Inasmuch as the Megillah begins with the statement that Ahasuerus reigned over a territory from *Hodu* (India) to *Kush* (Ethiopia), the *tarnegol Hodu* is eaten on Purim.

Incidentally, here is a piece of trivia. Allegedly, there were some Jewish sailors in Columbus' crew, and when they saw the multicolored turkey, it reminded them of a parrot, *tukey*

in Hebrew. They, therefore, gave "turkey" its name. Sounds logical, but I won't vouch for it.

Purim Masquerade

Masquerade on Purim is traditional, but what is the origin of the custom?

Various reason have been suggested. Here are a few, all dealing with the concealment of a masquerade.

(1) As we noted in the reason for hamantaschen and *kreplach,* their symbolism is that the Divine Hand in orchestrating the miracle of Purim was *concealed.* That is why G-d's Name is not mentioned even once in the Megillah, although it, too, is concealed in a number of acronyms. The masquerade is another symbol of this. The real person is *concealed* behind a mask and costume.

(2) The Talmud says that the decree to exterminate the Jews was a punishment for their bowing to the statue of Nebuchadnezzar. However, inasmuch as they did not truly worship the statue but bowed to it only out of fear, and their devotion to G-d was *concealed* within them, so also, the decree was to arouse their fear so that they should do *teshuvah;* G-d's intent was not that the decree should ever be implemented. His intent was *concealed,* hence the *concealment* of the masquerade.

(3) Esther *concealed* her Jewish origin.

(4) When Ahasuerus accused Haman of unbecoming intentions on the queen, his "face was *covered*" with shame.

(5) A folk tale:

The Jewish festivals all gathered together. Passover spoke up: "We all have Hebrew names: Pesach, Shavuos, Succos, Rosh Hashanah, Yom Kippur, Chanukah. What is 'Purim' doing here? There is no Hebrew word, *Purim*. The word *pur* is a Persian word for the 'lots' that Haman cast. We don't want anyone with a non-Hebrew name among us." Purim was, therefore, ejected from the assembly.

But inasmuch as Purim wished to join the other festivals, it disguised itself so it should not be recognized, and joined the rest. Therefore, we disguise ourselves on Purim.

(6) The Torah relates that Moses' face was so radiant with Divine light that the Israelites feared to approach him. Therefore, Moses *placed a mask on his face* (*Exodus* 34:29-33). Every year, except during a leap year, this portion of the Torah is read on the Shabbos of the week in which Purim occurs.

Why the Name Purim?

ll other festivals are named after a significant point of the day. Purim is named after the *pur*, the lots that Haman cast to determine on what day to exterminate the Jews. What is so special about the lots that they merit the festival being named after them?

As anyone who has played Monopoly knows, how the dice fall is purely a matter of chance. One may land on Boardwalk or on "GO." However, Haman's lots were not a matter of chance, but G-d directed their falling on the 14th day of Adar. This gave Haman a false sense of confidence, because he thought that the month of Adar was unfavorable for the Jews, being the month in which Moses died. But the fact is that Adar is propitious for the Jews (it is also the month in which Moshe was born), and G-d designed that the *pur* should select Adar.

This *pur* was not a matter of chance. Rather, it was directed by G-d. We acknowledge this idea by calling the festival "Purim," just as we acknowledge the sparing of the Jewish firstborn on the eve of Passover with the name "Pesach" (skipped over). Both Purim and Pesach indicate G-d's role in our salvation.

Knowing Foreign Tongues

During the Haskalah movement, there was pressure placed on the Torah community to teach secular subjects. One *maskil* said, "Obviously, Jews are required to know foreign languages. The salvation of the Jews was the result of Mordechai overhearing the plot against the king. The conspirators must have been speaking in a foreign tongue, and if Mordechai had not studied that language, he would not have understood them."

A rabbi responded, "Just the reverse is true. If Jews had known foreign languages, the conspirators would not have spoken in Mordechai's presence, because they would have assumed that he understood the language they were speaking. It is because they knew that Jews did *not* know foreign languages that they were not on their guard to speak in Mordechai's presence. Mordechai, as a member of the Sanhedrin, was required to know all languages, but other Jews did not know foreign languages."

The Purim Rabbi

There are yeshivos and various chassidic groups that have a custom of designating an individual as the "Purim Rav." This Rav may take portions of the Megillah and through exaggeration and wit turn them into humor. For example, he might cite the verse in the Megillah which states that the courtyard of Ahasuerus' palace gardens was paved with shell and onyx marble. "Why," he asked, "was Ahasuerus not afraid that people would steal these precious stones?" He answered, "Because, as we know, Ahasuerus was a fool, and the Jewish proverb says: 'If a fool throws a stone into the garden, ten wise men cannot pull it out.' "

The Purim Rav would often give out rabbinic "summons" to raise money for *tzedakah*.

My father related that our ancestor, the *tzaddik* of Sanz, was known to be a Talmudical genius at a very young age. In his youth, he once participated in a Purim "*beis din*," which sent a summons to a Rav of a nearby village to come with all his belongings. Imagine their surprise when the Rav and his family came with a wagon loaded with all their belongings! The Rav explained that he owned a *Sefer Torah*, and because he thought it not respectful to transport a *Sefer Torah* for no valid reason, he convened a *beis din* that ruled that he did not have to take the *Sefer Torah*. He explained, "I saw the signature of this great Talmudic scholar on the summons. How could I refuse to comply?"

Someone asked the Purim rabbi why a hamantasch is three-cornered.

The rabbi answered, "Because it represents the three patriarchs — Abraham, Isaac and Jacob."

"But," the man asked, "inasmuch as the Megillah is the Book of Esther, and she was the heroine of Purim, wouldn't it be more appropriate for the hamantaschen to be four-cornered, to represent the matriarchs — Sarah, Rebecca, Rachel and Leah?"

"Yes," the rabbi answered, "but if hamantaschen were four-cornered, they would be required to have *tzitzis*!"

A Purim rabbi delivered a discourse on the Megillah. The text reads that after overcoming their enemies on the 13th day of Adar, *v'noach be'arbaah asar* (they rested on the 14th day). The rabbi asked, "How does Noach get into the Megillah? Noach is in the beginning of Genesis!"

The rabbi explained, "Haman wanted to build a gallows 50 cubits high. But where could he find a piece of lumber that long? It occurred to him that the ark of Noach was 50 cubits wide, so Noach must have had a 50-cubit beam.

"Haman went to Noach to get the beam. When he told Noach that he needed the beam for a gallows to hang Mordechai, Noach refused to give it to him, so Haman tried to take it by force. Noach took hold of the beam, and the two were in a tug of war. Haman was the stronger of the two, and he pulled the beam with Noach still holding onto it, so that he pulled Noach right into the Megillah."

The Eternity of Jews

In *Shoshanas Yaakov,* which is recited after the reading of *Megillas Esther*, we say, "You have been their salvation throughout eternity."

There have been many eras when Jews were exiled, banished and persecuted. As we say in the Haggadah, "In every generation they rise up against us to annihilate us, but the Holy One, Blessed be He, saves us from their hands." We have had many Hamans.

Sometimes those who trusted in G-d did not live to witness the salvation. When we do not see the Divine salvation, our faith is strained. Why did G-d not come to our assistance?

There is no logical answer to this question. But what is undeniable is that the survival of Jews throughout history is a testimony to Divine Providence. Mighty empires that were mightily established in their own lands are now mere archeological relics, whereas a handful of Jews, driven from their own land and wandering from country to country, are a living and thriving people. As the Sages of the Great Assembly said, "For a lone lamb to survive being surrounded by hungry wolves is the greatest testimony to G-d's power."

Shoshanas Yaakov continues, "You have been their hope in every generation (throughout eternity)." An individual generation may suffer, but our survival through eternity is a firm foundation of hope.

An Invincible Bond

Purim is celebrated, as we read, by "feasting, exchanges of gifts, and alms to the poor" (*Esther* 9:22).

The Talmud says that even when Jews deviated

from observance of the Torah, as long as they were united, they merited Divine salvation.

Too often, it is only the threat of an aggressor that binds Jews together. In the absence of an external threat, petty factionalism separates us from one another.

We celebrate Purim by assembling at festive meals, by giving *tzedakah* generously, and by exchanging gifts with friends. These are ways of increasing our unity.

It is certainly high time that we resolve our differences, or at least cling together in spite of them.

Another Purim Miracle

ne Purim, after completing the reading of the Megillah, the reader recited the blessing of personal thanksgiving, thanking G-d for having performed a miracle for him personally. The rabbi asked him why he had substituted the *berachah* for a personal miracle in place of the one for the national miracle.

The man responded, "The *Shulchan Aruch* requires that the names of the ten sons of Haman who were executed must be read in one breath.

"Although here the Megillah states that Haman had ten sons, earlier it recounts that he boasted about his great wealth and his many children. The Talmud explains that, in fact, Haman had far more than ten children. According to one opinion, Haman had over 200 children.

"Just think," the man said, "if they had executed all of Haman's children, and I would have to read them all in one breath; why, I would have died of asphyxiation!

"So, for me, it is a personal miracle that only ten of Haman's many sons were executed. That's why I made a *berachah* for a personal miracle."

Tongue in Sweet and Sour Sauce

This is a little different from the usual recipe. I have been making this for my Purim seudah for over twenty years. It was given to me by my friend Dina Goldberg, a balabuste in every area. It's always delicious. I've even frozen the sauce and added sliced tongue to the reheated sauce at the last minute, and it works just fine. This is perfect alone or served with a portion of sweet lukshen kugel, (see page 89).

1. Peel the carrots and cut into thin round slices. Place oil into a 4-quart pot and add the carrot slices. Sauté for 15 minutes until golden.
2. Dissolve the cornstarch in 1 cup water, mix with remaining water and ketchup, stir until smooth. Add to carrots along with raisins, lemon juice, and sugar to taste.
3. Simmer for 5 minutes.
4. Add thinly sliced tongue. Simmer an additional 20 minutes.

YIELD: 10-12 appetizer servings

Ingredients:

2 carrots
¼ cup oil
½ cup cornstarch or flour
3 cups water, divided
¼ cup ketchup
½ cup raisins
juice of 1 lemon
¼-½ cup sugar, to taste
1 pickled tongue, cooked and sliced thin

Knishes

Knishes with various fillings were a staple in every Jewish household. Well-seasoned potato knishes are a perennial favorite, but to my taste nothing compares to a piping hot kasha knish. Knishes can be made using store-bought flaky dough, but this dough is so easy to make it doesn't pay to buy it.

1. Prepare the dough: Sift the first four ingredients and place into a bowl. Make a well in the flour. Add eggs, then oil and water (if you prefer an eggless dough — use ⅔ cup oil in place of egg).
2. Knead on lightly floured surface until smooth and elastic. Cover and let rest for 30 minutes.
3. Divide dough in half for large knishes, in fourths for appetizer knishes.
4. Roll each piece out on a lightly floured surface — 15" long by 12" wide for large knishes. For small knishes, cut the dough in half lengthwise so there are two 15" by 6" rectangles.
5. Spoon filling ½" from the lower edge of the long side of each strip. Bring up the dough near the filling then roll over onto itself to enclose completely.
6. Carefully lift the knish roll and place on a lightly greased cookie sheet, seam-side down.
7. With a knife, make slits, spacing them as large or as small as you want the knish to be. Don't cut all the way through.
8. Brush with egg wash and sprinkle with sesame seeds if desired.
9. Bake at 375° for 30-40 minutes until golden brown.

Ingredients:

Dough:
2 cups flour
2 Tablespoons sugar
1 teaspoon table salt
1 teaspoon baking powder
1 egg, slightly beaten
½ cup oil
½ cup warm water

1 egg yolk, well beaten with
    1 Tablespoon water, for wash
sesame seeds (optional)

Filling recipes can be found on the facing page.

Knish Fillings

Standard knish fillings are a matter of preference. My kids love potato knishes with lots of fried onions and they don't mind if the onions are dark brown and noticeable. The amount of each filling is sufficient to fill the dough given on the facing page.

Potato Filling:
1. Sauté the onion in oil until it's to your liking. (My grandchildren love the taste of onions, but if the pieces are obvious they won't eat the knishes.)
2. At the same time, cook the potatoes in boiling salted water until tender.
3. Drain the potatoes well. Mash with fried onions and, if desired, egg, until smooth.
4. Add salt and pepper to taste.

Kasha Filling:
1. Cook kasha according to directions for whole-grain kasha on page 218.
2. Sauté onions in oil until soft and golden brown.
3. Combine kasha and onions.
4. Add enough mashed potatoes to hold the filling together but not enough to overwhelm it.
5. Add salt and pepper to taste.

YIELD: 2 large rolls, 10-12 slices each or 4 appetizer rolls, 12-15 slices each

Ingredients:

Potato Filling:
1-2 cups onions, diced
⅓ cup oil
5-6 potatoes (2½ lbs.), cubed
1-2 eggs (optional)
kosher salt to taste
½ teaspoon pepper, or to taste

Kasha Filling:
1 box of fine kasha
1½ cups diced onions
¼ cup oil
1-2 large Idaho potatoes, cubed,
    cooked, and mashed
salt and pepper to taste

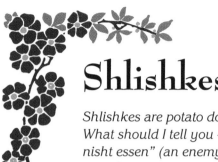

Shlishkes

Shlishkes are potato dough dumplings rolled in toasted bread crumbs. What should I tell you — as my mother used to say — "Ah soneh zull dos nisht essen" (an enemy shouldn't eat this). The recipe sounds more difficult to make than it actually is. I rarely make them — but that's because I like them so much. My daughter Adina doubles the recipe when she makes them for Succos. My niece Nechie Hirsch uses her husband's Bubby Hirsch's recipe and after she gave me the recipe, so do I.

1. Peel the potatoes and cut into 1″ chunks. Cook in boiling salted water to cover until tender. Drain.
2. Mash the potatoes until smooth. Add the eggs, flour, salt, and pepper, using additional flour as needed to make a smooth dough. Divide into 3 pieces.
3. On a floured surface, roll out into long ropes, 1″ in diameter. Cut diagonally into 1″ pieces.
4. Fill an 8-quart pot halfway with salted water. Bring to a boil. Add no more than 25 pieces of dough to the pot at one time. Bring the water back to a boil and when the pieces float to the surface, cook at a moderate simmer for an additional 10 minutes. Drain well and set aside.
5. Repeat with remaining dough, bringing water to a boil before each addition.
6. Sauté onion in oil until golden. Add seasoned bread crumbs and sauté until toasted. Toss with shlishkes.

YIELD: 6-8 side dish servings

Ingredients:

5-6 potatoes
2-3 eggs
1½ cups flour, plus more
   if needed
salt, if needed
pepper to taste

salted water for cooking
1-2 onions, diced
breadcrumbs seasoned with
   salt

Fluden

My mother was a Galitzianer — of Austro-Hungarian extraction. Obviously this didn't make her a Hungarian. This recipe is the way she made fluden. Is it authentic? Probably not — but it's delicious.

1. Put all the ingredients for the dough into a bowl (or the kneading bowl of your mixer) and knead until smooth. Cover the dough and place it in the refrigerator overnight.
2. Prepare a 18"x12" pan. Do not grease the bottom.
3. Preheat the oven to 350°.
4. Divide dough into 4 parts. Roll out each piece very, very thin to fit the pan.
5. Beat 8 egg whites until soft peaks form. Slowly add the sugar and vanilla and beat until sugar is incorporated and stiff peaks form. Using a spatula, fold in the nuts.
6. Transfer one layer of dough to the prepared pan. Smear with half the apricot butter. Top with second dough layer. Spread with nut mixture. Top with third dough layer. Smear with the rest of the apricot butter and top with the remaining layer of dough.
7. Bake in preheated oven for 50 minutes to 1 hour. Cool and cut into 2" squares.

YIELD: 40 2" square pieces

Ingredients:

Dough:
8 egg yolks
1½ cups sugar
½ cup shortening
½ cup oil
4 teaspoons baking powder
2 teaspoons vanilla
2 Tablespoons schnapps
½ cup water
6-7 cups flour

Filling:
1 lb. jar apricot butter, divided

Nut Mixture:
8 egg whites
1 lb. walnuts, chopped very fine
  or ground
1 teaspoon vanilla
1 Tablespoon sugar

Hamentashen

This traditional three-cornered treat is everyone's favorite Purim nosh. However, each favorite is slightly different or vastly different from the next person's. Hamentashen are made from any of the following doughs — yeast, yeast-no-rise, or cookie, all of them delicacies. And that's just the dough. The fillings vary even more: the traditional poppy seed filling, ground apricots, date-nut, apricot butter, prune lekvar, raisins and nuts, and a host of others. All of us have different memories of just what is the taste we remember. Here's a selection of ideas.

No-Rise Yeast Dough:

1. Using a glass measuring cup, proof the yeast in the lukewarm water, with a pinch of sugar.
2. Preheat the oven to 350°.
3. Mix the proofed yeast and the rest of the ingredients in the kneading bowl, using a dough hook, until a soft dough forms. Do not allow the dough to rise.
4. On a floured board, roll out the dough very thin (¼"-⅓").
5. With a plain or scalloped cookie cutter, cut into 2½" rounds.
6. Place a heaping teaspoon of filling (see page 242) in the center of each round. Bring the edges of the dough toward the center to form a triangle. The filling can show or it can be completely enclosed (see diagram).
7. Place on a greased cookie sheet (or line it with parchment paper).
8. Bake in preheated oven approximately 25-30 minutes until light brown.
9. Remove from the oven and transfer each hamentash to a rack for cooling.

Ingredients:

No-Rise Yeast Dough:
1 packet dry yeast
½ cup lukewarm water
pinch of sugar
2 sticks (1 cup) margarine
2 cups flour
2 egg yolks
2 Tablespoons sugar
pinch of salt

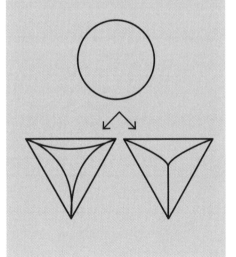

Yeast Dough:
1. Use the ingredients and follow the directions found for Babke (page 187, 299) or Yeast Rugelach (page 164, 165) to form a dough.
2. After the dough has risen, punch down and roll out to ¼"-⅓" thickness.
3. Cut with a plain or scalloped cookie cutter (or the rim of a glass) into 2½" rounds.
4. Put 1 Tablespoon of filling into the center of each round. Press the edges toward the center, forming a triangular shape.
5. Place onto a parchment-lined cookie sheet, leaving space for them to rise.
6. Preheat oven to 350°.
7. Let the hamentaschen rise for 30 minutes.
8. Smear with an egg wash; bake for ½ hour or until golden. Cool on rack.

Cookie Dough I:
1. Use the ingredients and follow the directions for Rolled Cookie Dough on page 213 to form a dough.
2. Preheat oven to 350°.
3. Roll dough to ⅛"-¼" thickness on a lightly floured board.
4. Cut into 2½"-3" circles.
5. Place a heaping teaspoon of filling in the center and bring edges to the center to form triangles.
6. Place hamentashen ½" apart on a lightly greased cookie sheet.
7. Bake for 15-18 minutes until golden brown. Transfer to rack to cool.

Ingredients:

Yeast Dough:
Any of the yeast dough recipes for yeast rugelach, babke or rolls will yield excellent hamentaschen.

1 egg yolk, well beaten with 1 Tablespoon water, for wash

Cookie Dough I:
Use the Rolled Cookie Dough (page 213), which will work just fine for hamentashen.

Cookie Dough II:

1. Cream margarine, shortening, and sugar together. Add eggs and beat until blended. (If the mixture curdles, add 1-2 Tablespoons flour.)
2. Stir in the liquid and the vanilla.
3. Fold in the flour, salt, and baking powder to make a soft dough.
4. Preheat oven to 350°. Line 2 large cookie sheets with parchment paper.
5. Divide dough into 2 or 3 pieces. On a lightly floured board roll out one piece to ⅛" thickness. Cut into 2½"-3" rounds.
6. Place a heaping teaspoonful of filling in the center of each round. Bring the edges to the center to form hamentashen. Transfer hamentashen to prepared cookie sheet. Repeat with remaining dough and filling.
7. Bake 18-25 minutes or until golden brown. Remove from cookie sheet and cool on a rack.

Filling II:

This is the filling my mother used and obviously the one I prefer.

1. Place the raisins and apricots in a saucepan with just enough water to cover. Bring to a boil. Lower heat.
2. Add the cinnamon, sugar, honey, and nuts. Simmer for 3-5 minutes, stirring constantly.
3. Let cool. Add just enough cornflake crumbs so that the mixture holds together and is not runny.

NOTE: This can be used immediately or prepared in advance and refrigerated.

YIELD: 45-60 hamentashen

Ingredients:

Cookie Dough II:
½ cup margarine
½ cup vegetable shortening
1¼ cups sugar
3 eggs
1-2 Tablespoons flour, if needed
¼ cup orange juice or parve milk
1½ teaspoon vanilla extract
4 cups flour (approximately)
½ teaspoon table salt
2½ teaspoons baking powder

Filling I:
1 lb. lekvar or filling of your
   choice

Filling II:
¼ cup raisins
½ cup dried apricots, chopped
cold water to cover
½ teaspoon cinnamon
½-1 cup sugar, to taste
¼ cup honey
½-2 cups pecans or walnuts,
   finely chopped but not ground
2-6 Tablespoons cornflake crumbs

Nuant

This recipe evokes all the flavor of Rabbi Twerski's memories. He recalls nuant as being sticky. There are recipes that call for the nuant to be cooked to a hard-boil stage and result in a confection that is more like a brittle, but this softer consistency is the one most frequently used.

1. Cook sugar and honey over medium-low heat, stirring constantly with a wooden spoon until the sugar dissolves.
2. Add nuts and cook, stirring frequently until mixture is very thick and chewy.
3. Remove from heat and spoon a ¼"-½" thick layer onto a wet board or an oiled cookie sheet. Let cool for 10 minutes, until firm but not hard.
4. Using a sharp knife dipped in hot water, cut into squares or diamonds.
5. Store in an airtight container at room temperature.

VARIATION: This mixture can be dropped by spoonfuls onto an oiled cookie sheet.

NOTE: Do **not** make nuant on a humid day.

YIELD: about 48 pieces

Ingredients:

1 cup sugar
2 cups honey
4-6 cups chopped walnuts, pecans, or almonds

Burning chametz in a small village, 1925

Pesach

From Bondage to Freedom

Most people probably think of Passover as an "Independence Day" celebration. If so, it seems to be a bit of overkill. Independence Day is usually a one-day event, with parades, picnics, patriotic speeches and fireworks. Why have an Independence Day celebration for seven days (eight days outside of Israel)? Furthermore, cleaning the house two weeks in advance, scrubbing down the kitchen and changing all dishes and utensils seems a bit much for an Independence Day celebration.

"O.K.," you may say, "but that's how Jews do it." Fine. But every Shabbos when we recite the Friday night *Kiddush* we say that Shabbos is in commemoration of the Exodus from Egypt, and so is every festival. *Tefillin* and *tzitzis* are daily reminders of the Exodus, and many of the mitzvos are related to the Exodus. No one celebrates Independence Day 7/24/365.

The true meaning of Passover was revealed to me by a young man who recovered from a severe drug addiction. When his father began reciting the Haggadah, saying, "We were slaves unto Pharaoh," the young man interrupted him. "Father," he said, "can you truthfully say that *you* were a slave? You can talk about your ancestors being enslaved, but you were never a slave. *I* can say *avadim hayinu*, that I was a slave. As long as I was addicted to drugs, I was a slave to them. I had no freedom. I was not free to choose what to do. I had to do whatever the drugs demanded I do. I did things in my addiction that I never thought I could do, but I had no choice. I was a slave, and today I am free."

This was a flash of insight to me. Drugs are not the only addiction to which people are subject. A person who cannot control his anger, greed or lust is very much a slave to them. A person who will stop at nothing to achieve fame and recognition is very much a slave. A compulsive gambler is a slave. A person who does not want to get cancer or heart disease, yet cannot stop smoking, is a slave. An obese person who cannot stop overeating is a slave. There are countless ways in which people are enslaved.

The message of Passover is that we must strive to be free, to break the bonds of *any* kind of compulsion or coercion. Liberty should be so dear to us that we do not allow ourselves to be under the tyranny of any destructive habit. Passover is much more than an Independence Day celebration. It teaches us to repudiate all varieties of enslavement and to reclaim the dignity of being free.

That is why we must repeatedly be reminded of the Exodus. We are constantly subject to becoming enslaved.

The Exodus was entirely the work of G-d. To liberate ourselves from enslavement to destructive habits, we must indeed pray and invoke Divine help. However, we must begin with sincere and dedicated effort, and we will then merit the Divine blessing of true, personal freedom.

Work and Fun

es, Passover is *loads* of work for adults and *lots* of fun for kids. Passover is really a children's Yom Tov. The ritual of the Seder, beginning with the Four Questions, is to attract the attention of children, so that they should learn about the Exodus.

One never outgrows one's identity as a child in relation to Passover. According to halachah, even if a person is old and totally alone, he must begin the Seder with asking the Four Questions. Asking of Whom? Why, G-d, of course. We are never without a Father. *If one is not in the company of children, one becomes the child himself.*

The Haggadah states, "In every generation, a person must view himself as having personally participated in the Exodus from Egypt," emancipated from slavery. Just as the individual can recapture his childhood, so must the nation re-experience its infancy. Individually and collectively, Passover is a rejuvenation.

It is one of the ironies of life that as children, we rush to grow up, and when we finally do grow up, we wish we could be children again. Passover allows us to be both child and adult.

I recall the excitement of cleaning the house for Passover. I would help with carrying out the many volumes of my father's library and on the porch in the open air shaking the books to dislodge any crumb of bread or cake that might have fallen among the pages while someone was reading the books at the table. I would also help carry up the Passover dishes from the cellar. The most beautiful dishes were always set aside for Passover. In my study I have a plate from our Passover set.

I had a tiny silver wine cup that was all my own.

The night before Passover, we followed my father around the house as he carried the beeswax candle, searching for any *chametz* (product of leavened dough) that might have escaped the vigorous cleaning of the past few weeks. My mother had followed the tradition of placing ten little pieces of bread in hidden places around the house, to make sure that my father thoroughly searched all the rooms. Not until he had accounted for and retrieved all ten pieces would the search be completed. Of course, I had accompanied my mother when she hid the pieces, but I never revealed the hiding places to my father. That would have spoiled the fun! The following morning my father made a huge bonfire, and we watched as he threw in whatever *chametz* he had found in the search.

Some utensils used all year round may be used for Passover if they are rendered kosher by a halachically prescribed *kashering* process. My father would put these utensils into a huge metal tub of boiling water, then throw in a red-hot brick that would send up a geyser of water like Old Faithful. What fun that was!

On the morning before Passover, we could not eat a *chametz* breakfast upstairs, because everything had been made ready for Passover, so we ate doughnuts and coffee in the basement. Over the past decades, I have savored hundreds of doughnuts from a variety of bakeries. None equal the exquisite taste of the doughnuts we ate in the basement on the morning before Passover.

I was fortunate in having a special treat, because on the day before Passover, we baked our own matzah for the Seder. Nothing in the world is as exciting as baking matzah (especially when you're 8 years old).

The evening before the Seder night, we would drive out to the country, where there was a fresh-water spring, to fetch water for baking the matzah. My father would look at his watch, and we would wait until precisely the moment of sunset to begin filling the glass jugs, because that is when the water is coolest, as it must be to prevent the flour from becoming fermented by warm water. Did you ever taste delicious water? Try the spring water on the night before the Seder. (It helps if you are 8 years old.)

After we brought the jugs into the house, the men would form a circle and dance to a lively tune, chanting the verse, "You shall fetch water with joy from the wells of salvation" (*Isaiah* 12:5), while balancing the jugs on their shoulders. The actual baking of the matzah did not begin until noontime the following day, corresponding to the time of the Paschal offering in the days of yore. Inasmuch as I was not yet Bar Mitzvah, I was not permitted to participate in the actual baking, but there were plenty of things for me to do. I cleaned the rolling pins with sandpaper and delivered fresh sheets of butcher paper to the men who were rolling the matzah dough.

All this was supervised by Reb Elya, a Jerusalemite who would visit us every Passover. Reb Elya was the sweetest man on earth, but on the day before Passover he underwent a metamorphosis and was an absolute tyrant when it came to matzah baking. Everything had to be done with haste and precision, lest anyone cause a momentary hesitancy in preparation of the dough that might, *G-d forbid*, become *chametz*. Beware! Reb Elya's voice thundered across the room, instilling the fear of G-d in everyone.

A voice would ring out, "A matzah for the oven!" as one of the men neared completion of his matzah dough. I would repeat, "A matzah for the oven!" running to tell Reb Saul to prepare the long pole with which he would transfer the matzah into the oven.

After the baking was finished, the men joined hands and danced in a circle. This was true joy. We had just completed preparation for the once-a-year mitzvah of matzah. "Next year in Jerusalem," we all declared.

We returned home with the package of freshly baked matzah, to the once-a-year menu of fluffy potato dumplings and borscht. I have never tried to repeat this menu during the year. It couldn't possibly be the same.

The long day was exhausting, but a child has infinite reserves of energy. Yet, sometime during the Seder, particularly after a few sips of sweet wine, I would get drowsy and sit next to my father on the big couch, which my mother had draped with a golden bedspread and padded with huge pillows. I would rest my head on my father's lap, and his chanting the melody of the Haggadah was my lullaby. I would drift off to a sweet sleep, which could have been experienced only one other time in the history of the universe: that of Adam in Paradise.

It is now almost seventy years since those days. I sit on the draped couch, and my great-grandchildren put their heads on my lap and enjoy that sweet sleep. I am transported back in time, and am once again a child, falling asleep on my father's lap.

Abandoning the Chametz

R' Koppel Likover, grandfather of the Seer of Lublin, earned his livelihood by selling spirits — wine and liquor. When Passover arrived, he would sell his stock to one of the non-Jews in the village.

One year, a conniving citizen of the village instructed all the villagers not to buy R' Koppel's spirits before Passover, because then he would have no option other than to make them *hefker* (ownerless).

On the day before Passover, R' Koppel sought in vain to find someone to buy his *chametz*. He had no choice other than to leave the doors of his house wide open and announce that he was relinquishing the ownership of his entire stock of spirits, and anyone who wished could help himself. He then packed up his things and went to spend Passover with a relative.

When he returned, the townsfolk greeted him with, "So! That's how you relinquish ownership, by putting vicious dogs to guard the entrance to your house?" R' Koppel had no idea what they were talking about. When he came home, there were two ferocious dogs guarding the house. When the dogs saw R' Koppel, they quietly slipped away.

R' Koppel contacted his Rebbe, asking what he should do about his stock of spirits, because they had been guarded during Passover so that no one had access to them. His Rebbe told him, "You had divested ownership of your *chametz* and made it *hefker*. That G-d arranged to have your spirits protected does not nullify the *hefker*, and you may take possession of them."

Nevertheless, R' Koppel disposed of all the spirits, saying that he did not wish to benefit from a miracle.

A Passover Miracle

I n Brisk there was a wealthy man who was a miser, and did not contribute to *tzedakah*. He was also a bit of a freethinker. The townsfolk complained about him to the Rav, R' Yosef Dov, father of R' Chaim of Brisk. R' Yosef Dov told them that he would take care of the matter at the proper time.

Before Passover, R' Yosef Dov solicited this man for *maos chittim* (money to buy Passover provisions for the needy) and

the man donated a paltry sum. As if to justify himself, the man added that he was skeptical about the Passover story. He did not believe in miracles.

R' Yosef Dov said, "You do not believe in miracles? Why, I can perform a miracle right now. However, I will do so only if you promise to give 100 rubles to *maos chittim*." The man agreed to do so, if indeed the rabbi would perform a miracle.

"All right," R' Yosef Dov said. "I want you to take four 25-ruble notes and put one at each corner of the table. I will say just one word, and the four bills will promptly be in the bowl in the center of the table."

The man's curiosity was whetted. He placed a 25-ruble note at each corner of the table. R' Yosef Dov then said, "Chaim'ke!" The young Chaim quickly gathered the four notes and put them in the bowl. The man protested. "That is no miracle!" he said.

R' Yosef Dov said, "That's not a miracle? Why, getting 100 rubles from you for *maos chittim* is nearly as great a miracle as the splitting of the Reed Sea!"

No Need to Search

B efore Passover, Rabbi Isaac (R' Itzel) of Slonim went to the house of a wealthy miser to collect money for *maos chittim*. The miser was in the process of cleaning his clothes for Passover, and had turned the pockets of his garment inside-out to remove any possible crumbs of *chametz*.

When the miser turned down the Rebbe's request for *tzedakah*, R' Itzel said, "I can save you work. You are not required to check your pockets for crumbs."

"How so?" the miser asked.

"Because," R' Itzel said, "the halachah is that if there is a deep recess in the wall, a person is required to search for *chametz* only as far as his hand can reach. It is obvious that your hand never reached into your pockets, so you don't have to check them."

The Importance of Tradition

In the Haggadah there is a mnemonic of fifteen terms that describe the order of the Seder. Traditionally, the children would read the mnemonic and explain it. Chassidic Rebbes were very insistent that this practice be observed, because, they said, the mnemonics were also prayers.

For example, the child would say, "*Kaddesh* — when the father returns from shul, he dons the white *kittel* and chants the *Kiddush*." Father means G-d, our Heavenly Father. When G-d returns from the synagogues where Jews gathered for the Passover Eve prayers — and in spite of their being exhausted

by Passover preparations, prayed to Him with devotion and then sat down to the Seder commemorating His deliverance of them from Egypt — He clads Himself in white (representing the attribute of *chesed*, lovingkindness), and renews the *kiddushin*, the bond of betrothal with Israel.

Similarly, the mnemonic for *karpas* is, "One takes the *karpas* vegetable, dips it into salt water, recites the *berachah* '*borei pri ha'adamah*,' and has in mind to absolve us of the need to make the *berachah* on the *maror*." The hidden meaning: to free ourselves of *maror*, of all bitterness.

Chassidic Rebbes said that many traditions contain hidden meanings, and that is why they must be assiduously maintained.

Matzah Shemurah; 18-Minute Matzos

Because of the extremely exacting prohibitions against even infinitesimal amounts of *chametz*, some people have very strict practices regarding the matzah they use.

The word *shemurah* means "guarded or watched." According to halachah, taking heed to avoid dough becoming *chametz* should begin from the grinding of the wheat, to make sure the flour does not come in contact with moisture. Many people follow a more stringent standard, that the watchfulness against contact with moisture should begin from the time of the grain harvest. If flour that was adequately watched is not available, one may use flour that one knows was not processed in a way that exposed it to moisture.

The halachah states that it takes 18 minutes for a mixture of flour and water to become *chametz*. Therefore, some mass-production matzah bakeries stop the machines every 18 minutes and clean them, to check and make sure that no particle of dough remained in the equipment. (These are sold as "18-minute matzos.")

Many people will eat only matzos that are baked by hand, without any mechanical equipment. These are sold as "handmade matzos."

Gebrokts

The laws governing *chametz* on Passover are unusually restrictive, making *chametz* a more serious prohibition than other forbidden foods. For example, if a tiny piece of nonkosher food falls into a pot of kosher food, and the proportion of kosher to nonkosher is greater than 60 to 1, the food may be eaten, because the nonkosher food is nullified. However, if a tiny crumb of *chametz* falls into a huge vat of *Pesach'dige* food, and the proportion is greater than 1,000,000 to 1, nonetheless, the entire vat is forbidden.

Flour that comes into contact with liquid can become *chametz*. However, if the flour is baked into matzah, it can no longer become *chametz*. This is why there are sundry matzah products that may be mixed with liquid.

However, what if a tiny grain of flour failed to become saturated with water when the matzah dough was kneaded? It never became dough, hence it never became matzah. While it was indeed baked in the oven, it did not become matzah. If it subsequently comes into contact with liquid, it may become *chametz*.

Granted, this is a far-fetched scenario. However, because of the unique severity of *chametz* on Passover, and since there is no nullification of *chametz*, some people take the precaution of not allowing matzah to come in contact with liquid. How can they have *knaidlach*? They can't! (Well, they can — potato *knaidlach*.) They do not use matzah-meal, cake-meal, or any other matzah preparation. They cannot enjoy a matzah-*brei*, the delicious fried matzah-egg delicacy. Matzah that has come in contact with liquid is referred to as *gebrokts*.

A major segment of Torah-observant Jews do not restrict *gebrokts*, and the chicken soup at the Seder is served with *knaidlach*. Among chassidim, many families have accepted the restriction of *gebrokts*, to the point that if a crumb of matzah falls into a bowl of soup, they will set the bowl aside and not use it for the rest of Pesach!

One man asked R' Yitzchak Meir of Gur what he should do with a pot into which a piece of matzah had fallen. R' Yitzchak Meir said, "I don't know. The *Shulchan Aruch* only gives instructions what to do if a crumb of *chametz* falls into a pot. It says nothing about what to do if a crumb of matzah falls in."

Two chassidim of the *tzaddik* of Sanz happened to be in Pressburg on Passover and ate at the table of the Chasam Sofer, who partook of *gebrokts*. When they were served soup with *knaidlach*, one chassid thought, "True, I never eat *gebrokts*. But how can I sit at the table of the Chasam Sofer and be more restrictive than he is?" and he ate the *knaidlach*. The other chassid thought, "I cannot break my *minhag* (custom) not to eat *gebrokts*," and so he abstained from the soup.

When they returned to Sanz, the *tzaddik* said to the chassid who had eaten the *knaidlach,* "You will be assured of a place in Gan Eden." To the chassid who abstained he said, "You had better stand near me by *davening*. Perhaps I can acquire forgiveness for your foolishness, sitting at the table of the *gadol hador* and trying to outdo him in *frumkeit*."

Outside of Israel, an eighth day of Pesach is observed, which is of Rabbinic rather than Scriptural origin. Therefore, on the last day of Pesach in the Diaspora, the restriction of *gebrokts* is generally waived.

Kitniyos

In the era of the *Geonim* (roughly 7th to 10th Century), an edict was issued restricting use of beans and peas (*kitniyos*) on Passover. The reason usually given for this restriction is that beans are sometimes ground into flour (e.g., soy flour), and although this flour cannot ferment and cannot become *chametz*, nevertheless, someone who sees that this kind of flour is used on Passover may not discern the distinction and may think that one may use any kind of flour, including those that can become *chametz*. This was a precautionary restriction, and it was specified that if there is an inadequate supply of food available for Passover, one may eat beans. There were, indeed, several times when food shortages warranted waiving the restriction on *kitniyos*.

When the *kitniyos* edict was promulgated, it was not universally accepted. Sephardic Jews did not accept this restriction upon themselves, and to this day, Sephardic Jews eat *kitniyos* on Passover. In Israel, foods containing *kitniyos* are clearly labeled, "For use only by those who eat *kitniyos*."

An obvious question is: Why are potatoes permitted? Inasmuch as potato starch has a close resemblance to flour, why doesn't it fall under the *kitniyos* restriction? The answer is that potatoes were not known to the Old World until they were brought from America. Hence, when the edict was issued, potatoes were not included. Inasmuch as *kitniyos* is halachically permissible and is restricted only as a precautionary measure, anything not included in the original edict remains permissible.

One halachic authority gave this response to the question, "We were not meant to starve on Passover. Elimination of potatoes on Passover is tantamount to starvation!"

The Kashering Day

I came across an article by a nostalgic writer who said that among the various Jewish holidays, one of the most important ones is not even listed in the Jewish calendar: the *kashering* day. He describes how, several days before Passover, his father would erect a foundation of stones, upon which he would set a huge cauldron and fill it with water. The children would bring wood, which would be set afire, and once the fire was raging, they would continue to throw branches into it. After the water came to a boil, people would bring pots and utensils to *kasher* for Pesach. He remembers feeling that just as the boiling water was extracting and eliminating all the *chametz* from the pots, he, too, was undergoing a purifying process.

My grandfather, the Rebbe of Bobov, once visited Baron Rothschild, who proudly showed him a separate house that was his Passover home. It was not used all year round, and never had any *chametz* brought into it.

My grandfather told the Baron that he was missing the point. Angels are perfect. They have no defects, and do not have to do anything to improve themselves. People are imperfect. We have faults that we must eliminate. The point is not to never have any *chametz*, but rather to be able to rid ourselves of the *chametz* we have. The idea is to have *chametz* in our homes all year round, and to completely eliminate it for Pesach so that not even a tiny crumb remains. Indeed, the prayer we say when we burn the *chametz* states, "Just as we have rid our homes of all *chametz*, so, Hashem, enable us to eliminate every remnant of the *yetzer hara* from our hearts."

I, too, remember my father *kashering* things for Pesach. Come to think of it, there was really no need for him to do so. We had enough *Pesach'dige* utensils. I think he did so to preserve the tradition of *kashering*, and perhaps to reinforce the feeling that we, too, should undergo a purifying process.

Wise Deductions

A *navon* is a wise person who can deduce the outcome based on present occurrences.

The day before Passover, a man asked R' Chaim of

Brisk whether it is permissible to fulfill the mitzvah of the Four Cups at the Seder with milk. R' Chaim promptly gave the man a substantial sum of money.

R' Chaim's wife asked, "Why did you give him so much money? He doesn't need that much money for wine."

"I know," R' Chaim said, "but if he could afford meat, he would not have asked whether he could use milk for the Four Cups. So, I had to give him money for meat as well."

An interesting incident occurred when R' Moshe Feinstein was baking matzos with his students. As they left the matzah bakery, one student remarked to R' Moshe that he had some concern about his matzos. R' Moshe quickly concluded that this student's concern was not based on any real problem, but that it was essentially a neurotic-type of worry, in which case logic would be of no avail, and the student would not be reassured that his matzos were fine. R' Moshe said, "I'll tell you what. Take my matzos and I'll take yours."

The student then said, "Oh, no, I'll keep my matzos." But, R' Moshe, understanding that the student would still not be free of a nagging doubt, insisted on exchanging the matzos with him, and the exchange was carried out.

There is an aphorism, "Where there is Torah, there is *chochmah* (wisdom)." How true!

Maos Chittim (Money for Matzah)

lthough the mitzvah of *tzedakah* is of the greatest merit all year round, it is of special importance before Passover, to assure that the poor will have adequate provisions for the festival. Every Jewish community has a pre-Passover *maos chittim* campaign. In some European communities, the local council would assess the citizens and determine what they should contribute.

R' Avigdor was the *gabbai* (collector) of the *maos chittim* campaign. He sent a messenger to R' Zorach, the town's wealthiest man, an intransigent miser, requesting that he contribute the 50 rubles for which he had been assessed. When the messenger returned with 20 rubles, R' Avigdor sent him back, saying that the needs of the poor in the community were very great, and nothing less than 50 rubles was acceptable.

R' Zorach came to the community council, and angrily demanded to know who does the assessing. The process was explained to him, but he said that no one can dictate to him how much he should give. At that point, R' Avigdor said, "If you do not remit 50 rubles, you will not get matzos from the matzah bakery."

R' Zorach flew into a rage. "I will not give 50 rubles, and I do not respond to threats. If I do not get matzah, then I will eat *chametz*," and slammed the door as he left.

As Pesach approached, the word in town was that R' Zorach was not making any preparations for Pesach — not cleaning the house and changing the kitchen utensils. The townsfolk put pressure on R' Avigdor to relent. "You cannot allow a Jew to eat *chametz* on Pesach," but R' Avigdor stood his ground. "I will personally assume responsibility for this sin," he said.

On noon of Erev Pesach, R' Zorach's servant came with 50 rubles, and R' Avigdor sent him his matzos. "I know how miserly R' Zorach can be," he said. "His money is as dear to him as his life. But no Jew will eat *chametz* on Pesach, even a miser.

"There was never a danger that R' Zorach would eat *chametz*. As dear as his money is to him, the mitzvah of matzah and the prohibition of *chametz* is even dearer."

The Festival of Matzos or Passover?

Were generally refer to this festival as Passover, whereas the Torah refers to it only as *Chag HaMatzos*, the Festival of Matzos. Why?

R' Levi Yitzchak of Berditchev explained that the term Passover refers to the fact that G-d "passed over" the homes of the Israelites when He smote the Egyptian firstborn. This was a manifestation of G-d's love for us. The term "matzah," on the other hand, is an allusion to the haste of the Israelites' departure from Egypt. "They baked the dough that they took out of Egypt into unleavened cakes, for they could not be leavened, because they were driven from Egypt and could not delay, nor had they made provisions for themselves" (*Exodus* 12:39). With no food other than the matzah, they strode into the arid desert with complete trust that G-d would provide for them.

In the Torah, G-d praises the Israelites for their trust in Him, hence the Torah refers to the festival with the praise of Israel — "the Festival of Matzos." We, on the other hand, wish to express our gratitude to G-d for His mercy in sparing the Jewish firstborn, and therefore we refer to the festival as Passover.

It might be well, at this point, to mention that the matzah we use today is different than the "unleavened cakes" our ancestors ate. We make the matzah into thin wafers because that is the safest way to assure that it will be baked thoroughly. Some Sephardic Jews have soft matzos, much like pita bread. They bake their matzah according to their unbroken tradition.

A Dramatic Seder

Among some families, there is an interesting custom. Just as the Seder is about to begin, there is a knock on the door. When the door is opened, a person is standing there with a knapsack on his shoulder. He is asked, "Where are you going?" and he responds. "I am leaving Egypt to go to the Land that G-d promised to our ancestors."

In the Haggadah we say, "In every generation one must see himself as if he left Egypt." We must identify with our ancestors and feel that G-d is liberating us. The enactment cited helps remind us of our obligation to think of ourselves as being freed from Egypt.

Nissim and Nissalach

n Passover we eat pastries made with nuts, not only because we cannot use flour, but for symbolism as well.

When I was a child, we used to play a game with hazelnuts, much like marbles. We would set up a board against a wall, then roll the hazelnuts up the board. As the nuts rolled down, they bumped into other nuts. All the nuts that were hit on your roll belonged to you. Of course, the winner was the one who got the most nuts. This was a traditional Passover game.

This tradition is based on the fact that the Yiddish word for nuts is *niss*, and the goal was to collect many *nissalach*. *Nissim* in Hebrew means "miracles." Hence, on the festival celebrating the great *nissim* of the Exodus, we play a game to accumulate *nissalach*. In addition to our *tefillos*, this is another way of asking Hashem for more miracles.

Who Is Like Your People, Israel?

 Levi Yitzchak of Berditchev was an inveterate advocate on behalf of Israel. One Passover eve, he asked his followers to bring him Turkish tobacco. Inasmuch as there was hostility between Russia and Turkey, possession of Turkish goods was considered treason and could warrant the death penalty. Nevertheless, they were able to find Turkish tobacco.

"Good," R' Levi Yitzchak said, "now I must have Turkish wool."

"That is impossible to get," his followers responded. "No one will admit to having Turkish wool."

"I must have Turkish wool before I go to the Seder," R' Levi Yitzchak said. Eventually, they were able to find Turkish wool.

"Wonderful!" R' Levi Yitzchak exclaimed. "Now, bring me a piece of *chametz* from any Jewish home in Berditchev."

When his followers returned empty-handed, R' Levi Yitzchak was ecstatic. "Master of the Universe!" he said. "The czar has a mighty police force, and they can shoot anyone who possesses Turkish goods. Yet, I was able to get Turkish tobacco and Turkish wool. You have no police force. No one is in danger of being shot. But 3,000 years ago You said that on Pesach we should have no *chametz*, and just look how Your devoted children abide by Your word. Now, Master of the Universe! Do Your children not deserve better than You have been treating them?"

Who Is Wise?

It is customary that at the Seder, one of the children "steals" the father's *afikoman* and holds it captive, surrendered only when the father ransoms it by granting the child's request.

When R' Yonasan Eibeshitz was a child, he stole his father's *afikoman* and requested a new suit as the price for returning it. The father promised him a suit. When the father distributed pieces of the *afikoman* to everyone at the Seder table, he said to the child, "You will not get any *afikoman* unless you release me from my promise."

The young Yonasan said, "I thought you might do that, so I took off a piece of *afikoman* for myself before returning it to you!"

Next Year in Jerusalem

My father would tell this story on Passover:

Gedaliah was a merchant. He had a non-Jewish friend who asked to be invited to his Seder, since he was curious about Passover.

As they read the Haggadah, Gedaliah translated it for his friend and explained the story of the Exodus to him. At the end of the Seder, when they proclaimed, "Next Year in Jerusalem,"

Gedaliah explained that we pray for the coming of Mashiach, and that next year we will be in Jerusalem.

The following year, the friend said that he had enjoyed the Seder immensely, and would like to attend again. When, at the close of the Seder, they said "Next Year in Jerusalem," the friend asked, " But isn't that what you said last year?" Gedaliah explained that even though our prayers for the Redemption had not been answered this year, we pray for it to come in the coming year.

When the next Passover approached and the guest again asked to be invited to the Seder, Gedaliah went to shul, opened the *Aron Kodesh* (ark of the Torah) and tearfully prayed, "Master of the Universe! Have mercy and send us Mashiach now. I am so embarrassed! How can I explain to my friend why we are not in Jerusalem this year?"

My father would say, "Even if we are not sufficiently meritorious to deserve Mashiach, he should come if for no other reason than to prevent our humiliation when the gentiles see that our prayers have not been answered."

Eliyahu HaNavi (The Prophet Elijah)

Eliyahu HaNavi is an important personality on Passover. Every Jewish child knows that during the Seder, following the *seudah*, the door is opened. Eliyahu enters and takes a sip from the *kos shel Eliyahu* (the cup of Elijah) that was prepared for him.

Although there is merit to this thought, it appears that the cup of Elijah has another source. The Jerusalem Talmud (*Pesachim* 10:7) says that the four cups of wine at the Seder correspond to the four expressions of deliverance from Egypt: "I shall take you out … I shall rescue you … I shall redeem you …and I shall take you unto Me" (*Exodus* 6:6-7). R' Tarfon says that there should be a fifth cup, corresponding to "I shall bring you to the land" (ibid. 6:8). There is a difference of opinion whether a fifth cup is necessary, and the issue will not be resolved until the ultimate Redemption, when Eliyahu will clarify it. Therefore, the fifth cup is the "cup of Eliyahu."

Various reasons are given for opening the door at the Seder. (1) We do it to show that this is a night of watching (*leil shimurim*), when we can feel safe even with our doors unlocked. (2) During the Inquisition, there were spies who checked whether the Jews who were forced to convert to Christianity were still observing the mitzvos; the door was opened to check whether there were any spies there. (3) There were blood libels in which the Jews were accused of using Christian blood in the matzos. Anti-Semites would kill a Christian child and throw the body in the doorway of a Jewish home. The door was opened to ascertain whether this might have happened.

But tradition has it that Eliyahu visits Jewish homes on the Seder night, and tradition is authoritative. The great R' Yehudah Landau (*Noda B'Yehudah*) would escort Elijah all the way to the street. In some homes there was a custom to have an ornate "Chair of Elijah" at the Seder, similar to the Chair of Elijah at circumcisions.

It is said that because Eliyahu was a zealot and said to God, "Your people have forsaken Your covenant," G-d assigned him to attend every *bris* to see for himself that Jews have *not* forsaken the covenant of Abraham. It is also related that Elijah said to G-d, "How can I go to every *bris*? You know that I am a zealot and cannot tolerate being in the presence of sinners!" G-d responded, "I will, therefore, forgive the sins of all who are present at a *bris*." Inasmuch as Eliyahu visits every Seder, we can be confident that on Passover Eve, our sins are forgiven as well.

My mother relates that when she was 6 years old, her father sent her to open the door, and she saw a shadow move across the floor. Say what you will. I believe her.

Kos Shel Eliyahu (Elijah's Cup)

here are many stories about the *kos shel Eliyahu*. Here is one of them: In Mainz (Magenza, Germany), there was a wealthy man who owned a *kos shel Eliyahu* that bore the inscription, "Gershom bar Yehudah," and was alleged to have belonged to the great 11th-century Talmudist, Rabbeinu Gershom. When this man died, each of his two sons, Reuven and Shimon, wanted the *kos shel Eliyahu,* and each one was willing to surrender all the inheritance in order to own it. There being no way to adjudicate this dispute, the *beis din* deliberated, and the *kos shel Eliyahu* was awarded to Reuven, with Shimon getting the entire inheritance. Although this was a fair decision, Shimon developed an intense resentment of Reuven.

Shimon prospered and greatly expanded his wealth, whereas Reuven was impoverished. There were times when there was no food for Reuven's children, but he would look at the cherished *kos shel Eliyahu,* and the distress of his poverty was assuaged.

When Passover arrived, Reuven could not afford to buy even meager provisions for the festival. At his wife's insistence, he went to Shimon, asking for a loan. Shimon said to him, "Brother, you suffer needlessly. I will give you our father's entire inheritance in return for the *kos shel Eliyahu,* and I will give you a beautiful gold goblet in its place." Reuven replied, "What! Surrender the *kos shel Eliyahu*? Never!" and he left empty-handed.

Before Passover, Reuven's children said to their mother, "How can we go to shul on Yom Tov in tattered clothes and without shoes?" Unable to bear the children's suffering,

Reuven's wife took the *kos shel Eliyahu* to Shimon, who promptly gave her a huge sum of money and a golden cup.

When Reuven discovered this, he was crushed. His children tried to console him, "You will see, Abba, that Eliyahu will be pleased with the golden cup." Although the children had new clothes and the Seder table was filled with sumptuous foods, it was all Reuven could do to maintain a semblance of holiday joy.

When the children opened the door to greet Eliyahu, the golden cup suddenly disappeared, and in its place was the *kos shel Eliyahu* with the inscription, "Gershom bar Yehudah." Reuven was ecstatic with joy. "Look what Eliyahu has brought me! My father's *kos shel Eliyahu.*"

At Shimon's home, when the door was opened for Eliyahu, the *kos shel Eliyahu* suddenly disappeared, and in its place stood the golden cup.

The following morning, Shimon went to Reuven's home, and found the *kos shel Eliyahu* on the table. He embraced Reuven and said, "It is clear now that Hashem wants you to have our father's *kos shel Eliyahu.* It is truly yours. Forgive me for my unkindness to you," and the two brothers tearfully embraced.

For the second Seder, Shimon and his family joined Reuven, and they shared the *kos shel Eliyahu,* which glowed brilliantly. After Passover, Shimon gave half his wealth to Reuven, and a loving relationship was re-established.

Is this folk tale true? Of course it is true, even if it never actually occurred.

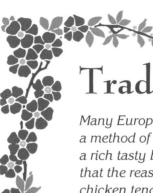

Traditional Falsche Fish

Many European Jews did not use fish in any form on Pesach. They devised a method of using ground chicken that was shaped into balls, poached in a rich tasty broth, and served in place of gefilte fish. My friend Gitta says that the reason many people do not like falsche fish balls is because ground chicken tends to be dry. Her trick is to use schmaltz (or oil) both in the broth and in the ground mixture.

1. Place the sliced vegetables into a deep 8- or 10-quart pot. Add seasonings. Add water to 2 inches above the vegetables. Bring to a boil and let simmer at least 1½ hours. Taste the broth and adjust seasonings.
2. The proportion of puréed vegetables to ground chicken should be ⅓ vegetables to ⅔ chicken. Purée all the vegetables on the S-blade of the food processor.
3. Combine puréed vegetables with chicken and 1-2 eggs per pound of chicken. Add schmaltz. Mix well. If possible blend with hand blender until very smooth.
4. With wet palms, shape ¼-⅓ cup of the mixture into an oval or small ball. Place in simmering broth. Continue until all the mixture has been used. Poach in broth for 1 hour. Allow to cool in broth.
5. Using a slotted spoon, remove fish portions to a container. Refrigerate.

YIELD: Varies — 2 lbs. ground chicken mixed with the proper amount of the other ingredients yields 10-12 servings

Ingredients:

Poaching Broth:
2 carrots, sliced
1 parsley root, sliced
1 knob celery, sliced
2 large onions, sliced
1 Tablespoon schmaltz (see page 263) or oil
salt to taste
pepper to taste
sugar to taste

Ground Mixture:
(Read instructions for amounts.)
carrots
knob celery
onions
eggs
ground chicken
sugar
pepper to taste
salt
1-2 Tablespoons schmaltz

Horseradish – Chrain

To give an exact recipe for chrain is tricky. A lot will depend on the strength of the horseradish root — some are mild and some so strong they literally take your breath away. The next variable is the beets. Some beets are very sweet and some are not as sweet. Chrain is traditionally served with fish. My mother enjoyed the freshly made chrain as an accompaniment to chicken and meat. You can skip the first instruction by buying freshly ground horseradish from your kosher fruit store a day or two before Pesach.

1. Peel horseradish root and cut into 1" chunks. Process fine on the S-blade of the food processor with the lemon juice and a small amount (just enough to allow the horseradish to be puréed) of the beet water from the cooking. Do this in a well-ventilated area and try not to inhale through your mouth. The fumes from the horseradish are strong and will make you cough and your eyes tear.
2. Mix shredded beets, lemon juice, sugar, and salt in a bowl. Add the grated horseradish and mix thouroughly. (I do this outside on the porch and I make sure to wear rubber gloves. A strong horseradish can cause your hands to feel as if they are on fire).
3. Taste and adjust seasoning. Refrigerate in a tightly closed Ball jar.

NOTE: Chrain can be frozen.

YIELD: 1 quart

Ingredients:

1 horseradish root (about 2 lbs.)
4-6 cooked beets, shredded fine
a small amount of water that
    the beets were cooked in,
    as needed
juice of 4 lemons
¼-½ cup sugar
beet juice, as needed
2-3 Tablespoons kosher salt

Potatoes, Eggs, and Onions

This is one of my favorite Pesach foods. It's ideal for Erev Yom Tov lunch when there's not much around on which to fill up. It's delicious warm, cold, or anything in between and, once Yom Tov has come in, lovely on thin crisp matzoh.

1. Place the cubed potatoes in a pot and add water just to cover. Add salt and cook until potatoes are tender, about 10 minutes.
2. Drain well and return potatoes to the pot over low heat for a few seconds to dry. Set aside.
3. In a large bowl, peel and chop the hard-boiled eggs.
4. Add the cooked potatoes and onions and mash well. Add oil and seasoning. (Taste — the potatoes may have enough salt from the cooking water.)
5. Use immediately, let come to room temperature, or chill.

YIELD: 10 servings

Ingredients:

3-4 large potatoes, peeled and cubed
water
salt for cooking
4 hard-boiled eggs
1 onion, diced
3 Tablespoons schmaltz or oil
salt
pepper (optional)

Griben and Schmaltz

Nothing makes food taste like it did in Europe as much as the use of schmaltz. Its rich, mellow, soul-satisfying flavor has been rightfully dubbed "taam Gan Eden." You may not want to use it often but chopped liver (using beef or chicken livers) and mashed potatoes are definitely enhanced to an otherworldly level when made with schmaltz and griben. Your butcher may provide you with chicken fat if you ask nicely — but if not, you can save chicken fat and chicken skins in the freezer until you have at least ½ lb. of fat. At this point it's worthwhile to render the schmaltz.

1. Place the fat and skins in a heavy-bottomed pot. If the pot has deep sides, you won't have to clean up any splatter.
2. Cook over medium/high heat, stirring occasionally with a spoon, until the schmaltz melts and the skins turn light brown.
3. At this point add the onion and raise the heat. Cook until skins are dark brown and crispy and onions are browned. Salt lightly.
4. Strain. Store schmaltz and griben separately. The schmaltz can be stored in the refrigerator and used for months, but the griben should be used within a day or two, before they lose their crunchiness.

NOTE: Some people shred the skins so there are small pieces but the true maven loves large crunchy pieces. They will break when mashed anyway.

YIELD: will vary according to the amount of fat and skin used.

Ingredients:

8 oz. (or more) chicken fat
½-1 cup chopped onion
chicken skins
kosher salt to taste

Vegetable Soup

This recipe does not rely on any specific amounts. It really depends on how much you want. I usually make this for Erev Yom Tov. All the guests come early (their homes aren't Pesachdik) and everyone is hungry. Soup is filling and can simmer on the stove for hours and be ready whenever needed. The different textures — diced, shredded and sliced — will give the soup texture without benefit of a thickener. For an even more filling soup, serve with potato knaidlach (see facing page).

1. Place the diced vegetables and a small amount of oil into a 6-quart pot. Sauté for 10 minutes until soft, golden, and aromatic. Add the remaining vegetables and seasonings.
2. Add boiling water almost to cover and let simmer for one hour. Taste and adjust seasoning. Potato knaidlach can be added 5 minutes before serving.

YIELD: 10-12 servings

Ingredients:

2 onions, diced
2 celery stalks, diced
2 carrots, diced
3 Tablespoons oil
1 stalk celery, sliced
2 carrots, 1 shredded, 1 sliced
2 zucchini, 1 shredded, 1 sliced
1 turnip, shredded
1 parsley root
1 parsnip
5 potatoes, cubed
salt to taste
pepper to taste

Beet Salad

Beet salad is a refreshing side dish for any Pesach (or all-year-round meal). It can be made from the beets used in cooking the borscht, beets cooked in plain water, or even canned beets. It's fast and easy — but don't forget to wear gloves when handling the beets — they'll stain your hands a dark shade of red. (Rubbing the stain with the inside of a squeezed lemon helps lighten it.)

Both recipes call for the beets to be peeled and cooked. When they are no longer hard and can be easily pierced with a fork, remove from the pot. Let cool slightly. Shred or slice cooled beets, add remaining ingredients, and mix. Chill.

YIELD: 8-10 servings

Ingredients:

Beet Salad I — Sweet:
5 beets, peeled and cooked
juice of 1 lemon
sugar to taste (depends on how sweet the beets are)
salt to taste
less than 1 Tablespoon mayonnaise (optional)

Beet Salad II — Tart:
5 beets, peeled and cooked
1 onion, diced
salt to taste
juice of 1 lemon

Mayonnaise

In Europe, store-bought Pesachdik mayonnaise was not available. Many households, even today, adhere to the standards of the alte heim and use few, if any, processed ingredients. This Pesach recipe is not authentic to Europe but it is an added bonus for the Jewish housewife. I include it because mayonnaise is one of the ingredients in the Health Salad (page 268) and Beet Salad (page 269).

1. Put all the ingredients in the order listed into a 1-quart, wide-mouth Ball or Mason jar.
2. Insert a stick blender and blend the ingredients together until the mixture is the consistency of mayonnaise.

NOTE: Mayonnaise keeps in the refrigerator for one week.

YIELD: 1 pint

Ingredients:

1 egg
1 cup oil
1 Tablespoon lemon juice
1 teaspoon salt
¼ teaspoon pepper
pinch of sugar (optional)

Fast and Easy Carrots

This is a fast and colorful and tasty side dish for a Pesach meal. I often take the easy way out, and use this in place of tzimmes on Rosh Hashanah. It's not the same by far, but in a pinch it serves as meirin.

1. Put first four ingredients in a heavy-bottomed pot (**without** water). Cover tightly and simmer over low heat for 25-30 minutes until tender. (The carrots will release a lot of liquid.)
2. Dissolve the potato starch in water; add to the pot. Cook for an additional minute or two until thickened.

YIELD: 6-8 servings

Ingredients:

1 lb. carrots, sliced in rounds
2 Tablespoons oil
¼ cup sugar
pinch of salt

½ Tablespoon potato starch
⅓ cup water

Bletlach for Lukshen or Blintzes

This is still my family's hands-down favorite for the Sedarim. At the seudah, everyone is tired and full of wine, matzoh, and marror. But no one says "No" to a steaming hot bowl of chicken soup and lukshen. They'll refuse the main course, and ask for doubles of soup.

I remember as a teenager standing over a hot stove on the Seder night and making lukshen for that meal (never just a few — we had hordes of guests). Nowadays I make loads of lukshen first and freeze them.

1. Beat eggs lightly with the water. Beat in potato starch and salt.
2. Grease a frying pan by smearing it with a paper towel dipped in oil. Place over a medium/high heat. Spoon 1-2 tablespoons of batter into the heated pan, quickly tilting it so that the surface is thinly covered.
3. Fry over medium heat until set on one side, turn the leaf over, and fry a few seconds on the second side.
4. Turn onto a paper towel-lined plate. Repeat, stirring the batter so that the potato starch doesn't settle, and regreasing the pan every second time.
5. For Lukshen: Stack four leaves and roll up jelly-roll style. Using a sharp knife, slice as wide or as narrow as you like. The cut-up lukshen freeze beautifully.
6. For Blintzes: Use a 6"-7" frying pan and fry on one side. Use cooked side for inside of blintzes. Fill with filling of your choice and roll up. Fry the filled blintz for 2-3 minutes on each side until crisp.

YIELD: 12-16 bletlach, depending on the size of the frying pan

Ingredients:

6 eggs
1⅛ cups water
¼-⅓ cup potato starch
1 teaspoon kosher salt

oil for frying

Potato Chremslach

This is one of the recipes I learned from my daughter-in-law, Fraidle. I never thought I'd like these but my advice is, make more than you think you will need — they go fast.

1. Make a tasty mixture of mashed potatoes with lots of fried onions, salt, and pepper (see potato filling for knishes recipe, page 234). Make any amount you feel you need and refrigerate.
2. Prior to the meal, remove from fridge and shape into balls or flattened cakes (using 2-3 Tablespoons of mixture for each chremsel), then coat in potato starch.
3. Fry in oil on each side until crisp-brown.

YIELD: varies according to the amount of mixture

Ingredients:

potatoes, cooked and mashed
onions, diced and sautéed
salt to taste
pepper to taste

potato starch for coating
oil for frying

Onion Soufflé

This kugel is always a hit, even if (as sometimes happens) the soufflé deflates and looks as though it fell. I double this and get 3 5"x9" loaf pans. It can be made in a 9" round pan although it won't rise as high.

1. Preheat oven to 350°.
2. Beat egg whites until stiff. Set aside.
3. Beat yolks until creamy. Add the remaining ingredients and mix.
4. Fold whites into yolk mixture.
5. Pour into an ungreased pan.
6. Bake 30-35 minutes until lightly browned and puffed.

NOTE: This can be made in advance since it freezes beautifully. I warm it on a *blech* or by putting the pan near the spot where the heat vents from the oven. This way it warms through but does not dry out.

YIELD: 8 servings

Ingredients:

6 eggs, separated
2 cups fried onions (about 2 lbs. onions, diced, sautéed, and cooled to room temperature)
⅓ cup potato starch
½ teaspoon table salt
¼ teaspoon pepper
⅓ cup oil (there may be enough in the fried onions)

Cholent Kugel

The cholent usually made on Pesach consists only of meat and potatoes. It can taste delicious when a lot (and I mean a lot) of fried onions are used as a base. Adding this kugel to the cholent shortly before Shabbos makes it special.

1. Put all the ingredients except the potato starch into food processor fitted with the S-blade. Process until smooth. (This can be done by hand.)
2. Pour the mixture into a bowl, add the potato starch, and mix thoroughly.
3. Form into 1 or 2 logs: Spoon the mixture onto a piece of foil or parchment paper and shape into a cylinder. Close ends of foil or paper tightly.
4. Place the wrapped mixture into boiling cholent.

YIELD: 8-10 servings

Ingredients:

1 large carrot
1 large potato
small onion
1½ Tablespoons salt, or to taste
½ cup oil
¾ cup potato starch

Vegetable Kugel

This one is a winner. My cousin Eudice Nathan gave me the recipe. She got it from her cousin Ruth Kipust and in our house this is called Kipust Kugel. Some of my kids occasionally make this during the year but I save it strictly for Pesach.

1. Sauté the onions in oil until golden. Add the celery, peppers, mushrooms (if using), and carrots. Sauté until soft.
2. Preheat oven to 375°.
3. Place the eggs into a mixing bowl. Beat by hand and add salt and pepper to taste.
4. In a food processor, grate the potatoes using the fine shredder. Transfer to the egg mixture. Add the sautéed vegetables. Mix thoroughly.
5. Pour into a 9"x13" pan. Bake for 40-60 minutes, until browned and crusty.

YIELD: 1 9"x13" pan

Ingredients:

2 large onions, diced
3-4 Tablespoons oil
4 stalks celery, diced
2 green peppers, diced
½ lb. mushrooms, sliced or chopped (optional)
4 carrots, shredded
8 eggs
salt to taste
pepper to taste
8 large Idaho potatoes (4-5 lbs.), grated

Confetti Vegetable Kugel

I got this recipe many years ago from a good friend, Chana Karfiol. She was a warm and giving person who gladly shared the best she had. The finished kugel is colorful — hence the name confetti.

1. Preheat oven to 350°.
2. Shred the raw vegetables using the largest holes of a shredder.
3. Add the remaining ingredients and mix well.
4. Pour into a 9" round pan and bake 45 minutes to 1 hour, until crisp.

YIELD: 1 9" round pan

Ingredients:

2 carrots, peeled
1 zucchini, peeled
1 large raw Idaho potato, peeled
1 onion
1 large cooked potato, mashed
3 eggs
salt to taste
pepper to taste

No-fail Potato Kugel

This simple, delicious kugel is from my daughter Fraidle. She divides it and usually puts half in the cholent. But even when it gets eaten up right away, this kugel is always a winner!

1. Preheat oven to 350°.
2. Grate potatoes and onions in food processor using the S-blade.
3. Pour into bowl. Add remaining ingredients.
4. Pour into 9"x13" pan and bake for 1½ - 2 hours.

YIELD: 1 9"x13" pan

Ingredients:

5 lbs. potatoes
1 large Spanish onion
9 eggs
1 cup oil
salt to taste
pepper to taste

Cholent – Rabachts

In our house the longed-for Pesach cholent is a rabachts, which is a sort of potato kugel and is either loved or not — depending on your taste. This amount is perfect for a 6-quart pot.

1. Sauté the diced onions in a thin layer of oil until they are nicely browned.
2. Process the potatoes in the food processor using either the S-blade or the kugel blade.
3. In a large bowl, beat the eggs. Add the grated potatoes, sautéed onions, and salt and pepper.
4. Pour half the mixture into a 6-quart pot or a crock-pot. Add breast flanken and cover with remaining mixture. If using a regular pot, place it into a 300° oven for 1-2 hours so it starts to set all around and then place it on a *blech*.
5. Cook overnight and serve at the Shabbos afternoon *seudah*.

YIELD: 12-14 hefty servings

Ingredients:

2-2½ lbs. onions, diced
3-4 Tablespoons oil
5 lbs. potatoes, peeled and
   cubed
4 eggs
salt to taste
pepper to taste
2-2½ lbs. breast flanken

Chicken with Duck Sauce

This sauce makes a delectable topping for chicken. If you do not use all the ingredients on Pesach, the recipe can be modified to fit your needs. The sauce is enough to coat 8 quarters of chicken. If you choose to make less chicken, the leftover sauce can be stored in the refrigerater for later use.

1. Bring the first 8 ingredients to a boil.
2. Add margarine or frozen cottonseed oil. Set aside.
3. Place the chicken in a pan that can hold the pieces in a single layer. Sprinkle the seasonings of your choice — salt, pepper, garlic powder, etc. — on the chicken.
4. Smear the sauce on the chicken. Cover with foil and bake at 350° for 1½ hours or until chicken juices run clear.
5. If desired, remove foil for last 10-15 minutes of baking to allow the skin to crisp.

VARIATION: You can place cubed potatoes under the chicken for a complete meal.

YIELD: up to 8 chicken quarters with sauce

Ingredients:

Sauce:
1 cup orange juice
½-⅔ cup sugar
1 Tablespoon potato starch dissolved in 1 Tablespoon cold water or orange juice
1 teaspoon kosher salt
¼ cup red wine
garlic powder (optional)
dash of pepper
paprika (optional)
2 Tablespoons margarine (or 2 Tablespoons cottonseed oil, frozen)

Chicken:
8 chicken quarters, with skin on

Applesauce

We love applesauce as a dessert any time of year and especially with latkes on Chanukah. But my most-favorite way to eat applesauce is as a sidedish to pickled meat or boiled chicken on Pesach.

Ingredients:

water (see instructions)
½-1 Tablespoon kosher salt
10 large Macintosh or Cortland apples
sugar to taste

1. Cover the bottom of a 5-quart pot with 2 inches of water. Add salt (salt brings out the sweetness of the apples). If you are doubling this recipe, use a larger pot and fill it with 2 inches of water but do not increase the amount of salt.
2. Peel and core the apples.
3. Place pot over low heat and bring water to a boil.
4. Slice the apples and add to the boiling water, stirring occasionally. This way the apples become soft and the new pieces cook in the already softened sauce. By the time the last pieces are added the applesauce is done. The end product is a great applesauce that still has a few chunky pieces for texture.
5. Turn off the heat and taste. Be careful — applesauce retains its heat for a long time. If the taste is too tart, add sugar ¼ cup at a time, mix throughly, and taste again until it's to your liking.

NOTE: If you want perfectly smooth applesauce, pureé with a stick blender.

YIELD: 2-2½ quarts

Pear Dessert

This recipe can be made using any type of pear, but I prefer Bartletts or Anjous. They can be served in halves or slices. I prefer the halves for elegance but usually make slices for convenience and portion control. It's fast, easy, and refreshing after a heavy Yom Tov meal.

1. Halve or slice the pears. Place into a 6- or 8-quart pot.
2. Add all the remaining ingredients. Cover and refrigerate for 8 hours or overnight.
3. Remove from refrigerator and place on the stove. Bring to a boil.
4. Lower heat and simmer 30-45 minutes until the pears are tender.
5. Transfer pears and liquid to a container. Pears can be served warm or cold. Freezes well.

YIELD: 8-10 servings

Ingredients:

5-6 pears, peeled and cored
¾ cup red wine
⅓-½ cup sugar
2 cloves (optional)
⅛ teaspoon cinnamon
1-2 slices of lemon
water to barely cover the pears

Strawberry Fluff

This recipe works like magic. The single egg white fills the whole mixing bowl with light, fluffy, sweet ice cream.

1. Place all the ingredients into the large bowl of a mixer.
2. Beat on high until mixture fills the bowl.
3. Transfer to a container and freeze.

YIELD: 12-16 servings

Ingredients:

1 pint fresh strawberries, cleaned and puréed
1 egg white, unbeaten
½ cup sugar

Coffee Ice Cream

Ice cream made only from eggs, oil, and sugar often lacks the body of real ice cream. This recipe is rich and thick and tasty. Doubling this recipe yields a 9"x13" pan.

1. Beat yolks until thick. Add oil, sugar, and coffee. Beat for 15 minutes. Pour into a large bowl.
2. In a clean, dry bowl, beat egg whites until stiff. Add sugar and vanilla sugar. Beat until very stiff.
3. Using a spatula, gently combine both mixtures by folding them together.
4. Pour into an 8" square pan and sprinkle toasted walnuts on top.
5. Freeze.

YIELD: 8 servings

Ingredients:

6 eggs, separated
¾ cup oil
⅓ cup sugar
1 Tablespoon instant coffee granules dissolved in a little hot water and cooled
2 Tablespoons sugar
3 Tablespoons vanilla sugar
¼ cup toasted walnuts

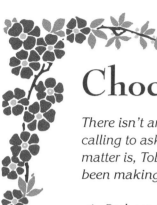

Chocolate Nut Sponge Cake

There isn't an Erev Yom Tov that goes by without my friend Toby Goldstein calling to ask "So what new recipes do you have for me?" The truth of the matter is, Toby gives me more recipes than I give her. This is one of hers. I've been making it for more years than I care to admit.

1. Preheat oven to 350°.
2. Beat 8 egg whites until foamy. Slowly add ½ cup sugar and beat until stiff. Set aside.
3. Beat 8 egg yolks and 1 whole egg until thick. Add ½ cup sugar and beat until incorporated. Add wine and then the rest of the ingredients. Beat together to form a thick batter.
4. Fold ½ the whites into the yolk mixture, then fold in the rest until completely incorporated.
5. Pour batter into an **ungreased** 9" or 10" tube pan.
6. Bake for 45 minutes to 1 hour.
7. Remove from oven and invert to cool.

YIELD: 12-14 servings

Ingredients:

8 eggs, separated
1 whole egg
1 cup sugar, divided
¼ cup sweet red wine
½ cup potato starch
½ cup ground filberts
4 oz. bittersweet chocolate, grated on the broad shredder

Super Duper Chocolate Cake

This excellent chocolate cake is the invention of Mrs. Martha Lax, my friend Shaine Hirsch's mother. I usually bake about 20-25 cakes each Pesach and for sure 8-12 of them are made from this recipe. Even if it falls — which can happen on Pesach — it's still delicious.

1. Preheat oven to 340°.*
2. Line a 9"x13" pan with parchment paper.
3. In a clean, dry bowl of a mixer, beat 6 egg whites until stiff. Set aside.
4. In a mixing bowl, beat yolks with sugar until thick and lemon colored. Add oil and beat well. Add remaining ingredients and mix. Add the 2 egg whites to loosen the batter and mix thoroughly.
5. Fold whites into the yolk batter.
5. Pour the batter into the prepared pan. Bake for approximately one hour or until an inserted toothpick comes out dry.
6. Cool on a rack.

*NOTE: This is not a typographical error. 350° is too high and 325° is too low.

YIELD: 1 9"x13" pan

Ingredients:

8 eggs, separated
  (keep 2 whites separate)
2 cups sugar
1 cup oil
½ teaspoon kosher salt
scant 1¾ Tablespoons instant
  coffee granules
¾ cup potato starch
vanilla sugar (optional)

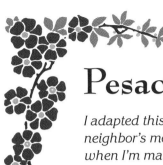

Pesach Nut Cake

I adapted this from an excellent nut cake recipe given to me by my neighbor's mother, Mrs. Sirkis. I hate to separate eggs, but I never mind when I'm making this cake — it's worth it.

1. Preheat oven to 350°.
2. Beat yolks with ½ cup sugar until thick and creamy.
3. Add potato starch and oil to the yolk mixture and beat until incorporated. Set aside.
4. In a clean bowl, using clean, dry beaters, beat egg whites until frothy. Slowly add ½ cup sugar and vanilla sugar and beat until stiff.
5. Fold whites into yolk mixture.
6. Fold in ground nuts.
7. Pour into **ungreased** 9" springform pan.
8. Bake for 40 minutes or until inserted toothpick comes out clean.
9. Remove from oven and invert to cool.

YIELD: 10 servings

Ingredients:

7 eggs, separated
1 cup sugar, divided
2 Tablespoons potato starch
3 Tablespoons oil
1 teaspoon vanilla
1 (6-7 oz.) package ground walnuts or any nut of your choice

A cheder in Warsaw, 1923

Shavuos

Z'man Matan Toraseinu: Not Mentioned in the Torah

Shavuos is the festival that commemorates our receiving the Torah at Sinai. This is clearly the most significant event in the history of the Jewish nation, and indeed, in our prayers we refer to it as "the time when our Torah was given." Is it not strange that the Torah makes no mention of this aspect of Shavuos, referring to it instead as *Chag HaBikkurim*, the Festival of the First-ripened Fruits? Why is this ceremony more significant than the giving of the Torah?

The Midrash says that *derech eretz*, proper behavior, is a prerequisite to Torah (*Vayikra Rabbah* 9:3). Ramban says that it is possible for a person to be in technical compliance with all Torah commandments, yet be a coarse person (*Leviticus* 19:2).

Only with refined *middos* (character traits) can a person acquire Torah (*Ethics of the Fathers* 6:6).

The ritual of *bikkurim* consisted of bringing the first-ripened fruits to the Temple in Jerusalem and expressing gratitude to G-d for His bounty. The works of *mussar* point out that *hakaras hatov*, acknowledging a kindness and expressing one's gratitude, is a cornerstone of proper *middos*. The first words we recite upon awakening in the morning are *Modeh ani*, thanking G-d for another day of life. We then recite a number of *berachos*, thanking G-d for our ability to see, to move about and to don our clothes. During the day we say *berachos* before and after partaking of food, as well as for our bodily functions. The acknowledgment of kindness and the expression of gratitude are central to Jewishness.

This is why the Torah emphasizes *bikkurim*, the ceremony of gratitude, as the focus of Shavuos. Without refined *middos*, one cannot acquire Torah.

Tainted Bikkurim Are Not Gratitude

The Talmud says that poverty stalks the poor. Wealthy people brought their *bikkurim* in golden and silver vessels, and these were returned to them. The poor brought their *bikkurim* in woven reed baskets, and these were retained in the Sanctuary.

R' David of Tolna gave this explanation.

"I once notified my chassidim in a certain village that I was coming to spend Shabbos with them. A cry of joy rang through the *beis midrash*.

"Chaim, a poor man, came home from shul elated. 'The Rebbe is coming!' he said. But after a bit, his mood changed to dejection. 'What is wrong?' his wife asked. 'You were just so happy about the Rebbe coming.'

" 'Of course,' Chaim said. 'But it is customary to give the Rebbe some money for his charities, and we have no money.'

" 'Don't let that worry you,' the wife replied. 'I'll do some extra baking and I'll sell the cakes, and you will have money for *tzedakah*.' Chaim's face lit up with joy, and the ruble he gave me was alive with good will.

"One of the town's wealthiest citizens came home from shul, downcast. 'What is wrong?' his wife asked, 'did anything happen?'

" 'No, nothing happened. It's just that the Rebbe is coming to town, and he is going to tap me for *tzedakah*. That will be 50 rubles down the drain.'

R' David continued, "To me, a single lively ruble is dearer than 50 dead rubles.

"Something similar happened with *bikkurim*," R' David explained. "A poor person, who had a few trees, came into the house jubilant. 'Some fruits have ripened, and I can take *bikkurim* to the *Beis HaMikdash*.' But then he became morose. 'What happened to suddenly make you so sad?' his wife asked.

" 'I don't have a decent vessel in which to place the *bikkurim*,' the man answered.

" 'Don't let that worry you,' his wife replied. 'I will sit down with our daughter, and together we will weave a reed basket that will be magnificent.' They deftly wove the basket with their hearts full of devotion to G-d.

"A worker in a rich man's orchard one day said to him, 'I noticed that some of the fruits have ripened.'

" 'So, what of it?' the rich man retorted.

" 'Isn't it the time to bring the fruits to Jerusalem?' the worker asked.

" 'Oh, for heaven's sake!' the rich man replied. 'That's an imposition. I can't afford to take time off to go to Jerusalem.' Then he added, 'Oh, well, I guess there's no getting out of it. But I remember that last year there were some people who showed off by bringing the fruit in silver vessels. I am going to bring mine in a gold vessel. Let them eat their hearts out.' "

R' David explained, "The reed basket that was woven with love for G-d was retained in the Sanctuary. The silver and gold vessels that were brought for spite were returned to their owners. G-d has no use for these."

The Greenery Stimulates Simchah

I t is customary to decorate the shul with plants on Shavuos. The *Mishnah Berurah* says that this is in commemoration of the greenery with which G-d surrounded the barren Mount Sinai.

But if so, why do we not blow shofar on Shavuos? The shofar was sounded at the giving of the Torah.

R' Yitzchak Silberstein answers that the reason G-d decorated Mt. Sinai with greenery is because its beauty elevated the hearts of the Israelites, stimulating *simchah*, to teach us that Torah can be acquired only through *simchah*. Indeed, the *Mishnah Berurah* cites a custom to distribute fragrant herbs on Shavuos, to bring about a pleasant atmosphere that will result in an attitude of good cheer. Therefore, although the shofar was sounded at Sinai, we commemorate only that which elevates our spirit (*Aleinu Leshabe'ach, Vayikra* p. 423).

In commemoration of the *bikkurim* ritual, Jews in Kurdistan had a custom of bringing fruit baskets decorated with flowers to the chief rabbi, where they would sing and dance. Yemenite Jews, clad in white, adorned with greenery and flowers, would bring baskets of grapes to the town elder.

Doing Withour Sleep

M any people observe the custom of staying up on Shavuos eve to study Torah. A reason for this practice is the Midrash that states that on the morning of the 7th day of Sivan, the Israelites slept late, and Moses had to arouse them to come to the mountain to receive the Torah. To compensate for our ancestors' delinquency, we stay awake all night until we read the account of the giving of the Torah.

How is it that the great generation under the tutelage of Moses slept late on this auspicious day? One commentary defends the honor of our ancestors. The Midrash says that before offering the Torah to Israel, G-d offered it to other nations. The Israelites were certain that other nations would accept the Torah, and therefore, they had no reason to expect it would be offered to them.

The Shavuos Cuisine

Shavuos is the easiest of all the festivals to observe. One does not have the laborious preparation of Pesach nor build a *succah*. However, it has been quipped, "Look at the Jewish *mazal!* Pesach you can eat *wherever* you wish, but not *whatever* you wish. Succos you can eat *whatever* you wish, but not *wherever* you wish. Shavuos has no restrictions. You can eat whatever you wish and wherever you wish, so … it lasts only two days (one day in Israel) instead of eight (seven in Israel)!"

As compensation, Shavuos is graced with delicious dairy foods.

Many reasons are given for the practice of eating dairy foods on Shavuos. (My father would say, "Why look for a *taam* (reason) for eating cheesecake? Taste it, and you will discover the *taam* (taste)." Here are several of the suggested reasons:

(1) In *Song of Songs* (4:11), Solomon says, "The sweetness of Torah drips from your lips, *like honey and milk* under your tongue." We, therefore, eat sweet dairy foods, which symbolize the sweetness of Torah.

(2) Milk is a complete food, containing most essential nutrients. Torah provides all the essential spiritual nutrients.

(3) Before Sinai, there were no laws regarding kosher meat. After the Torah was given, the meat that the Jews possessed had not been prepared in a kosher fashion, so they had no choice but to eat dairy foods. The first Shavuos meal was *milchig*!

(4) The heavenly angels protested the giving of the Torah to mere mortals, claiming that they (the angels) were more deserving. G-d said, "You did not observe the Torah. Did you not eat milk and meat together when you visited the Patriarch Abraham?" (*Genesis* 18:8). It was, therefore, by virtue of dairy foods that we triumphed over the angels and received the Torah.

(5) The mountain of Sinai is referred to as "a mountain of many ridges" (*har gavnunim*; *Psalms* 68:17). To symbolize Sinai, we eat cheese (*gevinah* is cognate to *gavnunim*).

If you use our recipe for blintzes, you will have true gourmet blintzes, not like those of Shepsel.

Shepsel was a porter, who barely earned enough to put bread on his table. One time, upon delivering a parcel to a wealthy man, Shepsel saw the man enjoying a tasty dish of blintzes. When he returned home he said to his wife, "Yentl, only the rich people can enjoy this world. I saw a rich man eat delicious blintzes that made my mouth water."

"You want blintzes?" Yentl said. "I'll make you blintzes, just like the rich people."

Having no eggs or refined flour, Yentl made a batter of coarse flour and water. Having no cheese, she filled the blintz with mashed potatoes. Having no fresh butter, she fried the blintz in recycled oil.

Shepsel tasted the blintz and promptly spat it out. "Those rich people are *meshuge* (insane). I can't understand what they find so good about blintzes!"

Pirogen

My mother made these for Shavuos and also during the Nine Days. Although time-consuming, this is an all-time winner.

The complete dough recipe is found under Kreplach on page 136. The method is almost identical, with minor differences. They are:
— In step 4: Cut the dough into rounds with a floured 2½-3″ cookie cutter. My mother used the rim of a glass, I use a scalloped edge cutter — it's prettier.
— In step 5: Use 1-2 Tablespoons of filling, and fold the circles to form half-moons.
— In step 7: Melt butter or margarine.
Dough instructions steps 1-3, 6, and 8 are identical.
Using a slotted spoon, remove the pirogen and drain in a colander. Then place in a frying pan or dish holding the melted butter or margarine. Drizzle additional melted butter over them. At this point they can be fried, baked for 15-20 minutes in a preheated 350° oven, or frozen. Follow directions for freezing in Kreplach recipe. Defrost and heat as above.

Potato Filling:
1. Cook potatoes in salted water for 15-20 minutes, until a fork inserts easily.
2. Drain well and return potatoes to pot. Briefly place over low heat to dry.
3. Mash potatoes with sautéed onion and seasonings. Taste and adjust seasonings.

YIELD: 60-70 pirogen

Ingredients:

Potato Filling:
6 potatoes (about 3 lbs.), peeled and cubed
water to cover
2 Tablespoons kosher salt
¾ cup sautéed onions, or more to taste
½-1 teaspoon pepper

Potato-Cheese Filling:
To every cup of farmer cheese add and mix well:
½ cup cooked mashed potato
1 onion, diced and sautéed
salt and pepper to taste

Cheese Filling:
Combine:
1½ lbs. farmer cheese
4 Tablespoons sugar or to taste
3 egg yolks
1 egg white
1½ Tablespoons vanilla sugar

Cherry or Blueberry Filling:
canned pie filling

Cheese Crepes for a Crowd

This recipe comes from Rabbi Twerski's daughter-in-law, Hendel. These blintzes are super rich and super delicious. If you have the time but don't have the crowd they can be frozen and used at your pleasure.

1. Combine crepe ingredients in a bowl and blend together.
2. Place a very lightly greased frying pan over medium heat. When it is hot, spoon in a thin layer (2-3 Tablespoons) of batter and tilt the pan to evenly coat the bottom. Fry briefly and turn out of the pan when slightly browned. Repeat with remaining batter, regreasing the pan as needed.
3. Mix the filling ingredients together. With the cooked side of the crepes facing you, divide the blintz filling evenly so that each crepe has the same amount of filling. Fold the sides over the filling and then roll up the crepe.
4. Fry on both sides until golden. May be eaten immedaitely or rewarmed in a 350° oven or even room temperature

YIELD: 35 blintzes

Ingredients:

Crepes:
7 eggs
3 cups flour
3 cups milk
½ cup sugar
2 teaspoons vanilla sugar
⅛ teaspoon table salt
½ cup oil
1 cup water

oil, butter, or margarine for
   frying

Filling:
1½ lb. farmer cheese
8 oz. plain cream cheese,
   whipped
8 oz. sour cream
½ cup sugar
1 packet vanilla sugar
½ cup confectioners' sugar

Streussel-Topped Kokosh Cake

This is my daughter-in-law Fraidle's recipe. The recipe makes 5 large loaf pans. They can all be baked at once or, after the kokosh has been shaped and placed into the pan to rise, freeze those you will not be using immediately. Remove from the freezer 2 hours before baking.

1. Prepare the dough: Proof the yeast in the warm water with a pinch of sugar.
2. Place the yeast along with the other dough ingredients into the bowl of a mixer and, using the dough hook, knead until a smooth dough forms.
3. Place the dough into a lightly greased bowl, turn to grease top, and cover with plastic wrap. Let rise for 2 hours.
4. Meanwhile, prepare the filling: Beat 3 egg whites with sugar until stiff. Beat in margarine and cocoa (the whites will fall and be gooey — that's OK).
5. Preheat oven to 350°.
6. When the dough is ready, punch down and divide into 5 equal parts.
7. Roll out each piece on lightly floured board into a small rectangle. Smear with ⅕ of the filling. Roll up each piece jelly-roll fashion and place in parchment paper-lined 4½"x10½" loaf pan. Repeat with the remaining dough.
8. Prepare the streussel by combining the ingredients to form crumbs. Sprinkle on the loaves. Allow the loaves to rise for 30 minutes.
9. Bake for 30-45 minutes. Cool in the pan on a rack.

YIELD: 5 loaves, each yielding 10-12 slices

Ingredients:

Dough:
3 oz. fresh yeast
½ cup warm water
pinch of sugar
5 lbs. all-purpose flour (or a mixture of high-gluten and all-purpose)
2 whole eggs
5 egg yolks
1½ cups oil
1 stick margarine
½ cup sugar
1½ Tablespoons kosher salt
1½ cups light grape juice
2½-2¾ cups water

Filling:
3 egg whites
2 cups sugar
½ stick margarine, softened
¼ cup cocoa

Streussel:
1 stick margarine, softened
1 cup flour
½ cup sugar
1 Tablespoon vanilla sugar

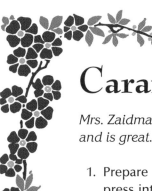

Caramel-Topped Cheese Cake

Mrs. Zaidman's recipe makes a cheese cake that looks great, tastes great, and is great.

1. Prepare the crust: Combine the cookie crumbs with the margarine and press into the bottom of three shallow 9″ round disposable pie plates **or** one deep 9″x 2″ round springform pan.
2. Preheat oven to 350°.
3. Prepare the filling: Beat eggs, add the rest of the ingredients one at a time, mixing well after each addition. Make sure the batter is smooth. Pour mixture into the crust.
4. Bake for 1 hour. Turn off heat; leave cake in oven with door closed for 1 hour to cool.
5. Meanwhile, prepare the caramel topping: Melt the chocolate in a double boiler. Set aside.
6. Dissolve the coffee in the hot water. Add the corn syrup and mix thoroughly over low heat until the mixture has a smooth texture and a caramel color.
7. Combine the chocolate and caramel and pour over cooled cheese cake.

VARIATION: Omit the caramel topping and top the cake with blueberry pie filling.

YIELD: 20-24 servings

Ingredients:

Crust:
1 lb. lemon cookies, crushed into crumbs
1 stick margarine, melted

Cheese Filling:
4 eggs
1½ lb. farmer cheese
2 (8-oz.) containers cream cheese
8 oz. sour cream
1½ cups sugar
2 scant Tablespoons vanilla sugar
5 Tablespoons cornstarch
2 cups milk

Caramel Topping:
3½ oz. bar white chocolate (Schmerling), not decorator chocolate
½ teaspoon instant coffee granules
3 Tablespoons hot water
1 Tablespoon corn syrup

Braided Yeast Cheese Cake

This is one recipe that I hesitate to make because it's so rich and so irresistible. Everyone loves it. I got the recipe from my daughter-in-law Reizi in Lakewood. It's not difficult and tastes even better than it looks.

1. Prepare the dough using a dough hook or by hand: Mix the first 4 ingredients together in bowl. Combine melted butter or margarine with water. Add to dry mixture. Add the egg and the rest of the flour. Knead dough. Put into greased bowl, turn to grease top, and cover with plastic. Let rise until doubled.
2. Prepare the filling: Mix first five ingredients until smooth. Add raisins.
3. Punch down the dough and divide into two pieces.
4. Roll one piece of dough into a 12"x15" rectangle (see diagram).
5. Spread half the filling lengthwise 4" wide down the center of the rectangle. (I like more filling so I use 1½ times the amounts given here.)
6. Cut dough crosswise on both sides of filling into 3" wide stripes, 1" apart. Place the strips (alternating one side, then the other) at an angle across the filling for a braided effect. Transfer the braid to a parchment paper-lined cookie sheet.
7. Brush braid with egg wash. Repeat steps 4-7 with second piece of dough.
8. Preheat oven to 350°. Let the braids rise for 20 minutes.
9. Bake for 20-30 minutes until golden.

VARIATION: Mrs. Zaidman spreads blueberry pie filling down the center, under the cheese mixture. What should I tell you — it's even better than better.

YIELD: 2 cheese braids, each yielding 12-15 slices

Ingredients:

Dough:
½ cup sugar
½ teaspoon table salt
2 packets (¼-oz. each) dry yeast
1 cup flour
6 Tablespoons margarine
  or butter, melted
⅔ cup warm water
2½ cups flour
1 egg

1 egg white, well beaten, for wash

Filling:
8 oz. cottage cheese
8 oz. cream cheese
½ cup confectioners' sugar
1 teaspoon lemon zest
1 egg yolk
½ cup raisins

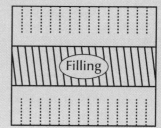

Coffee Cloud Cake

As you know by now — separating eggs is just not my thing. Nonetheless this cake is my all-time very favorite cake. The name says it all.

Cake:
1. Preheat oven to 350°.
2. Beat yolks with 1½ cups sugar until thick and creamy. Add vanilla.
3. Sift flour, baking powder, and salt together and add to yolks, alternating with the coffee, beginning and ending with the dry ingredients. Set aside.
4. In a clean, dry bowl with clean beaters, beat egg whites until foamy. Slowly add the sugar (½ teaspoon at a time) and mix until incorporated and whites form stiff peaks when beaters are lifted.
5. Fold ⅓ of the whites into the yolk mixture. Then fold in the rest of the whites and the ground walnuts or pecans.
6. Pour into an **ungreased** 10" tube pan. Bake for 60-70 minutes until a toothpick inserted into the center of the cake comes out dry. Remove from oven and invert pan over a bottle to cool.

Frosting:
1. Mix margarine, confectioners' sugar and non-dairy creamer until smooth.
2. When cake is cool, remove from pan and frost cake. Sprinkle with chopped nuts.

YIELD: 12-16 servings

Ingredients:

Cake:
6 eggs, separated
2 cups sugar, divided
1 teaspoon vanilla
2 cups flour
3 teaspoons baking powder
½ teaspoon kosher salt
1 Tablespoon instant coffee granules dissolved in 1 cup boiling water, cooled
1 cup ground walnuts or pecans

Frosting:
4 Tablespoons margarine
1¾ cups confectioners' sugar
7 Tablespoons non-dairy creamer

1½ cups toasted chopped nuts

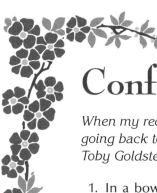

Confectioners' Sugar Crescents

When my recipe box is in a state of major disorder, I can always count on going back to my source for the original recipe. These were given to me by Toby Goldstein and she even added a variation to this crowd-pleaser.

1. In a bowl, cream the margarine, confectioners' sugar, and vanilla until combined.
2. Blend in the ground nuts and flour and knead gently to form a soft dough.
3. Wrap dough in plastic and refrigerate for 30-45 minutes.
4. Preheat oven to 325°. Line 2 cookie sheets with parchment paper.
5. Remove dough and shape by pinching off pieces that are slightly larger than a grape but smaller than a walnut. Roll into a 2" rope and curl to shape into a crescent. Place the crescents on the prepared cookie sheets, 1" apart.
6. Bake 20-30 minutes. The bottoms should be golden brown but don't allow the tops of the crescents to brown.
7. Remove from oven, dust heavily with confectioners' sugar and let cool. Dust with confectioners' sugar again.

VARIATION: Place 2 oz. of either semisweet chocolate or chocolate chips into a sandwich-size plastic bag. Immerse in hot water until the chocolate is melted. Remove, snip off the corner of the bag and drizzle the chocolate onto the cooled cookies.

YIELD: 4 dozen cookies

Ingredients:

2 sticks margarine (½ lb.), diced
½ cup confectioners' sugar
1 teaspoon pure vanilla extract
2 cups flour
½ cup ground almonds or
   filberts

sifted confectioners' sugar,
   for dusting

Torahlach

I got this recipe (and many others) from Mrs. Zaidman. I'm not sure this is authentic to Europe, but it's so charming and tasty that I couldn't resist including it.

1. Preheat oven to 350°.
2. Roll out the kindle dough very thin. Smear the surface with apricot jam.
3. Cut the dough into small rectangles 2½" wide by 1½" high. Place two pretzel sticks opposite each other on two sides of each rectangle. Roll both ends toward the center, leaving ¾" in the center with the jam exposed.
4. Place the Torahlech on a parchment paper-lined cookie sheet and bake at 350° for 15-20 minutes, until lightly browned at the edges.

YIELD: 25-30 Torahlach

Ingredients:

1 package frozen kindle dough, defrosted
apricot jam
1 package thin pretzel sticks